Retail Business Kit For Dummies®

Cheat Sheet

Common Retailing Terms

ad slicks: Camera-ready ad, usually on glossy paper.

add-on sale: Additional items a customer buys due to suggestive selling.

allowance: Any price reduction given for a multitude of reasons ranging from slightly defective merchandise to a late delivery.

beginning of the month inventory (BOM): Physical inventory in the store at the beginning of the month.

big box store: A major chain store focused on selection and price, usually very large with no frills.

bottom feeders: Customers who buy only clearance merchandise.

call tag: A specific freight carrier's written authorization for customers to return merchandise to the retailer at no cost.

charge back: Deductions on an invoice taken by the retailer for damages, freight allowances, shortages, and so on.

closeouts: Discontinued or clearance merchandise sold at a reduced price.

consignment merchandise: Merchandise the retailer does not own or pay for until it is sold.

deep and narrow: Large quantities of a small selection of merchandise.

dog: Slang term for merchandise that is not selling.

end of month (EOM): Term referring to either the payment of invoice due at the end of the month in which the merchandise was shipped or the amount of physical inventory in the store at the end of a month.

factor: A bank or finance company that buys the receivables from a manufacturer. The retailer then pays the factor for the merchandise rather than paying the vendor.

free on board (FOB): This is the point at which the shipping costs become the responsibility of the retailer rather than the vendor.

guaranteed sale: A vendor's promise to take back unsold merchandise and issue either a refund or a merchandise credit toward other goods.

hot items: Popular and quickly selling merchandise.

jobber: A distributor who buys merchandise to be resold to the retailer.

keystone: A price for merchandise that is double the wholesale price.

For Dummies: Bestselling Book Series for Beginners

Retail Business Kit For Dummies®

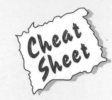

layaway: Storing merchandise for a customer for a later purchase, usually requiring a deposit and a time limit for the transaction.

letter of credit: Used on international purchasing, an agreement from a bank assuring a foreign vendor that it will be paid for the merchandise.

logo: A symbol of the written name of a business; used to represent the business.

markdown: The difference between the original retail price and the reduced price.

markup: The amount of money added to the wholesale price to obtain the retail price.

niche retailing: Selecting a highly defined specialty within a specialty.

off-price: Merchandise that is purchased for less than regular price.

open to buy: Budgeted amount of merchandise still open to be purchased for a specific time period.

profit and loss statement (P&L): An accounting report that highlights revenues, cost of goods sold, and net profit.

purchase order: The actual form used for placing an order.

rate card: The price list used primarily in the world of advertising.

resale number: A state-issued identification number allowing a retailer to buy merchandise without having to pay sales tax. This number and certificate are also used for admission into most trade shows.

run of paper (ROP): A newspaper advertising term used when placing an ad indicating that the ad can be placed anywhere within the newspaper.

show special: A price incentive offered by manufacturers to induce buyers to place orders at the show.

stock keeping unit (SKU): A number assigned by the store to identify the manufacturer, style number, size, color, and unit price of a piece of merchandise.

substitution: Occurs when a vendor substitutes one style for another on an open order.

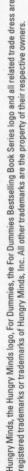
Hungry Minds™

For Dummies: Bestselling Book Series for Beginners

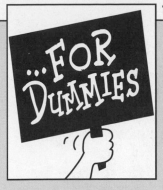 TM

References for the Rest of Us!®

BESTSELLING BOOK SERIES

Do you find that traditional reference books are overloaded with technical details and advice you'll never use? Do you postpone important life decisions because you just don't want to deal with them? Then our *For Dummies*® business and general reference book series is for you.

For Dummies business and general reference books are written for those frustrated and hard-working souls who know they aren't dumb, but find that the myriad of personal and business issues and the accompanying horror stories make them feel helpless. *For Dummies* books use a lighthearted approach, a down-to-earth style, and even cartoons and humorous icons to dispel fears and build confidence. Lighthearted but not lightweight, these books are perfect survival guides to solve your everyday personal and business problems.

Already, millions of satisfied readers agree. They have made For Dummies the #1 introductory level computer book series and a best-selling business book series. They have written asking for more. So, if you're looking for the best and easiest way to learn about business and other general reference topics, look to For Dummies to give you a helping hand.

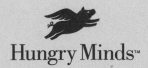
Hungry Minds™

1/01

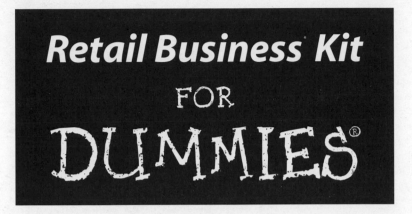

Retail Business Kit FOR DUMMIES®

by Rick Segel

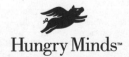

Hungry Minds™

Best-Selling Books • Digital Downloads • e-Books • Answer Networks • e-Newsletters • Branded Web Sites • e-Learning

New York, NY ◆ Cleveland, OH ◆ Indianapolis, IN

Retail Business Kit For Dummies®

Published by:
Hungry Minds, Inc.
909 Third Avenue
New York, NY 10022
www.hungryminds.com
www.dummies.com

Library of Congress Control Number: 2001089311

ISBN: 0-7645-5381-X

Printed in the United States of America

10 9 8 7 6 5 4 3 2

1O/RV/QW/QR/IN

Distributed in the United States by Hungry Minds, Inc.

Distributed by CDG Books Canada Inc. for Canada; by Transworld Publishers Limited in the United Kingdom; by IDG Norge Books for Norway; by IDG Sweden Books for Sweden; by IDG Books Australia Publishing Corporation Pty. Ltd. for Australia and New Zealand; by TransQuest Publishers Pte Ltd. for Singapore, Malaysia, Thailand, Indonesia, and Hong Kong; by Gotop Information Inc. for Taiwan; by ICG Muse, Inc. for Japan; by Intersoft for South Africa; by Eyrolles for France; by International Thomson Publishing for Germany, Austria and Switzerland; by Distribuidora Cuspide for Argentina; by LR International for Brazil; by Galileo Libros for Chile; by Ediciones ZETA S.C.R. Ltda. for Peru; by WS Computer Publishing Corporation, Inc., for the Philippines; by Contemporanea de Ediciones for Venezuela; by Express Computer Distributors for the Caribbean and West Indies; by Micronesia Media Distributor, Inc. for Micronesia; by Chips Computadoras S.A. de C.V. for Mexico; by Editorial Norma de Panama S.A. for Panama; by American Bookshops for Finland.

For general information on Hungry Minds' products and services please contact our Customer Care department; within the U.S. at 800-762-2974, outside the U.S. at 317-572-3993 or fax 317-572-4002.

For sales inquiries and resellers information, including discounts, premium and bulk quantity sales and foreign language translations please contact our Customer Care department at 800-434-3422, fax 317-572-4002 or write to Hungry Minds, Inc., Attn: Customer Care department, 10475 Crosspoint Boulevard, Indianapolis, IN 46256.

For information on licensing foreign or domestic rights, please contact our Sub-Rights Customer Care department at 212-884-5000.

For information on using Hungry Minds' products and services in the classroom or for ordering examination copies, please contact our Educational Sales department at 800-434-2086 or fax 317-572-4005.

Please contact our Public Relations department at 317-572-3168 for press review copies or 317-572-3168 for author interviews and other publicity information or fax 317-572-4168.

For authorization to photocopy items for corporate, personal, or educational use, please contact Copyright Clearance Center, 222 Rosewood Drive, Danvers, MA 01923, or fax 978-750-4470.

Library of Congress Cataloging-in-Publication Data

Hungry Minds™ is a trademark of Hungry Minds, Inc.

About the Author

Rick Segel, CSP (Certified Speaking Professional), seasoned retailer of 25 years, owned one of New England's most successful independent woman's specialty stores. He's currently a contributing writer for numerous national and international publications, a founding member of the Retail Advisory Council for Johnson & Wales University, and the online marketing expert for Staples.com. Rick is the director of retail training for the Retail Association of Massachusetts and is currently serving on the boards of directors for five corporations and associations.

Rick earned his CSP, the highest earned designation from the National Speakers Association, making him part of an elite group of less than 8 percent of the total membership. Rick is a past president of the New England Speakers Association and one of the most awarded speakers in New England. He has been a featured speaker in 43 states, on three continents, and has delivered over 1400 presentations. Rick is always one of the highest rated speakers at the conferences where he speaks.

Rick has authored five audio programs and two training videos (*Stop Losing Retail Sales* and *Soft Suggestive Selling*). He has written three other books: *Laugh & Get Rich*, published by Specific House, an insightful look at our entertainment-based society and how it affects the way we do business; *Driving Traffic To Your Retail Business*, published by Inc. Business Publishing; and *Romancing the Customer* due out in September 2001. Rick has appeared on over 100 radio and TV shows and he recently represented the retail community on an episode of the *Sally Jessy Raphael Show* titled "Buy It, Wear It, and Return It."

Rick's clients include McDonald's, Dillard's, Bentley Luggage, Gulf, Texaco, Shell Oil, Dunkin' Donuts, National Retail Federation, The New South Wales Economic Development Council in Australia, Yurekli Seminar Company in Turkey, San Francisco International Gift Fair, California Association of Nurserymen, Dallas Market Center, America's Mart in Atlanta, Ross Park Mall, Jewelers of America, the US Postal Service, National Main Street, Iowa Department of Tourism, The Plaza at King of Prussia, Golf Retailer, Hobby Industries of America, and hundreds of smaller businesses around the world.

Rick is one of the highest rated retail speakers in the world today. His upbeat "laugh and learn" anecdotal style makes him a crowd pleaser wherever he goes. Rick's services include:

- Writing, developing, and delivering customized training to all levels of retailers.
- Keynote presentations that educate, entertain, and motivate.
- After-dinner presentations that are fun and light but deliver a message that inspires.
- One-on-one coaching and teleclasses.

Rick would be delighted to speak at your next meeting, conference, or convention. For more information on keynote presentations, training, or consulting, contact Rick Segel at: Rick Segel & Associates, One Wheatland Street, Burlington, MA 01803; phone 781-272-9995; fax 781-272-9996; e-mail ricksegel.com; Web site www.ricksegel.com

Dedication

I would like to dedicate this book to my family, because without them this book would never have been written. First my three children and their spouses — Lori and Keith Osborne, Lisa and Mike Freson, and Andy and Lisa Segel. To my sister, Roz, whose encouragement made a difference. To the greatest in-laws anyone could ever have, Thelma and David Green, who spent 45 years in the retail furniture business and whose thoughts, beliefs, and ideas are sprinkled throughout this book.

The true inspirations for this book are my parents. My father never knew what type of retailer I became because his death was the trigger that catapulted me into the retail business. As different as we both were, many of our beliefs were very similar and I always regretted never having had the opportunity to work with him. To my mom, Sara "Ruth" Segel, who was quite a remarkable woman. She was brought up in poverty but died a success, both personally and professionally, having built one of the most successful independent women's apparel stores in New England. She was loved by her customers and admired by her competitors. We worked together for 25 years. We fought and argued but always put the customer first. There were so many things that she was so right about that one can only learn from experience. It's sad in a way to finally learn life's lesson and be ready to say, "Mom, you were right," and she wasn't here to listen. Mom, I know you are watching and I hope I have made you proud.

The last and the most important person in the whole world to me, whose name should also be on this book, is my wife of 32 years, Margie. Not just because we worked together in the store and in our training, speaking, and consulting business for the past 29 years. Not just because every word I wrote was reread and edited by her. Not just because she is a great partner in life and in business. Not because of all the highs, lows, and experiences we have shared together. Not just because I love her more than anything in the world. But because she is my very best friend.

I am a very fortunate man to have had all of these wonderful family members in my life to help create this book and make me what I am today. I hope you enjoy, learn from it, and are able to build your business with the same love and passion we have built ours. It is all about family.

Author's Acknowledgments

I feel like an Academy Award winner who has 100 people to thank and 60 seconds to do it. So please understand my rapid-fire approach. I want to thank John Hurst from the Retailers Association of Massachusetts who believed in me from the beginning and has supported our State Retail Awards program. To Melinda Gallant, the mall manager at Mashapee Commons and John Renz, the leasing agent, who were both invaluable in the research of this book. Melinda is not only a great mall manager from one of the most creative and unique shopping areas in the world but also a friend, whom I drive crazy with my phone calls from all over the country asking some of the weirdest questions while she is in the middle of a meeting.

I would like to thank Stacey Heiss, the director of education at Western Exhibitors for her unquestioned support and great ideas for educational programs that have been incorporated in this book. I would also like to thank Andrew Andionadis, whom I met at Western Exhibitors, a very effective consultant and trainer serving as the technical editor of this book. Thanks to Ryp Walters, from Over Coffee Productions for his help on the electronic marketing chapter. Nate Jessup, VP from Retail Technologies, maker of the popular Retail Pro Software whose input was invaluable to the production of this book. To Eric Zucker Esquire of Wakefield, MA for help with all the legal advise that is in this book. Debbie McDonough from Hasting Tapley Insurance, who served as my technical consultant advising on all insurance issues.

A special thanks to Sasha Davidson of Davidson and Sperry for a 20-year advertising education, the basis for my entire advertising education.

Thank you doesn't seem like quite enough to the two people who not only helped me on this book but inspired me to understand and appreciate the true meaning and awesome power of visual merchandising. So to Berit Gagne and Smilia Morvasch (two-time state award winning display artist whose work is demonstrated on the CD), thank you for your ideas and for all of the WOWs I received from my customers for all of those years. You guys are the best!

Another special thanks to Marilyn Censullo, my accountant, technical consultant and friend for all of the help and her unquestioned belief in me. She makes accounting exciting . . . I wish! But she does make accounting understandable and that's the most important thing any accountant can do. To my Aunt Marion Hurvitz, who worked 40 years in the retail business with dedication and pride in her work, contributed to this book in ways she'll never know. Thank you.

To Celia Rocks, my literary agent. She is the one person who made this all happen. She was the perfect matchmaker and the best of win/win all of the time. Celia, this is just the beginning. And finally to all of the people at Hungry Minds, but especially Marcia Johnson. You have made a process that could have been difficult one of the most wonderful experiences of my life. Marcia, thanks for teaching me what a great Editor/Project Manager really does — that's what you are.

Publisher's Acknowledgments

We're proud of this book; please send us your comments through our Online Registration Form located at www.hungryminds.com

Some of the people who helped bring this book to market include the following:

Acquisitions, Editorial, and Media Development

Project Editor: Marcia L. Johnson

Senior Acquisition Editor: Holly McGuire

Associate Acquisition Editor: Jill Alexander

Copy Editors: Tina Sims; Suzanna Thompson

Technical Editor: Andrew A. Andoniadis

Senior Permissions Editor: Carmen Krikorian

Media Development Specialist: Megan Decraene

Media Development Coordinator: Marisa Pearman

Editorial Manager: Pamela Mourouzis

Media Development Manager: Laura VanWinkle

Editorial Assistant: Carol Strickland

Cover Photos: © Gary Buss/FPG International

Production

Project Coordinator: Jennifer Bingham

Layout and Graphics: Amy Adrian, Jill Piscitelli, Heather Pope, Brian Torwelle, Betty Schulte, Julie Trippetti, Jeremey Unger, Erin Zeltner

Proofreaders: John Bitter, John Greenough, Angel Perez, Dwight Ramsey, Nancy Price, Marianne Santy, TECHBOOKS Production Services

Indexer: TECHBOOKS Production Services

General and Administrative

Hungry Minds, Inc.: John Kilcullen, CEO; Bill Barry, President and COO; John Ball, Executive VP, Operations & Administration; John Harris, CFO

Hungry Minds Consumer Reference Group

Business: Kathleen Nebenhaus, Vice President and Publisher; Kevin Thornton, Acquisitions Manager

Cooking/Gardening: Jennifer Feldman, Associate Vice President and Publisher; Anne Ficklen, Executive Editor; Kristi Hart, Managing Editor

Education/Reference: Diane Graves Steele, Vice President and Publisher

Lifestyles: Kathleen Nebenhaus, Vice President and Publisher; Tracy Boggier, Managing Editor

Pets: Dominique De Vito, Associate Vice President and Publisher; Tracy Boggier, Managing Editor

Travel: Michael Spring, Vice President and Publisher; Brice Gosnell, Publishing Director; Suzanne Jannetta, Editorial Director

Hungry Minds Consumer Editorial Services: Kathleen Nebenhaus, Vice President and Publisher; Kristin A. Cocks, Editorial Director; Cindy Kitchel, Editorial Director

Hungry Minds Consumer Production: Debbie Stailey, Production Director

◆

The publisher would like to give special thanks to Patrick J. McGovern, without whom this book would not have been possible.

◆

Contents at a Glance

Cartoons at a Glance

By Rich Tennant

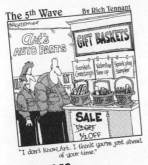

The 5th Wave — By Rich Tennant

"I don't know, Art. I think you're just ahead of your time."

page 303

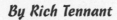

page 199

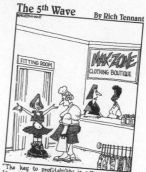

The 5th Wave — By Rich Tennant

"The key to profitability is selling accessories. We sell tons of dark glasses to parents who don't want to be recognized."

251

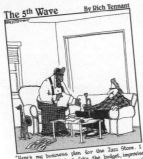

The 5th Wave — By Rich Tennant

"Here's my business plan for the Jazz Store. I think we should just fake the budget, improvise the marketing and make up the long range goals as we go along."

page 97

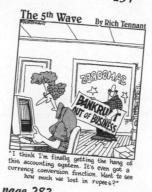

The 5th Wave — By Rich Tennant

"I think I'm finally getting the hang of this accounting system. It's even got a currency conversion function. Want to see how much we lost in rupees?"

page 283

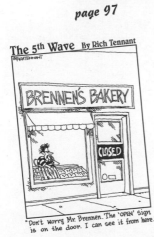

The 5th Wave — By Rich Tennant

"Don't worry Mr. Brennen. The 'OPEN' sign is on the door. I can see it from here."

page 135

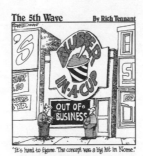

"It's hard to figure. The concept was a big hit in Nome."

page 51

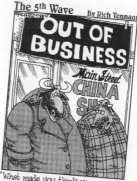

The 5th Wave — By Rich Tennant

"What made you think you were the one to own and operate a china shop, I'll never know."

page 7

Cartoon Information:
Fax: 978-546-7747
E Mail: richtennant@the5thwave.com
World Wide Web: www.the5thwave.com

Table of Contents

Introduction

●●●

*R*etailing today, especially specialty independent retailing, is on the threshold of a major explosion. Don't let some of the headlines scare or confuse you. Some retailers have always failed — that's the natural attrition of the retail industry. But you don't have to. The marketplace is more fertile now than ever before and there is always room for creative, knowledgeable retailers with a different way of looking at the world and customers. That's the reason for this book: to share with you what has worked, what it takes to be successful, and some of the secrets from the pros. Let this book be your manual but don't stop asking questions. It's generations of "whys" that has made retailing what it is today.

About This Book

Retail Business Kit for Dummies is truly a how-to manual for starting and running a retail business. It covers every aspect of the retail business from the original dream all the way through to the day-to-day operations of an established store. Rarely will you read a "How-To" book that is written with the passion and emotion of this one because rarely does a "how-to" author get the opportunity to reflect on his life's work — to focus on all of the little details that fill the day of a retail professional.

Every point or idea has recalled a whole set of scenarios and/or experiences that I have actually lived through — mistakes made, lessons learned, and triumphs celebrated. The purpose of this book is to share many of these experiences so that you can benefit from them in an easy to understand format.

Retail is detail is an old expression you'll find sprinkled throughout this book. What it means is that to be a successful retailer, you must focus on many detailed tasks. If you have a great location, wonderful merchandise, super advertising, but your sales staff can't sell, you have a detail that needs attention. Most successful retailers become great because of their attention to details. That's the reason I've filled this book and CD with checklists and formulas that address a multitude of these details.

I have learned, and you will as well, that the successful retailers are not the ones who break onto the retail landscape with the biggest stores, the most expensive store designs and fixtures, or even a large advertising campaign. No, the true winners are those retail businesses that address all of the little things in concert with a vision and mission for their business.

Who Needs To Read This Book?

The targeted readers of this book are as varied as the world of retailing itself. They range from the salesclerk who has just been offered ownership of the store to:

✔ Anyone who has ever considered a career in retailing.

✔ Anyone who has ever thought about opening her own business.

✔ Anyone who has a desire for independence and for being his own boss.

✔ Anyone who loves working with people.

✔ Anyone who loves the merchandise they are selling.

✔ Anyone who gets a rush shopping for merchandise.

✔ Anyone who gets excited every time they see new arrivals in a store.

✔ Anyone who is so creative they can vision a better way and a burning desire to express their creativity.

✔ Anyone who wants to share work, as well as a life, with a friend or family member.

How This Book Is Organized

Retail Business Kit for Dummies is organized into eight parts, and the chapters within each part cover specific topic areas in detail. In addition, the CD-ROM serves as a reference that puts numerous samples of relevant retail forms at your fingertips for quick retrieval. The CD was designed to be used in conjunction with the book and you'll find references to CD elements throughout the book, but it can also be used on its own. You don't have to read this book straight through. Open it up anywhere and you'll be sure to find gems of retail wisdom to help you make your business a success.

Part 1: Testing the Retail Waters

This is the part that will help you determine if retailing is right for you and if you are right for retailing. It presents many of the pros and cons of retail and offers strategies to help you turn your dreams of running your own store into a reality.

Part II: Settin' Up Shop

This is the fun stuff because this part covers some of the "glamorous" reasons why you might want to go into the retail business — buying merchandise, choosing your store's location, and planning your store design. The chapters in this part provide real how-to information to help you complete these tasks successfully.

Part III: The Details of Retail: Shufflin' Papers

Every business needs a plan, and the first chapter in this part guides you through the procedure of creating a workable business plan that will serve as your blueprint to success. Business is also about crossing every *t* and dotting every *i*, so the second chapter focuses on helping you determine the legal structure of your business. This part wraps up with a chapter that addresses various tax issues and introduces you to many of the permits, registrations, and local requirements you'll face when you decide to open your business.

Part IV: Running Your Business

The chapters in this part get down to the nitty-gritty and focus on the day to day stuff — how to actually run your store on a daily basis. The first chapter in this part guides you through the process of establishing specific store procedures so that your business will run smoothly. The second chapter covers getting the merchandise you want to sell, including how to buy it and how to control your spending. Finally, every business is only as good as its employees, so the last chapter in this part is devoted to helping you find, hire, and keep a terrific staff. And in case I forgot anything, I've also included a chapter on all kinds of "what if" scenarios — from shoplifting to legal and insurance issues.

Part V: Spreading the Word Without Going Broke!

You'll be amazed at all the available options for letting the public know who you are and what you do. The chapters in this part introduce you to numerous ways for increasing your store's profile in the community. You'll read about ways to get people talking favorably about your store — word-of-mouth advertising — and tips for running exciting promotions and profitable sales events.

Part VI: Selling Made Simple

The chapters in this section are designed to help you master the art of selling, whether face to face or on the Internet. They present selling strategies that will keep your cash register ringing and offer tips for displaying merchandise in a way that compels customers to buy it.

Part VII: Taking Care of Business

To be a successful business person, you can never rely on the phrase, "My accountant handles that." The chapters in this part explain how you can (must) use your financial reports to guide many of your business decisions, ensuring that your store will be profitable for years to come. I've also included information about computerized software packages that can help you manage your financial reports. You just have to use the data they generate to run a profitable business.

Part VIII: The Part of Tens

This final part is made up of five lists that highlight some of the basic themes of retailing. From debunking some common retail myths to remembering keys to retail success, the chapters in this part offers tips on wowing your customers and avoiding common retail pitfalls.

Don't forget to check out the Appendix that tells you how to use the CD in the back of this book.

Icons Used in This Book

 The paragraphs marked by this icon represent a generally good idea or suggest a way to do something better or more efficiently.

 This icon indicates an area of concern or offers a tip on how to avoid trouble.

 Well, this icon just marks the information you don't want to forget.

Occasionally, I talk about retail matters that are a bit technical in nature. This icon lets you know you can skip the information if you only want the basics.

The paragraphs marked by this icon are intended to alert you to materials on the CD that are relevant to the discussion at hand.

These short tidbits of knowledge capture poignant points for you to remember and quote based on my many years of retail experience. They are random because there is no order or sequence in the numbering. The key message is in their name: *Retail Rules!*

You can't spend 29 years in an industry without accumulating a rich collection of stories and experiences that not only entertain but also deliver a point. These slices of life give you a chance to look at the retail world as some others have experienced it. Hopefully, you can learn from their successes and mistakes.

Part I
Testing the
Retail Waters

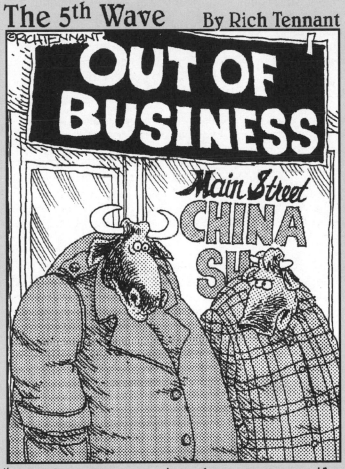

The 5th Wave   By Rich Tennant

"What made you think you were the one to own and operate a china shop, I'll never know."

In this part . . .

This is your fact-finding mission. Here you will determine if retailing is right for you and if you are right for retailing. This is your glimpse behind the counters of the retail industry with all its challenges and opportunities. This is the one part of the book where dreams and ideas matter — where you're encouraged to develop your vision of what you want your business to become then explore ways to turn those dreams into realities.

The first step toward this goal is understanding that the most important brand you will ever carry is the name over your front door. The chapters in this part show you how to develop your store's brand so that the name of your business really means something in the marketplace. They also help you identify who your ideal customers are so that you can set up your business to serve them and so that you can determine if you have enough of them to make your business work.

You also learn about the 8 Point Retail Filter that can serve you well for as long as you are in the retail business. It's simply the 8 most important considerations in everything you do — product, pricing, profitability, presentation, procedures, promotions, people, and brand. As you make various business decisions, you must ask yourself how they will affect each one of these.

Chapter 1

Retailing: How It Really Works and How It Can Work for You

. . . .

In This Chapter

▶ Exploring the dynamic nature of retail

▶ Getting started in the retail business

▶ Assessing your "retail readiness"

▶ Introducing strategies to guide your retail decisions

. . . .

From the challenge of finding the right merchandise, to the thrill of buying it, to the excitement of unpacking it and showing everyone (especially the customers) what you bought, *retailing can be one of the most exciting and exhilarating experiences you will ever have.*

Nevertheless, between 12 and 17 percent of all new businesses fail within the first two years. Why? Because people don't spend enough time learning about the business to find out whether it's right for them. This doesn't have to happen to you. The retail business is a wonderful business — *if* you're the right person for it. In this chapter, I give you an idea of what the retail business is all about so that you can decide for yourself whether retail is right for you.

Looking at Some Advantages to Starting a Retail Business Now

Is this the golden age of retail? You bet it is! Society is more accepting of change and innovation today than ever before — there are no limits to creativity where retailing is concerned. No more of the "that's-the-way-we-always-do-it" mentality! In fact, this generation is used to change — it accepts it, it expects it, and it wants it.

Retailing is a way of life with boundless opportunities. Downtown areas are coming back as viable places to shop. Malls and strip centers that offer competitive leases abound. States are adopting financing packages that are designed to help businesses get started and stay open. More merchant organizations than ever can help the new retailer compete in the marketplace. And the Internet not only offers valuable retail business information and opportunities, but it also allows you to market to and communicate with your customers at virtually no cost.

Today's retailing world is made up of people with many different talents, skills, and approaches. The new kids on the block don't always have the finest college education, nor do they always come from major cities of the world. (After all, even the now-mighty Wal-Mart originated in Bentonville, Arkansas.) But in the retailing world, ordinary men and women can become extraordinary. The new kids can either push the established and already successful stores to become better, or they can put those old stores out of business. Great stores (big or small) thrive, and there's plenty of room for great stores. The time is ripe for new success stories!

Setting Up a Retail Business

The essence of retailing is buying something and reselling it for a profit. What you sell, where you sell it, how you price and display it, and who you sell it to are all factors that help make retailing an extremely interesting challenge. The old retail business expression *"Retail is detail"* is as true today (or more so) as it was 50 years ago. And as bright new entrepreneurs enter the retail arena, each one brings a new detail to retail — a new wrinkle in the way to do business. *Retailing is about change, and if you like change, you will love the retail business.* In fact, creativity is the giant-slayer of businesses that are too set in their ways to change.

But although retailing can be a lot of fun, if you want your business to succeed, you need to make sure that you've tightened a few serious nuts and bolts. To help you do this, here's a handy to-do list of the five basic steps that you must take to create a successful retail business.

1. **Plan your business.**

   First of all, develop a business plan that forces you to document every aspect of your business (I show you how to do this in Chapter 8). And early in the planning stage, define what kind of business you want to open and what's going to make you special (as I discuss in Chapter 2), what kind of merchandise you want to carry (see Chapters 5 and 12), and what type of customers you want to attract (see Chapter 4).

You must also decide where to locate your business for optimal success (see Chapter 6) and how to design your store to make it attractive to customers (see Chapter 7). And before you get too far along in your planning, make sure that you determine the structure of your business (see Chapter 9) and obtain the necessary permits and registrations (see Chapter 10).

2. **Validate your ideas.**

Ask everyone you know what he or she thinks about your idea for a new retail business. Show them your business plan, but be prepared for negative feedback — even your family or your closest friends will often give you the classic, "It will never work." (Perhaps they are jealous that you are trying something that they wish they could try their hands at.) No matter. You must ask their opinion — they may bring up some important points that you've overlooked.

Now is the time to talk to as many professionals as possible. Contact your local state retail association and the trade show or association that services your industry. Many of these groups can refer you to people who will give you an honest opinion. Obviously, now is also the time to share your business plans with your friendly banker. Even if you don't need to borrow money, showing her your plans won't hurt. After your plans have been validated by the appropriate authorities, it's time to execute them (the plans, not the authorities!).

3. **Orchestrate your grand opening.**

Your next goal is to open the store. You must set two dates — one for the "soft" opening and the other for the big splash. For the soft opening, simply open the doors to your business, and whoever comes in, comes in. Doing this gives you a chance to work out the bugs before your grand opening event that includes the ribbon-cutting, the opening party, and — of course — the grand opening sale. No matter how hard you try, preparations usually aren't complete by opening day and opening a store that is so un-ready that it looks unprofessional is the kiss of death for any new business. Your grand opening might be short term in duration, but its effect can last forever. (For information on managing grand openings, promotions, and sales, see Part V.)

4. **Create your routine.**

During your first year, you will establish the way your business does things — your policies and procedures. Are they working in practice? Keep a pad of paper by your cash register, and every time you think about a better way to do something, document it. As your business grows, this habit (which requires little effort to create but years to duplicate if you don't start early) will become an invaluable tool. (For how to run your business from day to day, see Part IV.)

5. Grow your business.

When the newness of the experience starts to wear off and the startup phase is complete, it's time to focus on growing your business. You must now concentrate on advertising (see Chapters 15 and 16.), building your brand, buying the right merchandise (Chapters 5 and 12), and attracting the right personnel (Chapter 13). To maintain your success, you must master the art of selling (see Part VI). And in order for your business to stay afloat, you must keep on top of its finances (see Part VII). As you've probably already figured out, this is the step that never ends!

I've included links to state retail associations and trade show association Web sites on the CD to make it easy for you to do some research.

If anyone succeeds in talking you out of your new venture, your conviction wasn't strong enough to make it work in the first place.

Deciding If Retail Is Right for You

So is the retail business right for you? Or should I say, are excitement, change, and constant improvement right for you? If the answer is "yes," retail is right up your alley. The following questions can help you think more deeply about whether or not retail is for you.

Do I like to sell?

Retailing is selling! But don't worry, the days of turning the customer upside down and shaking him till the money comes out are over. Your advertising, your displays, and the contact you have with your customers are all part of the selling process. (The customers think it's good service, but you're really trying to sell them your product.) If the idea of selling scares you, beware. Retailing is selling — no matter how you disguise it.

Do I like to buy?

Retailing is shopping. If you find shopping to be a pain, though, you better find yourself a good buyer — or you better not go into the retail business. You have to know what your competition is doing. You're not looking to steal their ideas, but their ideas can certainly inspire some great ones of your own.

Do I like dealing with and serving people?

Retailing is a people business. As a retailer, you must deal with emotions both high and low — many times, you must deal with irrational people, rationally. If you welcome this challenge, you may be right for retail.

Do I like to network?

Retailing is establishing contacts. When I ask myself what made me successful, I realize that I couldn't have made it without all of my business contacts who've helped me over the years. Through them, I can learn which merchandise is selling and which has "slowed up," who has the best buys, and where the best seminars are. My contacts are also there for me when I get a little down in the dumps. Sometimes it's nice to have a friend around.

Can I motivate people?

Retailing is motivating your staff. Can you inspire your employees to man the ship and get things done when you're not around? If so, not only can you be a successful retailer, but you may also have the ability to own multiple stores — perhaps even an entire chain! The ability to motivate others is a skill that winners have.

Do I mind sacrificing my schedule to accommodate my customers?

Retailing isn't a Monday through Friday, nine to five job. You must be in the store when your customers are there — you have to be when and where the action is. Don't worry, you can still have a normal life and schedule — it's just that your normal will be a little different. (You get used to it.)

Do I like to plan?

Retailing is planning. You must plan your buying trips and what you will buy on these trips. You must plan your budget. Plan your staff. Plan when to change your displays. Plan your time on the selling floor. Get the picture? Planning is just part of the business.

Do I like to learn new things?

Retailing is constant learning. It doesn't take place in the classroom, but at trade shows — looking at merchandise, listening to salespeople, going to seminars and workshops, and reading trade publications. You must keep up with what's happening in your industry. There is nothing worse than a stale retailer.

Do I like displaying, arranging, and changing merchandise to make it look appealing enough to buy?

Retailing is displaying your merchandise in the most attractive way possible. The ability to arrange a selling floor to make the merchandise say, "Buy me!" is one of the most valuable talents a retailer can have. If you don't possess this ability, find someone to do it for you.

Do I know (or can I learn) some basic accounting to understand how I'm doing financially?

I know what you're thinking: "I'll have my accountant handle that." Sorry to tell you this, but there are a few basics that you yourself must learn to do weekly and monthly. It's not that bad, so don't get nervous — just accept the fact that you must master a few basic accounting skills.

If most of these questions excited you, you will make a great retailer. If, as you read them, you thought, "I can do that," you have retail in your blood. And if you know why there are eleven questions instead of the standard ten, you even think like a retailer: Every good retailer always gives a little extra — it's the thirteenth doughnut that keeps your customers coming back.

But if you're thinking, "I just want to open a small gift shop and sell souvenirs — all this can't apply to me," you need this book more than you think you do. If you think that having some old fixtures from a store that closed and knowing a company that can supply you with some merchandise are good enough reasons to go into the retail business, think again.

Rick's Random Rule #691: Good enough isn't good enough!

Reviewing some reasons for opening a store

Often, people open stores for the wrong reasons. What are your reasons? Are they valid? And just what is a valid reason, anyway? After all, what's right for one person may not be right for another. The following list gives some common reasons for opening a store.

- ✔ **Tapping into your creativity.** A store can provide an outlet for artistic expression. Every display tells a story, and the owners take painstaking efforts to make sure that it's perfect in every way. These retailers don't necessarily like dealing with the finicky nature of a customer — but their displays act as silent salespeople that consistently make the registers ring. Those who love what they do and who work hard (but never think of it as hard work) almost always succeed.

- ✔ **Interacting with people.** Opening a store can give you the opportunity to interact with customers and meet plenty of new people. People who open stores for this reason thrill to the challenge of developing new customers. Many don't even work for the money — some are even semi-retired, but the prospect of turning a "looker" into a "buyer" is enough incentive for them to open a store.

- ✔ **Relishing the excitement.** Having a store can provide you with the excitement of buying the merchandise for it. Wielding the buying power and having access to the latest merchandise is a thrill. Wouldn't everyone love to attend the electronics or toy show in Las Vegas? Of course they would — it's fun! *And it's fun to run a store.*

- ✔ **Creating a job for yourself.** If you are a manufacturer or a designer, opening a store can enable you to sell your merchandise directly to the public. In this way, you can create a visibility for your product that may not have been possible through the traditional channels. Or if, like the Jewish immigrants during the early part of the twentieth century, you're finding it difficult to get a job, opening a store can be a way around this obstacle. Many Jewish immigrants who opened their own small retail shops went on to become the giants of the retail industry.

✔ **Taking the reins.** To those who have worked in retail their entire life, opening a store can fulfill their dreams of owning their own business. These people already know the ins and outs of retailing and only need to learn the backroom functions. In my opinion, this is one of the best reasons to open a store.

✔ **Making money.** Running a store can make you money — in many cases lots of it — while keeping you close to home. Many people who started with very little have gone on to make millions in the retail business.

Rick's Random Rule #52: Successful retailing is just creativity and practicality stuffed into one shopping bag.

The reasons to open a store are many, but the key is to know and recognize *your own reasons.* Be aware, however, that your reasons for owning a store will probably change as you are exposed to more aspects of the retail business. And they will probably change as your life situation evolves. For example, my mother originally opened a store because she needed to support a family but had a problem finding a job. Mom ended up staying in the retail business until she was 82 — not because she still couldn't find a job, but because she loved the excitement of the buy and the thrill of the sale.

Understanding how retailing will affect your lifestyle

When you think of retail, do you think about all the hours that stores are open? "For Pete's sake," you may ask yourself, "how much can a fellow work?" Well, I have good news and bad news.

First, the good news — you *can't* work all the hours that the store is open. You just can't, and if you think that you're going to in order to "sacrifice" at the beginning, you're crazy. I'm all for sacrifice, but I'm definitely not for torture!

The fastest way to an unhappy life and career is to work seven days a week. It hurts the business. You aren't fresh, you become short-tempered, and you start to feel like a rat on a treadmill. I recommend that retailers work five days a week and take the other two off. The businesses whose managers do this are much healthier, and their staffs are happier and more creative. Getting out of the store helps your business by getting your mind moving and inspiring new ideas.

A major advantage of retail is that your business is usually local; thus, you don't have to travel. Sure, there's the occasional buying trip — but at least it's not every week. You'll probably only have between two and six of these per year.

And the best part about the retailing lifestyle is that you won't ever have to stand in line on your days off. Nothing is ever crowded — when you're running your errands and doing your shopping, almost everyone else is at work! It's great: When the whole world is shopping, you are working. And when the whole world is working, you can go shopping!

Now, here's the bad news. You will not work the normal Monday through Friday, nine to five schedule because that's not when people shop. Working on Saturday is a must — in most retail businesses, it's the busiest day of the week. The same could be said for Sunday (but with fewer hours). The bottom line is simple — you must be in the store when you're doing the most business for two reasons:

- ✔ You need to meet, greet, and get to know the customers.
- ✔ You need to know why certain items sell or don't sell.

Will you have to work long hours? Probably so, but so will anyone who's starting a new business. Can you be in the retail business *and* lead a normal life? Absolutely! Yes, there'll be times when you'll have to put in your hours, but for the most part you'll be able to live a very normal life. So how many hours a week should you work? Up to 50 hours — and that's enough! Make an exception only if you're planning something out of the ordinary, such as a promotional event or a sale.

Retailing is a marathon, not a sprint. You must pace yourself.

So why retail? Why not? Retailing is fun, exciting, and ever-changing. It's also collegial — as a retailer, you are part of a group. The group may include neighboring stores, your state association of retailers, or the state and national associations of retailers in your industry (such as the Jewelry Retailers, Convenience Store Retailers, Appliance Retailers, and so on). These groups all offer trade shows, educational seminars, and member benefit programs — best of all, being in these groups allows you to network with others who do exactly what you do.

The retail business can be the most exciting business in the world. The income potential, the lifestyle advantages, the thrill of the buying process, the challenges, the contact with people, and the sheer pride of owning your own store are what make retail a wonderful career option.

Sure, you'll get frustrated and question why you entered the retail industry — but you'd feel this way starting any new venture. New things are always difficult in the beginning. Change is difficult, but change is good. So get excited, and enjoy your journey. It's all out there for the taking — if you're up to the challenge. Have fun!

Using the "8-Point Retail Filter" to Guide Your Decisions

So, if you've determined that you want to go forward with setting up a retail business, you're going to need some specific success strategies. In various places throughout this book, I refer to what I call the "8-Point Retail Filter." This filter is, in fact, a list of the eight basic elements of running a retail business. In every single consulting assignment I've ever undertaken, I have found that any store problem can be traced back to one of these eight elements. Unless every area is running efficiently, your business will have problems. On the other hand, if you address these eight points consistently and thoroughly, your business will succeed.

Retailers use this list to analyze the workings of their businesses; that's why it's important for you to be able to identify the eight points and use them to evaluate your business. The 8-Point Retail Filter helps you understand the retail business, focus on the details of retail, and set goals to bring your business to the next level. Be sure to sift every retail decision through this filter.

In the list that follows, I briefly define each point in the filter and then pose questions for you to ask yourself whenever you make a decision that pertains to your business. In other chapters, I provide additional questions based on this 8-Point Retail Filter that are more specific to the discussion at hand.

- **Product.** As you probably guessed, this is the stuff that your store sells. What kind of product will your store carry? Are there any special lines of this product that you'd like to carry in the future?

- **Presentation.** This is what your store looks like, inside and out. Don't fall into the trap of just letting this aspect of your store "happen." What feeling will your store's atmosphere convey? How will you display your product?

- **Procedures.** This is how your store is run. Over the years, innovative procedures have produced revolutionary concepts (such as drive-thrus, supermarkets, superstores, and e-tail sites) that have changed the face of retail. How will you do the everyday things you do? What goals will you work towards in this area?

- **Pricing.** This is how much you sell your product for. Will your store be a discount store, a premium price business (a la Tiffany's), or something in between? How often will you have sales?

- ✔ **Promotion.** This is how your store advertises and markets itself to the public. How are you going to tell the world you exist? Will you have non-sale promotions, as well as price promotions?

- ✔ **Profitability.** This is how much money you make from selling your product. Don't leave this to your accountant — it could put you out of business. When do you plan on turning a profit, and will you be drawing a salary? What system will you use to remain informed of your profitability?

- ✔ **People.** This is the staff you hire to do everything from sweeping the floors to ringing up the cash register to filing your taxes. Your success depends on the team you put together. Who will you hire, and what will their roles be? Who will train your staff?

- ✔ **Brand.** This is how your store distinguishes itself from others like it. Brand often plays a major role in why a customer chooses one store over another. What will customers associate your store with? How will you promote your brand?

Goals are powerful tools that must be evaluated with a big splash of reality. Many times, goals need to be examined by a fresh set of eyes — just be careful where you get your advice.

He had high hopes

A couple years ago, Bud, the owner of an expensive home furnishings store, called me for help. He told me that his new 6000-square-foot store was on track to do $3 million in sales during its first year. Frankly, I was impressed. "What do you need me for?" I asked.

Bud replied, "My break-even is $5 million." I asked Bud why he had planned that aggressively and what his alternative plan involved. He answered that he had never *planned* to be that aggressive because he'd always believed that he would be able to break even. But now, because he had spent all of his money outfitting his store, Bud was desperate.

Bud's sales goals were so high that they set him up for failure — and fail he did. Although his store was doing $500 in sales per square foot (which is well above the national average for stores that have already been in business a while), he needed to do much more than that just to break even! He set goals that were just too high. Therefore, any plan to meet these goals would never have worked.

Chapter 2

Defining Your Vision: It Starts With a Dream

Show me a successful entrepreneur, and I'll show you a dreamer. What is *your* dream? Who are you, and what do you stand for? Your dream will serve as the foundation of your business. Thus, if you want to succeed in starting a retail business, you must first define your vision. The questions that I ask you in this chapter are designed to help you express your dream and formulate the words that you'll live — and do business — by.

Getting Focused on Your Dream

Too many businesses fail because they lack focus. Defining your vision can give you the focus that you need and is critical to the success of your business because it helps you

- ✔ Know what type of business you're going to run — down to the smallest detail. (And once you understand what kind of business you are, never stray from it!)

- ✔ Express your business ideas in a *signature line,* a short statement that represents the mission and vision of your business — and lets your customers know what to expect when they walk through your front door.

- ✔ Understand what your store means in the marketplace. (If you are fuzzy about the details, everyone else will be, too.)

✔ Identify the paths that will lead to the success or failure of your business. (For example, if your mission is to cater to a price-conscious customer, don't locate your store in an upscale premium mall — doing so would be bad for your business.)

Rick's Random Rule #53: Stand for something or fall for anything.

As you start to solidify your dreams, take into account your employees (or future employees). Always share your business dreams with them — they're the torchbearers of your dreams, and, as such, they need to understand your dreams. Regard your employees as customers, doing all that you can to keep them happy and invested in your business — in this day and age, attracting customers is much easier than attracting effective employees!

What came between me and my Calvins?

I used to own a moderately priced women's specialty store just outside of Boston. In the 1970s, we carried a line of dresses for the mature woman. That line of dresses was one of the most profitable lines in our store. After all, mothers were our specialty.

On one particular buying trip to my usual supplier of clothing for mature women, I noticed an entire wall that was stacked to the ceiling with jeans. I asked the salesperson about it, and he explained that his boss had made a deal with a new designer. Surprisingly, he remarked, the jeans were selling well — despite the fact that the designer had put his name on the outside of the pants.

Anticipating that he'd try to sell me some of the jeans, I told him that I'd buy a dozen pairs. "I can't do that," he said. "Those are all sold. All I have to do is ship them." These jeans were popular, he said, and they had to be purchased in New York. This was amazing to me — I guess I got a little carried away with the hype. I went to New York and ordered, not one dozen, but *seven* dozen pairs of jeans.

A month later, the jeans arrived at my store. They sold for $38 apiece, a pretty steep price for jeans at that time. One of my employees, concerned

that we had so many pairs, suggested putting a couple of them in the front window. Within ten minutes of putting the jeans on display, high school kids started to come into the store, asking about the jeans. At one point, every dressing room contained a kid that was trying on these jeans. During the next hour and a half, we sold nineteen pairs.

Nevertheless, at closing time, I called the owner of the jeans store across the street and sold him the rest of the jeans at my cost. Why? Because I knew my customers — and they certainly weren't 19 years old! My store just wasn't big enough to handle two totally different types of customers, and I knew that dumping the jeans was the right thing to do. I was able to make that decision because I knew who I was, and I had a crystal clear understanding of the mission of my business. And to have tried to cater to two distinctly different customers would have sent mixed messages to the public about what my store was all about.

The quick buck today can cause irreparable damage later. You will be constantly tempted with fads that are here today, gone tomorrow. Stay the course, build your brand, and never forget who you are — or who you're serving.

Brainstorming to Gather Your Ideas

Brainstorming is an effective strategy to help you take notions and vague ideas and put them into more concrete terms. Take time to do this, not only by yourself but also with others — you need to have very definite ideas about your vision. Enlist the help of your friends, associates, and other business people you respect. Brainstorming sessions with these people can help you gather your ideas and add new ones that you may not have thought about before.

Brainstorming to define your vision involves three steps: self-talk, bouncing, and free flow.

Talking to yourself

Right now, you're probably in the first stage of brainstorming, the *self-talk* stage. Perhaps you've had a dream for a long time, and the time is getting ripe for you to act on it. Commit your ideas to paper so that, in the future, you can go back to your notes and determine whether you've kept true to your original dream.

It's always a good idea, and especially during the formative stage, to carry around a notebook or cassette recorder to capture great ideas.

Resist the urge to think of all the reasons why your dream won't work. Don't indulge in negative self-talk like, "Oh, it'll never work; what am I thinking?" especially if you've had a bad day. Remember that the winners in the retail business are those who overcome negative self-talk and plunge ahead with their dreams — in spite of any defeats or setbacks. You can't succeed if you don't try.

Getting feedback

The second stage of brainstorming involves *bouncing* ideas off a friend or colleague. Ask what they think of your ideas. Ask whether they think your ideas will work.

In this stage, you're gathering information, using a very unscientific survey to gauge others' reactions to your ideas. Many times, you can determine whether people think your idea is good by monitoring their reaction when you tell them about it. Generally, the wider their eyes get, the more they like your idea. If you get this kind of response, consider it a favorable indicator that you should go ahead and pursue your dreams.

Beware of the folks who tell you, "It will never work." I often wonder how many people must have said to the founder of Starbucks Coffee, "You are going to sell coffee for how much? That's crazy!" It's a good thing that he really believed in his dream; otherwise, I wouldn't be able to drink my Grande Decaf Latte.

Letting it flow

In the *free flow* stage, you focus on coming up with — or expanding on — an idea, a solution, or a game plan. For this brainstorming session, gather a small group of people who are interested in helping your business succeed.

During this session, you can use the questions that I present in the following section to help focus the thoughts of those in the group. Be sure that you allow follow-up questions such as "What do you mean by that?" or "Tell me more about that." Keep in mind that *every idea is a good idea*. Ideas or suggestions that seem to be out in left field can often spawn great ideas.

Squeezing Your Dreams into a Signature Line

Crafting a *signature line,* a key phrase that defines your business, is a critical element to the success of your business. This phrase is an expression of your business's values; in a nanosecond, it communicates exactly what your business stands for. In this fast-paced, high-tech age, when you don't have more than an instant to present your brand, your signature line determines the way consumers perceive your business — for better or worse. (To find out how to create your own signature line, see the following section.)

Capturing an (often) abstract dream in one short phrase can seem an impossible task. To help you identify the key words or phrases that are central to your business vision, I've designed the Nifty Fifty, a series of questions that I use in my own consulting sessions. (Keep reading. You'll find it later in this section.)

If you haven't opened a store yet, you may not be able to answer all of the questions. That's okay, just answer them to the best of your ability. (Depending on how far along you are, you may have to substitute the word "would" for "do.") As you respond, look for words or phrases that come up time and again in your answers. Take note of the times that a response is accompanied by the thought, "Of course, what other answer could there possibly be?" A strong reaction like this indicates that the subject at hand may be close to the core of your business vision, making it a likely candidate for inclusion in your signature line.

Discovering what's important to you: The "Nifty Fifty"

1. In an ideal world (where money was no object), what would your store look like?

2. Because money is always an issue, what does your store actually look like?

3. How can you improve your store design?

4. What kind of merchandise do you carry?

5. Where do you buy your merchandise?

6. Do you like to carry expensive merchandise?

7. Do you let the merchandise you carry determine the type of customer you want to attract?

8. Are you customer-focused?

9. Describe your ideal customers:

   What do they look like? (If you have more than one type, describe each one.)

   What kind of merchandise do they buy?

   What kind of car do they drive?

   How many children do they have?

   Do their children attend public school?

   Do they belong to a country club?

   Do they belong to a bowling league?

   What price range is attractive to them?

10. Why do you consider them to be your best customers?

    Do they spend a lot of money in the store?

    Do they come into the store frequently?

11. How do you communicate with your customers?

12. If a customer put something in layaway, and the item was subsequently marked down, how would you handle the situation?

13. How would you handle employee theft?

14. How would you handle an employee who wanted to take time off for their daughter's ballet recital during the busy Christmas season?

15. Who's more important: your customers or your employees? Why?

16. Do you believe that you should treat all customers the same?

17. Do you believe that you should treat all employees the same?

18. What does quality mean to you?

19. What criteria would you use to classify a store as average, weak, or a leader?

20. What expectations do customers have when shopping at a store that's similar to yours?

21. What expectations do customers have when shopping at a store that's similar to yours but is considered to be weak or poorly run? What makes that store weak?

22. How do you plan on making your store different from that weak store?

23. What expectations do customers have when shopping at a store that's similar to yours but is considered to be strong or well run? What makes that store a leader?

24. How do you plan on making your store the same as that strong store?

25. What good ideas does that store use that you could implement at your store?

26. What type of store do you normally shop at?

27. What type of store would you love to shop at?

28. What makes your store different? If it's not different, why isn't it?

29. Why should someone buy from you rather than from your competition?

30. Why should customers go into your store rather than buying merchandise online?

31. What is the ultimate benefit that your customer receives by shopping at your store?

32. Do you want to make a difference in your community? In your industry? In your customers' lives? If so, how?

33. How important are social issues to your business?

34. Do you believe in getting involved with charities or with community organizations? If so, why?

35. In today's business world, do you feel as if you have to compromise your values in order to succeed?

36. What do you want customers to say about your store?

37. What do you want non-customers to say about your store?

38. What do you want your friends or family to say about the store?

39. What do you want your fellow merchants to say about the store?

40. What do you want customers to say about you?

41. What do you want your fellow merchants to say about you?

42. What do you want the community to say about you?

43. What do you want customers to say about your employees?

44. What is the one thing that customers will talk about after being in your store?

45. Fill in the following blanks:

    The sales help were so _____.

    They have the best _____.

    They are the place to go for _____.

46. What makes people talk about your store?

47. More blanks to fill in:

    It's so _____ to find what I am looking for.

    I _____ the way the store looks.

    It took _____ to get what I needed and leave.

48. How important is it to show a profit in your first year?

49. Where would you like your business to be in 3 years? In 5 years? In 10 years?

50. Where would *you* like to be in the same time frames — professionally and financially?

Save your responses in a folder and review them annually (perhaps on the anniversary of your store's opening) to monitor any changes in your answers or attitudes. During your first year in business, you may want to review your responses quarterly.

You can find a copy of The Nifty Fifty in the Miscellaneous Forms folder on the CD. Print it out and use it for future analysis.

Evaluating your responses

If you answered the questions in the preceding section honestly, you probably know a lot more about yourself and your business than you did before. Your responses indicate what is important to you and what isn't — what your business is going to emphasize, and what it isn't.

Consider your responses in the context of the 8-Point Retail Filter (which I introduce in Chapter 1):

✔ **Product.** Will the merchandise you carry be the most important aspect of your business?

- ✔ **Presentation.** Will the way that your merchandise is presented and the overall look of your store be your most distinguishing factor?

- ✔ **Procedure.** Will the way that you provide service to your customers be the element that sets your store apart from your competitors?

- ✔ **Pricing.** Will the price of your merchandise determine your focus?

- ✔ **Promotion.** Will your advertisements be what your customers talk about?

- ✔ **People.** Will the type of people that you hire and the training that you make available to them become your focus?

- ✔ **Profitability.** Will profitability determine your business decisions? (You have to say "yes" to this one!) Financial considerations can prevent you from doing things that could change your focus. I always wanted a big clock in front of my store that everyone would talk about. However, because the clock cost $18,000, I never got it. See what I mean?

- ✔ **Brand.** All of these considerations make up your brand and help you and your customers identify your business and understand its position in the marketplace.

Does every business have a signature line? No, but they should. Having a signature line costs hardly anything (unless you hire a professional to write with you — notice that I didn't say *for* you), but the benefits of having an effective signature line are tremendous. A signature line is more than just an advertising slogan: It communicates who you are and what you do — and what your customers can expect from you.

Recognizing effective signature lines

I've compiled a list of some of the best signature lines ever written. Undoubtedly, they have served as inspiration for countless businesses around the world. Let them help get you thinking about a phrase that could define your business.

- ✔ American Airlines: *Doing what we do best*
- ✔ Budweiser: *This Bud's for you*
- ✔ Burger King: *Have it your way*
- ✔ Chanel: *Share the fantasy*
- ✔ De Beers: *A diamond is forever*
- ✔ GE: *We bring good things to life*
- ✔ Motel 6: *We'll leave the light on for you*
- ✔ Oscar Meyer: *I wish I were an Oscar Meyer wiener*

Creating your own signature line

When you're creating your signature line, don't forget that these words will appear on *everything* that is related to your business. And they'll be among the first words out of your mouth when you describe your business to others. With your responses to the Nifty Fifty that I presented earlier in this chapter in hand,

- Reread the questions and your responses, trying to capture a mood or feeling.

- Circle or underline words, phrases, or themes that are repeated.

- Think about what characteristics of a business would benefit your customers, and write them down.

- Write a phrase that conveys the mission of your business. This phrase should be one that

    • Is made up of less than 8 words.

    • Can be placed after your logo every time your logo appears (at least until it becomes an inextricable part of your brand).

    • Is memorable or can be repeated often enough that it gets remembered. (What good is a fabulous signature line if you don't use it?)

At this point, you may be thinking, "It sounds to me like a signature line is really an advertising slogan." But what's wrong with advertising who you are and what you stand for? Nothing! Think of the following signature lines and the impact that they've had on their respective businesses:

- *Hallmark . . . When you care enough to send the very best.* Hallmark just sells paper and ink, but, with this signature line, they convey a sense of excellence and position themselves as the best in their industry.

- *FedEx . . . When it absolutely, positively, must be there on time.* Unquestionably, Federal Express stands for speed and efficiency.

- *Ford Motor Company . . . Striving to make the world a better place.* Although Ford is having some problems with tires, I think that, in the end, their signature line will pull them through.

- *The Ritz-Carlton Hotel . . . Ladies and gentlemen serving ladies and gentlemen.* I think that that says it all.

Rejuvenate your business with a signature line

Several years ago, I was approached by Ed, a frame store owner. Unfortunately, his store, which did wonderful work, had an otherwise nondescript reputation. He wanted me to help him come up with an attention-grabbing signature line. For starters, I had him go through the same Nifty Fifty questions that I present in this chapter.

When Ed finished answering the questions, we looked at his responses. Several words and phrases stood out: "quality," "precision," "fussy customers," "customers who appreciate my painstaking efforts." Most of his customers were artists, explained Ed. Jokingly, he added, "They're the only type of people who understand what I do."

With this information, Ed and I developed a signature line for his store: *Where the artists go for framing.* The phrase provided Ed with just the focus he needed. He put that line on everything — his signs, his receipts, his advertising, and everything else that had his store's name on it. The store's signature line became part of the store's name. Nine months later, Ed called to tell me that his business was better than ever — his store's profitability had soared.

Years later, I worked with a restaurant that was trying to change its image — from that of a stodgy old establishment to that of an offbeat, funky joint that served interesting foods. The restaurant's owners wanted to get the community talking about it, so they adopted the signature line: *From the naked tomato to the stuffed potato.* The phrase had attitude and shock value, and it worked. I think that the word "naked" did it.

Chapter 3

Branding: Making Your Business Memorable

*B*efore you can build a brand, you must know what a brand is. A *brand* is a name or a symbol of identification. For example, "Gap" is the *name* of a store — as such, it's part of that store's brand. Gap's logo is also part of its brand. Your store's name and logo are the basic building blocks for creating your store's brand — your image.

What association do you make when you see Gap's logo or hear its name? Quality? Hipness? Gotta have it? Gap's brand derives its power from the positive associations that it creates among consumers. Remember that a brand becomes whatever consumers associate with it. So be careful what people think about you — your reputation is also a component of your brand!

Learning What You Need to Know about Branding

In the last few years, the concept of brand (or *branding*) has dominated the pages of almost every business publication — it has become part of everyday business vocabulary everywhere. But, in actuality, branding is as old as business itself. To survive in today's crowded marketplace, you must develop name recognition for your store. There is no room for error. When you advertise your business, your brand has to be consistent. Branding simplifies your message so that it doesn't get lost in a maze of information overload.

So what does a brand do? First of all, it breeds familiarity — and familiarity represents trust. You've heard people exclaim, "Hey, I've heard of that!" as if to say that, because they've heard of it, it must be good. Is this reputation always deserved? Not necessarily. But consumers tend to think that if a business has a recognizable brand, its product must be okay.

Cashing in with a strong brand

A strong brand name adds value to your merchandise by suggesting that it's worth purchasing. And products with strong brand names can often even demand higher prices. *Brand equity* is the amount of extra money that someone is willing to pay for a product just because it is a "brand name" product or because it comes from a store with a "name." Think of the products that you pay extra for every day — the following examples show the power of brand equity.

- **Frank Perdue** was the first to brand the chicken that he sold to supermarkets. He branded *dead chickens!* Perdue chickens are more expensive than other kinds of chicken — but they sell.

- **Intel** branded something that most people have never seen or touched and don't really know what it does. But customers feel secure when the computer they buy sports an "Intel inside" sticker. People are willing to pay extra for an Intel chip because of what the brand represents. ***Note:*** The computer I am typing on right now doesn't have an Intel chip in it — and, obviously, it works just fine.

- **Mrs. Fields** branded her chocolate chip cookies. Most people who buy the Mrs. Fields brand can expect the cookies to be full of chocolate chips and other premium ingredients, to be baked to perfection, and to remind them of Grandma's baking. However, plenty of people make chocolate chip cookies better than (or at least as well as) Mrs. Fields does — but *she* branded hers, so they fetch a higher price than unbranded cookies.

- **Evian** branded water! Water's my number one most favorite thing ever branded. You can't go anywhere without seeing someone carrying a bottle of Evian. It costs more than regular tap water, but it sells. Perhaps it's because Evian water makes you think of elegant lunches or bubbling springs in the French countryside. These are powerful associations, but neither of them have anything to do with thirst.

- **Orville Redenbacher** branded expensive popcorn . . . need I say more?

My message is this: In order to distinguish your store from all others (and thus, attract lots of customers), you need to develop your store's brand into a name (or image) that means something in the marketplace.

Rick's Random Rule #98: Whoever owns the brand, holds the purse strings.

Making your business your brand

A big mistake many new retailers make is to focus on the brands they carry, and not on their *own* name. Because different manufacturers and lines will fall in and out of favor, build your business with an eye on establishing your store name as a recognizable brand. If you do this, your store will stay strong — regardless of fluctuating trends.

Promote your store's name, not the name of a manufacturer. Repeat this phrase 100 times, write it on the blackboard another 100 times — and before you go to sleep every night, say it again. (I know I am being a pain about this, but it's *that* important.)

Your goal should be to carry merchandise that is unique to your store. People go to Tiffany's because of the quality and style of its merchandise. People go to Burger King because it "flame broils" its burgers, not because it gets its meat from Oscar Meyer or Hebrew National. The flame-broiling is what distinguishes them from their competitors — what builds their brand. The following stores have huge brand recognition — and they've built their names by carrying their own brand of merchandise.

- Talbots
- Banana Republic
- Disney Store
- L.L. Bean
- Lands' End
- Restoration Hardware
- Pottery Barn
- Crate & Barrel
- Abercrombie & Fitch
- Godiva Chocolatier (my favorite)

You may be thinking, "That sounds good, but these are all big stores with lots of money available to create their own lines and labels — I'm too small to do that." Wrong! Many designer lines are made up of purchased items. The high profile retailers in the list above purchase merchandise from manufacturers and sales reps just like you do, they just go on to make those items a part of their *own* collection.

Rick's Random Rule #804: The most important brand you can carry is the name on your front door.

A 60-second history of branding

Around the turn of the twentieth century, the largest retailers in the United States were A&P and Sears Roebuck. These stores carried their own brands — A&P products and Craftsman products. The richest people in America were retailers.

But then manufacturing companies like Kellogg's, Proctor & Gamble, General Mills, and Black & Decker started advertising directly to consumers. This direct advertising initiative raised consumer awareness of their products.

And this awareness, in turn, forced existing retailers to start carrying the manufacturers' merchandise — customers were demanding it. The shift was on: The purse strings, or profits, were moving from retailer to manufacturer.

Over the last 20 years, however, the purse strings have started to shift back to the retailer. Why? Because retailers have figured out that if they promote and feature their own store brands, they can earn extra profits.

The bottom line: You have to establish your business's identity — that is, create a strong name — so that your store itself becomes a recognizable brand. If you do this, your business will be a success. Without a strong name, the most your business is worth (if you decide to sell it) is the amount that you can generate with a "going out of business" sale. Even at that point, however, the stronger your store name, the better the sale. For more on the running sales, flip to Chapter 18. For now, let's learn how to build your brand.

Understanding brand associations

Branding is a game of associations. When you think of McDonald's, you have a whole set of associations such as fast food, inexpensive, good place to take the kids, delicious French fries, clean — I could go on and on. As a retailer, you need to control the associations the public makes with your business as much as possible.

The following is a list of the most common brand associations and the reactions they elicit from customers:

- **Familiarity.** "I've heard of them!" (This one's still number one with me!)
- **Reliability.** "You can count on them."
- **Service.** "They'll be there to help if something goes wrong."
- **Quality.** "Their stuff really holds up over time."
- **Consistency.** "I know they'll have it." (Whatever "it" may be.)
- **Security.** "You're safe doing business with them."

✔ **Value.** "You will always get your money's worth at their store."

✔ **Speed.** "If you're in a hurry, go there."

✔ **Strength.** "Their products are powerful and dependable." (For example, Ford cars are "Ford tough.")

I could go on and on about the emotions that are associated with brands. Now it's time to take a little of what you know about brands and brand associations and put this knowledge to work.

To help you focus on a brand for your store, think of your brand as your store's image — it's what attracts customers. You have to make sure your brand is unique and recognizable. To help you clearly define your brand, ask yourself the following questions that are based on the 8-Point Retail Filter (See Chapter 1 if you need a refresher on the 8-Point Retail Filter):

✔ **What price category do I want my business to fall into? Discount? Middle-of-the-road? High-end? (Price).** The price range of the merchandise in your store affects your image (and ultimately your brand).

✔ **What type of products do I want to sell? (Product).** The products you choose to carry define your brand.

✔ **What kind of employees will enhance my store's image and reflect my dedication to customer care?" (People).** Your employees are central to your brand (this is especially true in a smaller store).

✔ **Do my procedures make it easy for customers to buy from me? For sales reps to enjoy doing business with me? (Procedure).** The way that you do business contributes to your store's reputation — remember, your reputation is your brand.

✔ **Does my store's public paper accurately reflect the brand I'm trying to create?" (Promotion).** The type of advertising and promotion you do determines your store's image. Your *public paper* (newspaper ads, promotional flyers, catalogs, store display signs — even sales receipts) are the tools with which you build your brand.

✔ **Is my brand strong enough that people feel confident doing business with me? If not, what can I do to strengthen it? (Profitability).** The strength of your brand offers your customers the security of knowing that they're dealing with a reputable (and profitable) business.

✔ **Does every visible thing related to my business accurately reflect the image of my store? (Presentation).** This covers everything from your logo design to your store's "look" — from interior displays and fixtures to your exterior signage and your windows.

Use your responses to these questions to help you define your store's image — your brand.

Taking Steps To Build Brand Power

The strategies that I present in this section can help you establish your business as a brand that reflects the merchandise you sell, the service you provide, the uniqueness you offer, and the kind of customer you want to attract.

Finding a niche

In this age of specialization, consumers are more than willing to pay extra money to deal with a specialized professional — someone who really knows his or her business, a real expert. In fact, the more you specialize, the better you get at what you do (and the more customers will travel farther or pay extra to do business with you). Establish your business as the expert in a particular retail niche, and customers will come.

The first business to discover a niche usually becomes very wealthy. Look for your niche. It's probably right under your nose.

Understanding who your customer is

When considering what kind of customers you want to attract to your business — your *ideal* customers — think about their income level, their education level, their lifestyle, and the media they are exposed to — especially the magazines they read. All this information helps you determine how best to build your brand to appeal to your ideal customer.

If you really want to know your customers, find out what they're reading! The variety of magazines and books on people's shelves reflects their various wants and needs. This makes them good indicators of what the people who buy them are really like.

Creating a logo

A truly great logo is one that is both a powerful image *and* a specific representation of your business — not just a pretty picture. It can be simply your name presented in a distinctive font, a symbol that represents your business, or a combination of these. Some examples of effective logos include

- Shell Oil Company's shell
- Texaco's Pegasus
- McDonald's golden arches

> ✔ NBC's peacock
>
> ✔ The Boston Celtics' leprechaun

These are effective logos because the public immediately recognizes them as representing their respective businesses. When you're designing your logo, remember to keep it simple (so that it's easy to recognize) and be sure that it reflects your business. Understand that different fonts elicit different emotions — some fonts are very formal while others are more casual. A good graphic designer will know the difference. But before you turn this project over to a graphic designer, you must do some homework.

First, determine the look and feel that you want to create. Think of the types of people you have defined as your ideal customers. What would appeal to them? What stores do they already shop at? Collect logos that appeal to you. Next, present your ideas to your graphic designer and let her create a sample logo for you. Finally, show the proofs of this new logo to friends, colleagues, enemies, family members, professionals, retailers, or anyone else you can think of and gather their opinions.

Rick's Random Rule #267: When you listen to advice, remember that brilliant people can make stupid mistakes. Make your own final decisions.

Owning a word or phrase

You can really make your brand stick in the minds of your customers if you can find a word or phrase that specifically represents your business, yet has a broad and catchy appeal. "Mothers are our specialty" is the expression that I used very successfully in my store (we sold mother-of-the-bride dresses) for more than 23 years. I included this phrase in all my advertising. The public came to accept my store, my employees, and me as the "experts" on mother-of-the-bride dresses.

Be careful not to crown yourself a "specialist" of a manufacturer's brand or of a faddish item. You could be building brand equity in an item that will eventually die out. You may have a nice run, but you'll have to look for a new "specialty" sooner or later. Go for longevity — invest in yourself!

Creating trade dressing

Trade dressing simply refers the colors that you use to represent your business. If I asked you, "What colors are used by Coca-Cola?" you would know — red and white. What are Pepsi's colors? Red, white, and blue. Kodak? Yellow and black. The *...For Dummies* books? Also yellow and black. You get the idea.

Pick your colors and use them on everything that you possibly can. On all of your packaging, on your signage (inside and out), and in your ads. You can try to include your trade dressing in the interior of your store, but the colors that make great packaging and signage rarely make for good interior design. Yellow and black are great colors for bags but terrible for a store interior.

Becoming an expert

Part of building your brand is to become the leader in your chosen retail niche. You want your business to be the first thing that pops into people's minds when they think about the products that you sell. In order for this to happen, you must work to become the recognized expert in the field.

Do your homework

Because of the Internet, becoming a recognized expert is not as difficult as it used to be. Today, you have access to unlimited amounts of information with just a few clicks of your computer mouse. Be sure that you do your homework and study your category thoroughly. Try to attend every seminar that your industry offers. Know more than your peers. If you spend just 20 minutes a day reading about your industry, you can be an expert in less than 18 months. How can you be an authority in such a short time? Easy — it's simply because your competition isn't studying up like you are.

Obtain credentials

If your association, such as the Jewelry Association or the Photo-Marketing Association, offers any type of certification program, get certified. It adds to your credibility — and that can only help your business. Although your customers may not know what your certification means, the fact that you are certified can inspire trust.

Spread the word

Once you have achieved "expert" status, share your accomplishment with the world. Contact the different media outlets, and let them know that they can call on you to comment on various issues that affect your industry. Send out a press release every time you go to a trade show to share with the public all the insights you gained from your trade show experience. Soon people will be coming to you for your expertise.

Share your knowledge

You can strengthen your brand and underscore your expert status by conducting seminars in your store. The public wants to know about whatever you sell. You don't have to attract a big crowd. Actually, small groups of four to six people are perfect. Be sure that you teach your customers things that they want to know.

At my store, we gave seminars on how to be the perfect mother-in-law. After all, mother-of-the-bride dresses were my store's specialty. These seminars attracted the type of customer I wanted and helped establish me as an expert on mothers. It was a win-win situation.

If you own a gift shop, teach a class in your store on how to select the perfect gift. If you have a hardware store, give classes on how to fix stuff. And if you own a jewelry store, think about this: Because every guy feels stupid buying a ring, how many wouldn't love to take a class on how to buy the perfect diamond for their sweetheart? (*Note:* To avoid a security disaster, keep the gems locked up and teach the class with the help of some good pictures or a PowerPoint presentation instead.) Share your knowledge — doing so builds your brand power.

Providing consistency

Your logo, your fonts, your signature line, and your colors must be the same every single time you use them. You may make some substitutions (such as using the name "Coke" rather than "Coca-Cola"), but don't change your logo or typeface. If you vary the elements of your store's presentation such as your logo or color scheme, you undermine the power of your brand.

Make sure that your brand looks the same every time. Consistency builds brand power more than anything else. Consistency builds brand power more than anything else. Consistency builds brand power more than anything else. Consistency builds brand power more than anything else. Got it?

Protecting your brand

Anything that you do in your business must be good for the brand that you are building. If you say that your salespeople are professionals, yet you fail to train your staff, you hurt your brand. If you say that you're efficient, yet your store is messy, you hurt your brand. If you say that you care about giving back to the community, yet you're caught littering, you hurt your brand.

Everything that you do (or that your staff does) affects your brand. Even posting a simple handwritten paper sign in your store affects your brand. If all your signs are handwritten on paper, no problem. But if making a handwritten paper sign was just a shortcut, you hurt your brand.

Chapter 4

Getting to Know Your Customers Before You Even Have Any

. . . .

In This Chapter

▶ Recognizing the value of knowing your customers

▶ Defining various types of customers

▶ Identifying *your* customers

▶ Figuring out what motivates your customers to buy

. . . .

To save money and increase your sales (and, thus, be successful), you must *know* your customers — know what they like and what motivates them to buy. Your store may have elaborate displays, distinctive packaging, and a great location, but if you and your staff don't know your customers, your store will fail. If, however, you take the time and effort to truly know your customers, your store — even if it's ugly, uses brown paper bags, and is in a terrible location — can succeed.

Successful stores know what merchandise their customers like and what merchandise their customers absolutely won't buy. Having a staff that is familiar with nearly every customer — what she bought the last time and what turns her on or off — is key. Because these stores know their customers, they can avoid getting stuck with merchandise that won't sell, and they can save money on advertising.

In this chapter, I help you define your ideal customer so that you can figure out what motivates *your* customers to buy.

Toyota's triumph: Going undercover to uncover what customers want

Prior to developing a new luxury car, Toyota sent engineers to live in the most affluent areas of North America for a nine-month period in an attempt to gain a deeper understanding of its ideal customer. The engineers' mission was to monitor the lifestyle of Toyota's targeted potential customer population. What did those potential customers value? Where did they dine? How did they spend their discretionary income? Toyota wanted to build and sell a luxury car in the United States, so it needed to design one that would appeal to its U.S. customers. The engineers' observations led to the creation of the Lexus.

Recognizing the Customer Types

Knowing who your customers (and your potential customers) are prevents you from depleting your precious resources marketing to people who will never buy from you. And the first step in the process of discovering who your customers are is to know what *kinds* of customers are out there in the first place. Doing this couldn't be easier — all you need to do is familiarize yourself with these customer types:

- ✓ **Non-customers** will never (or rarely) ever buy from you, regardless how great the merchandise (or the deal on it) may be. For example, if you sell maternity clothes, don't market to men and women over 50.

- ✓ **Prospective customers** *could* buy from you. They haven't yet, but they may do so in the future.

- ✓ **Near-customers** have come into your store at least once and may even be on your mailing list. Whether they bought something or not, you just don't have much information about them.

- ✓ **Customers** have purchased something from you, and they return to your store regularly (at least, that's your goal).

Rick's Random Rule #213: The more you know about your *potential* customers, the easier it is to make them your *customers*.

Identifying Your Ideal Customer

To attract the customers that will help your business succeed, you need to know everything about them: age, place of residence, clothing style, car preference, family situation, hobbies, and so on (and understand that you can have more than one type of ideal customer). You can then make sure that your vision for your business matches your vision of your ideal customer. In this section, I present a couple of tools that can help you identify what kind of people you want your business to cater to.

"Sensing" your customer

A creative interpretation of your five senses — sight, sound, touch, smell, and taste — can provide an easy means of identifying your ideal customer. These tools of identification are the easiest to use and the easiest to remember. The key to using this tool to identify your customer is that all your sensory responses should be in alignment giving you a consistent message.

Looking 'em over

When you picture customers coming through the front door of your store, what do you see? Use your sense of sight (real or imagined) to help you envision your ideal customer.

- ✔ **Personal appearance.** What do your ideal customers look like? Do their jeans sag to their knees, or do they wear neatly pressed suits? Do they have strands of pearls around their necks, or do they sport nose rings?

- ✔ **Personal possessions.** What kind of things do your ideal customers own? Do they drive a luxury car, or do they get around in a broken-down jalopy? Do they struggle under the weight of a worn backpack, or do they carry an executive briefcase?

Getting an earful

Use your sense of sound to help you imagine your ideal customer. You can consider this sense in the following two ways:

- ✔ **Speech.** What do your ideal customers sound like when they speak? Do their voices seem refined, or do they sound uneducated?

- ✔ **Music.** What kind of music do your ideal customers listen to? Do they buy Nine Inch Nails CDs, or do they love their old Barry Manilow records?

Touching on it

People often remark that something "just feels right." As a retailer, you want to attract the customer that feels right to you — and you want your store to feel right to that customer. Also, keep in mind the feel of anything (fabric, metal, glass, china, and so on) that your ideal customers could be associated with.

Sniffing around

Because we associate particular smells with certain types of customers, you need to know what you want your ideal customers to smell like — and what smells you want your ideal customers to like.

- ✔ **Customer scent.** What fragrance emanates from your ideal customers? Are they "ripe" from hard physical labor, or have they just sprayed themselves with expensive perfume?

- ✔ **Store aroma.** What will your ideal customers think of the way your store smells? Will they be attracted to it? Think of a bakery or of a leather goods store — their smell is part of their ambiance.

Making it palatable

For the purposes of this discussion, taste refers to the preferences of your ideal customers — and you want to attract customers with distinct tastes. (I know that "taste" used in this way isn't really one of the senses, but let me stretch here a little). What kind of merchandise, service, setting, location, selection, price, and ambience do your ideal customers prefer? Do your customers' tastes match *your* tastes? If so, you can be sure that you've identified your ideal customers.

"Filtering" your customer

The 8-Point Retail Filter (which I introduce in Chapter 1) is another tool that you can use to identify your ideal customer. Push your ideas of your customer through the 8-Point Retail Filter as follows:

- ✔ **Product.** What type of customer is likely to buy the merchandise that you plan to sell? Is there another store in the area that carries similar products? If so, what type of customer does that store attract?

- ✔ **Presentation.** What type of customer would feel comfortable in your store's atmosphere — be it trendy boutique or bargain warehouse?

- ✔ **Procedure.** What kind of customer would be drawn to your store's procedures you plan to implement — be they time-saving or customer-pampering?

- ✔ **Pricing.** What kind of customers would be attracted by the prices that you plan to set for your merchandise?

- ✔ **Promotion.** What type of customer would respond to the advertising that you're planning — be it price-slashing or image-boosting?

- ✔ **People.** What type of customer is likely to relate to your personnel, who share your business vision?

✏ **Profitability.** What type of customer will enable you to afford the cost of implementing your business plans — whether they include unique displays or extra business hours?

✏ **Brand.** What type of customer is likely to be attracted to your brand — whether it focuses on value or status?

Take a minute to write down a few words that describe what this customer is like. I'm not saying that you can't change your mind at this point — but if you do change you mind, be sure to do so consciously. Different types of customers can sometimes look equally appealing, so unless you're sure of what customer you want to attract, you could be fooled. Once you've determined what kind of customer you want to serve, never waver — doing so will weaken your brand!

Know thy customer, save thy business

A few years ago, a downtown organization asked me to give a workshop on how to run a sale. Part of my responsibility was to personally invite local business owners to participate.

I decided to stop by a hobby shop that had one of the worst locations in town. The store's wooden floor was old and creaky, and although its walls were plain, they were loaded with merchandise. The store was crammed with customers who were buying the most expensive stuff — model airplanes. The store's owner took pride in telling me that his hobby shop, which stocked all kinds of miniature engines for the planes, also carried more than 1,000 different types of airplane tires. Talk about finding a niche!

I invited him to the upcoming workshop, but he surprised me with a few questions of his own. "If I run a sale," he said, "will I have to mark down some merchandise?" "Yes," I replied. "The plan is to attract a lot more people, so I'll probably have to put on more help, won't I?" he asked. I nodded. "With more people coming into my store," he persisted, "I'll probably have a lot more shoplifters, so I should have some extra help to watch for that, shouldn't I?" I responded, "Possibly." "Why would I ever want to do that?" he exclaimed.

I answered that he probably had some slow sellers that he'd like to get out of the store.

With a dead serious expression, this shop owner replied, "Why would anyone want to reduce prices, increase shoplifting, *and* pay for more help? I'd rather just tell my customers when they come in that I have some things that I want to move, and that I'm willing to give them a discount on the stuff. I'll save a lot of money, and my customers will appreciate the discount. I'm going to pass on your workshop."

He was right. He knew his customers, and he knew that a sale wasn't going to bring them in — his customers were not motivated to buy by price alone. He knew his customers so well that his buying was precise; thus, he didn't have a lot of excess merchandise to dump. As he told me, "My *inventory* is my advertising. Customers are drawn by my selection of hard-to-find model airplane parts. My markups are reasonable, and customers come from all over to do business with me."

If a high-powered retailer were to take over this store without taking the time to understand its established customer base (and their reasons for shopping at the store), the new owner would very likely clean up the store — and ruin the business. Knowing your customer is paramount to the success of your store.

Figuring Out What Motivates Your Customers to Buy

Individual customers are motivated differently. For example, if I were to ask you to name today's top ten retail stores, you and I can both be sure that not many of them would be discount stores. It's not that you shouldn't be price-conscious — you just need to make sure that low prices are not the only reason people buy from you. If that were the case, you'd be vulnerable to every new competitor whose prices are lower than yours.

Rick's Random Rule # 22: The more you know about your customers, the easier it is to sell to them.

There's a retail spin you can put on the Golden Rule: rather than treating everyone the way that *you* want to be treated, you should treat everyone the way that *they* want to be treated. Most people want it their way (Burger King built a business around that philosophy) — and you better know what their way is! In this section, I help you to further define your customers by showing you what motivates different customers to buy.

Ten ways to lose a customer

One way to determine what motivates customers to do business with you is to look at a few reasons why retailers lose customers. The following list presents the top ten reasons customers give for not wanting to return to a store. The interesting thing about this list is that price is not even on it.

1. The store personnel (or even the owner) were on the telephone when I needed assistance.

2. The store was inconvenient in a number of ways.

3. The store (and/or the staff) was dirty or smelly.

4. The store just didn't have what I wanted.

5. The sales clerks had no product knowledge.

6. I had to wait in a long line.

7. The store didn't have the advertised merchandise in stock.

8. I was ignored by the sales clerks.

9. The sales clerks were pushy.

10. When I was ready to check out, there was no one at the cash register.

Other reasons that people might not return to your store include the following: inconvenient store hours, insufficient parking, an ungenerous return policy, difficulty finding things, no signs to direct you or to tell you what a product does, too far away, cluttered, not enough merchandise, and no prices on the merchandise.

Price is not the only factor that can turn people off. Yet more than 70 percent of the retailers I have consulted believed that the only reason that a customer would shop at their store is because of their low prices. Don't fall into the same trap!

Selling to the eight buyer types

So why should someone buy from you? In 20 years of analyzing what motivates a customer to come into a store (and eventually buy something), I've identified eight types of buyers. If you know where your ideal customers fit in, you'll know how to motivate them to buy something from your store.

How low can you go?

Although no one ever wants to overpay, a *price buyer* is almost obsessed with finding the low prices. A price buyer will drive two miles out of his way to buy gasoline because it's two cents cheaper there. Or she'll stop at three or four different supermarkets to get the lowest price on milk.

You can motivate price buyers by

- ✔ Designating a markdown section in your store. Add new merchandise regularly and make additional markdowns on a weekly basis. Your price buyer will become loyal to this section of your store — providing that it has the lowest prices, of course.

- ✔ Offering weekly (or even monthly) promotional items.

- ✔ Advertising your sales directly to them. Make sure that they're on your mailing list and categorized as price buyers. They'll always come to your sales — you can even have sales just for them.

You can't build a business with price buyers as your primary customers. They will never be loyal to you or to your store: They are only loyal to the lowest price. Try to be known for more than just price (even if you're a discount store).

Do you have the coolest merchandise?

Doing business with *WOW! buyers* is fun. They're interested in the latest and hottest items — the brand-new gadgets that everyone else says "WOW!" to. These type of buyers love to shop smaller stores because that is where they are most likely to uncover a treasure that no one else has even seen. Although WOW! buyers don't exactly want you to take advantage of their eagerness by charging them an arm and a leg, they are willing to pay a premium for the excitement of being the first to have a certain item.

You can motivate WOW! buyers by

- ✔ Featuring your newest merchandise in both your displays and your advertising.

- ✔ Building a reputation (and a brand) as the place to go for the unusual.

✔ Making sure that you start selling something new before the now-hot merchandise is carried by all the other stores. When everybody has the item, it loses the WOW! factor.

Can I depend on you?

Trust buyers rank security as one of the most important factors in shopping at a business or buying a product. This sense of trust creates loyalty. Trust buyers want to do business where they feel secure. They gravitate toward the businesses that advertise that they have been in business a long time, or that have "three generations of the same family to serve you." Trust buyers tend to favor brand names because they represent dependability, reliability, and familiarity.

You must work hard to develop the name of your business for trust buyers. The advertising slogan, "The quality goes in before the name goes on," especially appeals to trust buyers.

You can motivate trust buyers by

✔ Locating your store in a good neighborhood. Make sure that you have adequate lighting in your store and in your parking lot so that your customers feel safe.

✔ Implementing a generous refund policy. Trust buyers want to know that you stand behind what you sell.

Note: If you have a Web site, and you want trust buyers to purchase from you over the Internet, make sure that your site is secure. If it isn't, trust buyers may reject your business altogether.

Can you save me a hassle?

If you can save *convenience buyers* a little time, you can own them. The bigger your selection of merchandise, the more attractive your business is to them. Selection is a timesaver — convenience buyers don't want to travel to a whole bunch of stores to gather the items they need.

When you own a niche or a category, you have *category dominance*. For example, my store's specialty was mother-of-the-bride dresses. Within that narrow niche, I carried a broad assortment of manufacturers and styles. If you needed a dress for your daughter's wedding, I was the retailer with the most merchandise. (Customers would often tell me, "I sure am glad that I came here first. You saved me so much time!" And when they told others about my store, they probably said, "Don't waste your time going anywhere else!") Every Saturday, three dressmakers performed on-the-spot alterations. If you bought a dress for an event that night, we could alter it immediately. The service was not free, but rarely did anyone complain about the price. My customers were willing to pay for the convenience.

You can motivate convenience buyers by

✔ Placing merchandise that goes together in the same area. For example, if you're selling circular saws, have the replacement blades close by.

✔ Having adequate and clear signage. Make it easy for your customers to maneuver around your store: If customers can't find what they're looking for, your store's not convenient.

✔ Establishing your store in a convenient location (This alone is not enough, though — plenty of stores that are in convenient locations are otherwise inconvenient).

✔ Developing your store policies and procedures with customer convenience in mind.

Will you give me the royal treatment?

Status buyers want you to make them feel important. Think of all of the people who have gold credit cards — the "gold" makes them feel important. Many of these people even register for platinum cards — despite a ridiculous annual fee — just for the status.

I admit that I sometimes succumb to the lure of status. I fly almost exclusively on Delta Airlines — and will even pay a little extra to fly with them — because they reward me with frequent flyer points, give me a separate line to check in, grant me advance boarding, and bump me up to first class if any seats are available. (By the way, in first class, the flight attendants call you by name.) Delta makes me feel important.

You can motivate status buyers by

✔ Addressing them by name. It doesn't matter how big your business is or how many customers you have, greet your customers personally as they enter your store and use their name as often as natural when conversing with them.

✔ Establishing a preferred customer list. Offer your preferred customers special, exclusive services.

✔ Developing a special relationship with them so that you can tailor your recommendations and services to them personally. (Actually, you should try to do this with every customer.)

Do you know more than anyone else?

Expert buyers want to do business with people who are the authorities in what they sell. Whether they need a watchmaker, glassblower, or furrier, they want to do business with stores that specialize in a specific area. When OJ Simpson was shopping for an attorney, do you think he was concerned about price, WOW! factor, convenience, or status? No way! He wanted an expert — and he was willing to pay extra for it. To attract expert buyers to your business, you must establish your store as the expert in your chosen retail niche.

Preferred customers can really pay off

I once worked with a jewelry store owner who decided to offer a private sale on a certain jewelry designer's line. In anticipation of the event, he purchased what looked like the most expensive invitations money could buy — they cost him $10 apiece. But he chose to send them out only to his best 78 customers. His cost per customer was exorbitant, but the return on his investment blew away any other mailing he had ever done: 47 of his best customers came into the store during the two-day event, and the majority of them bought something. He did more business with that upscale invitation than he had on his last three promotions — for which he'd sent out 6,000 postcards, one for each person on his mailing list. He knew what motivated his best customers, and the specialized advertising paid off.

Note: Don't confuse the expert buyer with the trust buyer. For example, I trust a local jewelry store to take care of my family's repairs, but when it comes to buying a new diamond for my wife's birthday, I want to go to a diamond expert.

You can motivate expert buyers by

- ✔ Doing what you do better than anyone else. Focus on one aspect of your business, study it for an extended period of time — and then specialize in it.

- ✔ Shopping at every manufacturer in your retail category and at every related retail store (at least as many as possible) to know what's going on in your industry.

- ✔ Establishing yourself as a source of information. Submit articles on what is new and happening in your corner of the retail market to local newspapers, magazines, and radio stations. After a while, reporters will probably start contacting you for this information, and you'll become the recognized expert. (For more on spreading your word in the media, see Chapter 15.)

Do you want to help others?

Caring buyers want to patronize socially responsible businesses. They're concerned about how you treat your employees, what you think about the environment, and how involved you are in your community. A recent *Forbes* magazine survey found that 66 percent of Americans consider a company's attitude or involvement in socially responsible issues when making a buying decision.

You can motivate caring buyers by

✔ Becoming a member of a professional association within your industry.

✔ Establishing a program that "gives back" to your community. Some retail associations give out an award for retailers that excel in the area of community service.

✔ Sponsoring a selected charity. For example, Denny's supports the Save the Children Foundation; McDonald's has its own Ronald McDonald houses. Supporting a cause shows that you care.

✔ Demonstrating that you care about your business's image, customer relations, and overall excellence by being selective in your choice of employees.

Caring (or cause) marketing can be a powerful tool. If you get involved with a cause (make sure it's not a political one) or a charity, do it for the right reasons. Customers will know whether you're just trying to manipulate them — and that will eventually hurt your business.

Can you show me a good time?

Entertainment buyers, the newest and fastest growing category of buyers, want to be entertained when they go shopping. In this day and age, when people spend entire days looking at computer screens, they view shopping as a social experience. Creating a fun shopping experience for your customers can separate you from the rest of the retail pack. You can motivate entertainment buyers by giving your store a fun, lively atmosphere.

Rick's Random Rule #894: There's no business that's not show business!

Staying in tune with your customers

If you remember one thing from this chapter, remember that if you don't know why certain customers should buy from you, those customers won't know either. If you don't sell what your customers want, your store won't even have a chance. But if you know who your customers are, you can be flexible to their changing moods, needs, and wishes — and form an established customer base that will set your business on the road to success.

Part II
Settin' Up Shop

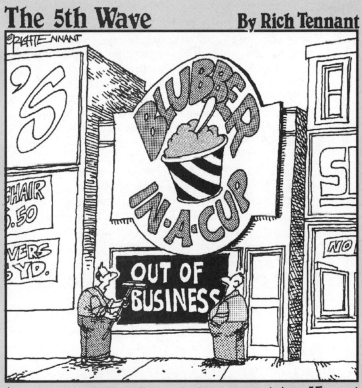

The 5th Wave   By Rich Tennant

"It's hard to figure. The concept was a big hit in Nome."

In this part . . .

This is where the fun really begins because this part covers some of the initial concrete steps you need to take to set up your store. It covers finding sources to get your merchandise from, and offers tips on how to do business with various types of vendors. This part also includes information on selecting the right location for your store and designing what your store will look like. It's just like deciding where you want to live and how you're going to decorate your new home.

Along with the joys of finding merchandise, choosing a location, and creating your store design come the rules that start to take the guesswork out of these processes. This part covers many of the do's and don'ts of working with vendors, negotiating leases, and designing your store in a way that compels customers to buy.

Chapter 5

Choosing Your Merchandise: What to Buy and Where to Find It

. . . .

In This Chapter

▶ Determining the right merchandise for your store

▶ Figuring out where to get it

. . . .

How do you determine the type, quality, and price level of the merchandise that you buy for your store? You could consult market research studies, surveys, and consultant's findings and observations, but what you really need to consider is *"What do you like?"* Do you like expensive, moderate, or lower-priced merchandise? Are you conservative or a little offbeat? Do you want to carry what is hot — the latest fad, — or do you like more traditional things? Do you want to be a high-volume business, or do you want to have a small store so that you can spend time caring for every customer?

Your job will be easier if you sell merchandise that you really believe in and that matches your style and personality type. However, you also have to think about what kinds of items your customers will like. Retailers often face a dilemma: You go into business because you want to carry a certain type of merchandise; you like it and you want to carry it, but what happens if your customers don't like it? Your have a few choices:

  ✔ You can wait for new customers.

  ✔ You can try to reeducate your customers — convince them to like the merchandise.

  ✔ You can abandon the merchandise you like and sell what your customers like.

  ✔ You can provide a combination of merchandise.

You not only have to decide what merchandise to carry, but you also need to know where to find it, whom to buy it from, and how to make the deals — without getting snookered! The information in this chapter is designed to help you do all of these things like a pro.

Before you can choose the type, price, and quality level of the merchandise for your store, you have to be absolutely certain about who you are — what kind of store you want yours to be. See Chapter 3 if you're not clear on this.

Rick's Random Rule #87: If there is no passion in the plan, then there is no power to produce. And without power and passion, there will rarely be any profits.

Doing Your Homework

In preparing this chapter, I interviewed store owners, salespeople, manufacturers, and distributors for their opinions about how a retailer should determine the right merchandise for a store. The one line I kept on hearing over and over again was "Retailers have to do their homework." It sounded like good advice, so I asked them what they meant by that. Their response was almost unanimous again: "Shop!" One retail veteran said, "The biggest mistake a retailer makes today is not shopping other stores and manufacturers. Shopping is to the retailer what research is to the lawyer. How is the retailer going to know what he likes until he sees what is around?"

Shopping helps you form opinions. If you see something you like but it is carried only in discount or off-price stores and you want to open a better-priced, high-service store, you better think twice — avoid the cheap stuff. The opposite is true as well. You don't want to put high-end merchandise that requires delicate treatment in a self-service, off-price store.

Be sure to shop as many manufacturers and resources as possible. New retailers often tell me that they have a friend who knows someone who can get them all the merchandise they need. That scares me because, especially at the beginning, you need to know who is selling what and who is right for you. Not every manufacturer or even distributor is right for everybody. So how do you know what merchandise is right for you? Ask yourself the following questions before buying anything.

- ✔ What other stores in your area carry what you want to carry?

- ✔ How successful are those stores? Are they growing and are they expanding?

- ✔ What store would you most like to be? Who would you model?

- ✔ What kind of merchandise do they carry? What are the names of the lines?

- ✔ Where are those stores located? Are they in downtowns or malls, or are they freestanding stores? Are the areas similar to yours?

> ✔ What is their business model? How do they do business? Do they discount?
>
> ✔ What type of socioeconomic areas are these stores in? Are the residents sophisticated and well educated or less educated?
>
> ✔ What is the demographic and lifestyle information of people in your area? Are they "earthy crunchy" or slick and hip? Modern or traditional?
>
> ✔ Are their customers similar to the customers in your area?

If you're wondering why I'm talking about everything *but* merchandise — location, customer types, and retail models — the reason is as basic as business itself, and it's all interwoven. To be a successful retailer, you have to identify a customer or market need and then carry the merchandise that fills the need. For tips on gathering demographic data and researching other businesses in your location, see Chapter 6.

Finding the Merchandise

You've done your homework. You've shopped around, and you have a pretty good idea of the type of merchandise you want to carry in your store. Now you need to know where to go to buy the merchandise — who you should buy it from. This section introduces some key terms used to refer to the people who are involved in selling merchandise to retailers. It also tells you where to find them and how to do business with them. This section covers different industries, and some terms may be more common in some industries than others.

Buying from manufacturers

The manufacturer is the company that produces the product for sale. Notice that I said producing rather than making. Many manufacturers arrange for subcontractors, who are often in foreign countries, to make the merchandise they sell.

If you hear the term "a complete vertical operation," that means the manufacturer doesn't subcontract anything and is in complete control of the manufacturing process. Vertical operations are very rare today because this is the age of specialists.

If you know the name of a manufacturer you want to do business with, search the Web for the company's site. The site probably can give you all the contact information you need. You can send an e-mail or call customer service and ask for the best place to buy the company's products and find out the requirements for opening an account. If customer service can't answer that question, the representative will usually refer you to the proper party. Manufacturers are always looking for new business, but they may have minimum buying requirements or may already have too many accounts in an area. They'll let you know if you qualify. The following list describes some settings where you can do business with manufacturers:

- ✔ **In the manufacturer's showroom:** Most manufacturers have permanent showrooms somewhere — near their facility or more likely in the larger market places such as New York, Los Angeles, Dallas, or Atlanta.

- ✔ **In your store:** Salespeople will come to your store and show you their line. Some salespeople like doing business this way, while others prefer to see store owners at trade shows.

- ✔ **At a trade show:** Every industry has a trade show where salespeople display their samples at booths and take orders for shipping. Some are regional shows, while others are national. To find out about shows in your industry, contact the National Retail Federation (www.nrf.org). The site provides links to every industry where you can find lists of trade show times and places. You can also visit www.about.com for great retail information. Just enter the search term "retail."

- ✔ **Web sites:** The trend is on to shift more buying over to the Web. I recommend this form of buying only after you have developed a relationship with the company and you know what you're buying. First establish a relationship and review the merchandise in person, then buy as much as you want via the Web, the phone, a catalog, and so on.

Manufacturers sell their merchandise through different channels with different names. In the following sections, I introduce some of the more common ones.

Direct salespeople

These people work exclusively for the manufacturer. They can work on commission, but many larger manufacturers put their direct salespeople on salary with a bonus, company car, and benefits. The way these salespeople get paid sometimes affects their motivation when you negotiate and deal with them. These salespeople focus on selling their manufacturer, and their company's policies often limit their ability to negotiate.

Manufacturer's representatives

These independent contractors work for one or more manufacturers strictly on commission. The range in commissions paid is from 4 percent to as much as 20 percent. The more popular the line, generally the smaller the commission. If the manufacturer is new and the representatives — "reps" for short —

are well established, they're usually paid at the top end of this scale. The major advantage to doing business with a manufacturer's rep over a direct salesperson is that you can buy six or seven lines from one representative and become an important account.

The reps can also have more flexibility in policy because they can say to the manufacturer, "This is a good account of mine, and she wants to return something." The manufacturer may not accept the return from you, because you may not be that important to the manufacturer, but the rep probably is and has the authority to accept the return.

I've never discovered a resource that lists only independent representatives. The closest thing to such a listing is a trade show directory that includes an alphabetical list of the salespeople or reps with all of the lines they represent. Many trade shows are starting to put this information on their Web sites, but doing so is not universally standard practice yet. The following list presents tips for buying from reps in a variety of locations.

- **In your store:** If a manufacturer's rep represents multiple lines, he is more apt to visit your store than a direct salesperson would be. However, depending on the amount of lines that the reps carry and the industry that they're in, you may be buying from pictures or catalogs.

- **In permanent showrooms:** This is a mixed bag. Not all reps have permanent showrooms. Many of them work out of their homes. The location of their office depends on how big their business is. Sometimes you can meet them at the manufacturer's showroom. If the rep has a showroom, it is usually located at a trade center in regional capitals.

- **At trade shows:** This is where most reps do the largest part of their business. If possible, try to make an appointment during the show. However, if you're new to the business, doing so can be difficult.

- **Over the Internet:** This alternative, as of this writing, is less developed on the rep level.

The sub-rep

This salesperson works for a manufacturer's representative. You can find sub-reps in the same locations as the direct representative, and doing business with them follows the same rules as with the direct rep. The sub-rep's role is usually just to make sure that sales calls are made to the stores.

The repping firm

The business of some manufacturer's reps grows so large that they form their own companies and have large staffs of employees. These firms always have permanent showrooms and offices, generally at the trade center.

Working with distributors

Distributors are companies that purchase merchandise from the manufacturers for the sole purpose of reselling it to smaller businesses. They buy from many different manufacturers and then consolidate the shipping so that the stores the distributors sell to get only one delivery rather than many deliveries from a variety of manufacturers.

In most cases, you won't pay more to get merchandise from a distributor than from a manufacturer because distributors are so big that they can work on very favorable terms with the manufacturer — they buy in huge quantities. Doing business with distributors is great because it's like one-stop shopping. Relationships with distributors are generally consistent and long term.

In general, distributors aren't listed in the Yellow Pages. You discover them when you contact manufacturers and they tell you that you're too small to do business directly with them. The manufacturers will refer you to a distributor. Their offices are in industrial parks or commercial areas. They warehouse merchandise they get from manufacturers, so they need a lot of space.

Often a manufacturer does business with many distributors, and the person who refers you may have a favorite. Ask what other distributors the manufacturer uses and talk to as many distributors as possible. Remember that you're making a long-term commitment so you want to make sure that you'll be happy with the distributor for the long haul.

The best source to find distributors is by networking with other retailers. Ask them whether they use a distributor, who else they talked to before choosing that distributor, and who they recommend for a business like yours. You may even make a friend.

Finding out about importers

Importers buy and sell foreign-made merchandise. Although they don't actually produce the merchandise, they function almost the same way a manufacturer does. The rules for buying from importers are the same as buying from manufacturers. Directories of importers are available, but don't waste your time. Many of these importers look for businesses that can purchase in large quantities, something that a new business may not be able to do. Instead, look for imported merchandise to buy through normal channels, such as distributors or jobbers. You can even ask the importer to recommend one.

Introducing jobbers

These companies are similar to distributors in many ways, and some people confuse the two. The main difference is that a jobber company can also sell some of the goods directly to consumers. Unlike a relationship you would develop with a distributor, you have no long-term commitment to jobbers. You can buy from them once a week or once a year. Generally, jobbers have contacts with a few key manufacturers where they are able to get favorable prices. Here are two factors to consider when you do business with jobbers:

- **Price:** If the jobber gets a good deal from the manufacturer, you could pay less than the actual manufacturer is selling it for. If the jobber doesn't get a good deal, you may pay more. To know whether you're getting a good price from a jobber, you have to know the manufacturer's price.

- **Merchandise:** Sometimes you may not get the best merchandise from the manufacturer's line. The jobber may be trying to sell merchandise that didn't sell as well as the manufacturer expected. The jobber may have gotten a great deal from the manufacturer (for taking the duds off their hands) and is passing the unpopular merchandise on to you at a reduced price.

One big advantage to working with jobbers is that they have all the merchandise in stock, so you can have immediate delivery. Jobbers do most of their business on a cash-and-carry basis — something most manufacturers never do. Some jobbers have salespeople on the road, but generally you must go to their facilities to buy the merchandise.

Jobbers traditionally have locations near, but rarely in, trade marts. When looking for a jobber, understand that many refer to themselves as *wholesalers* and not jobbers. In some markets and industries, you can find a listing of wholesalers, but that is more of the exception than the rule. They do not have any strong association, and competition is fierce among wholesalers, so rarely will one refer you to another.

You can find good jobbers by asking salespeople or other retailers about jobbers they know, use, or recommend. Also, check out www.retailindustry. about.com on the Web for listings. But the best way to find good jobbers is to talk to the other buyers or store representatives when you visit a jobber. Ask them for recommendations and find out what other jobbers they use. One day I was at a jobber's and had a cup of coffee with a buyer from a store in Texas who referred me to three jobbers I never knew existed. Those three resources, who specialized in buying off-price merchandise, became the main source for my promotional and sale merchandise. Network — it works!

Participating in buying groups

Buying groups are associations of retailers who have joined together to buy as a unit to get better deals from manufacturers. "United we stand" might be a good battle cry for buying groups because individually they don't have much clout with the manufacturers, but combined they're a powerful force. If you ever have an opportunity to join a buying group, I strongly recommend doing so. You pay dues to belong, but the savings are tremendous. Many of these groups offer educational seminars, and they exchange advertising ideas as well.

Watch for ads in trade journals for these groups, but the vast majority increase their membership via referrals from other members or manufacturers. These associations are generally located in office settings, rather than retail environments.

Introducing buying services

These services function in a similar way to a buying group, but they vary in that the buying office is not owned by the members but rather is owned by a company that has to make a profit to survive. You pay a monthly fee to belong to a buying service. In return, they inform you about hot merchandise and industry trends — vital information when you're new to the business. Buying services can also negotiate additional discounts for their members and they offer additional credibility in the marketplace.

One word of caution: many times the manufacturers that buying services recommend are the companies that support the office financially as well. Manufacturers pay the buying office a fee to sell their merchandise to the stores. They also pay the service to feature the manufacturer's merchandise in a circular or catalog. These are legitimate charges, but you have to be aware of how buying services make money.

Sometimes a buying service won't recommend a manufacturer if that manufacturer doesn't support the service (pay for their attention), even though the manufacturer may be great. Having said all of that, I still recommend joining a buying service or at least talking to one or two before you rule them out. Their buyers know the market, and the service is a great source of information — who's making what and for what price, and who can deliver the merchandise on time.

Because salespeople and trade associations know a lot about buying services, they're a terrific source of good referrals. Some industries have directories of these services, but going through all the listings can be a real waste of time. All you need is one referral because when you interview the service, you ask for references of satisfied clients. Ask these satisfied clients what other buying services they have interviewed or used and why they selected the service they did.

Sometimes a buying service may be too big or too small for your needs and will recommend other services. You have to be a good fit. Watch for ads in trade journals for openings of new services. Many times a strong buyer going off on her own is the one opening the service. Such a person needs clients and can offer you great service. She may be new in the buying service business but very experienced as a buyer.

Considering consignment merchandise

Manufacturers in some industries offer consignment merchandise. This is merchandise that you don't really own until you sell it, which means that you don't have to pay for it until it is sold. Also, if it's not selling, you can return it to the manufacturer. There are two problems with this kind of arrangement:

- ✔ You can have merchandise in your store that you would never buy in a million years, but because it's on consignment, you leave it there. Offering merchandise that doesn't reflect you or your customer can hurt your business. Now it sits there forever.

- ✔ You still have to pay for the goods when they're sold. Consignment does allow you to fill up the store without having to pay for the merchandise up front. If you're working with a tight cash flow, consignment can work, but don't lower your standards just to get free inventory.

The consignment arrangement seems to work best in the craft, gift, and fur industries. Craft and gift businesses work well on a consignment basis because many artisans do wonderful work but don't do the volume of business that warrants working with salespeople or reps. Furriers are also used to working on consignment. Their prices are so expensive, and maintaining an inventory can tie up too much money.

The best and most common way to find consignment people in the craft, art, and gift areas is to shop the major craft fairs. You can see their merchandise firsthand and discuss how a consignment agreement might work. As for furriers or any one selling very high-ticket items, ask whether they do consignment. Some will.

Never allow the craftsperson or artist to tell you how to price the merchandise. A retailer has the right to sell merchandise at any price he chooses. Suggested retail pricing, or telling you what to sell something at, isn't allowed by manufacturers, and a crafter is a small manufacturer. Just find out what the artisan wants for the item when it is sold. You determine your selling price. You — not the artisan — are the retailer. Some crafters want you to work on 20 or 25 percent commission, but that's not enough of a markup to survive today.

Chapter 6

Location, Location, Location: Finding the Right Place to Do Business

In This Chapter

▶ Looking at your location options

▶ Considering all the issues when choosing your location

▶ Working out an agreement with your landlord

▶ Understanding the finer points of leases

*T*his chapter is about finding the right location for your business. However, I could call this chapter the matchmaking chapter. It's about finding the right match for you and your business — the location that will enable you to do the maximum amount of profitable business in the way you want to do it. You need to find the location where you fit in the best — a place where your customers can find you, your customers appreciate what you do, your neighbors are pleased to share the location with you, both you and your landlord can make money (the proverbial win-win scenario), and you and your employees want to work.

Exploring Your Location Options

Different types of businesses do well in different types of locations. In some cases, a business can do more business in one location but make more money in another. Beauty salons are a good example. They do well in mall locations, but renting a mall location is expensive. When stylists have their own established clientele, they don't need the extra traffic that a mall brings, so they probably don't need to pay a premium for a mall location.

You have lots of location types to choose from. As you consider where to settle, keep the following two factors in mind:

> ✔ **The distance between your business and your customers' residences or workplaces:** Determine how far your customers are likely to travel to reach your kind of business. Most people want a dry cleaning shop to be close but are willing to drive a bit to get to a jeweler, for example.

> ✔ **The degree of independence you want for your business operations:** Your freedom to set your own store hours, to close one day a week if you want to, or even to decorate as you please depends on the location you choose.

Retail locations generally can be divided into two categories: street locations, where merchants can operate with relative independence; and planned shopping centers, where merchants must adhere to the rules established by the center's management or association.

Rick's Random Rule #37: Everybody has to pay to get business. Either you pay a landlord a lot of money for a high-traffic location, or you pay a smaller amount on rent and spend more on marketing and advertising to bring customers to your store.

Downtown Main Street locations

Downtown shopping is on its way back, and a location right on Main Street may be the perfect place for your new business. If you set up shop on Main Street, you determine the time your store opens and closes — a freedom you don't get if you locate in a mall or controlled shopping area, where you have a contractual obligation to be open the hours that management instructs you to be open.

Most downtowns offer great opportunity for new and old retailers alike. This is due partly to the efforts of the local economic development councils and the National Main Street Center of the National Trust for Historic Preservation in Washington, D.C. These organizations offer such benefits as money for signs, low-interest loans, and educational programs that are funded with state or federal funds earmarked to help rebuild downtowns.

Downtown businesses are usually owner-occupied specialty stores that fall into two basic categories:

> ✔ **Convenience-oriented businesses:** These include drugstores, print shops, coffee shops, quick-food restaurants, and beauty salons. They generally provide services for the people who work or live in the downtown area.

> ✔ **Highly specialized niche businesses:** These include high-end apparel stores that provide personal service, gift shops, craft stores, computer service stores, jewelry stores, appliance stores, candy stores, and hobby stores. These retailers are generally experts in the products they sell and provide services that customers can't find anyplace else.

The major drawback to a downtown location is parking. Think about this before you sign a lease. Test how far your customers will have to walk to their cars at different times of the day, and see whether parking spaces are available at all during peak times.

Locations off Main Street

In many towns, the strongest businesses are on side streets. Although shops in these locations don't get the natural foot traffic that Main Street stores receive, fewer pedestrians can be a blessing in disguise. Most side street business develop their own established clientele and don't need the extra foot traffic of a Main Street location. And because side street locations generally cost less, businesses can spend more money on advertising and promotion. Often, side street locations have their own parking — a major consideration in locating in or near a downtown area.

The key to retail success on a side street is visibility. If you're thinking about a side street location, consider how much visibility the location offers (would people be able to see your store from Main Street?) as well as how much visibility your business requires.

Neighborhood locations

Neighborhood locations are the closest retail locations to where your customers live and work — they offer the feel of a village community. The "neighborhood" could be a financial district, court district, or medical district. You can also find plenty of neighborhood shopping areas near manufacturing facilities, truck terminals, farm co-ops, and even fishing docks. Because of the convenient location, you can expect shopping at your store to become a part of your customers' regular routines.

If you decide to locate in a neighborhood, take time to learn your customers' names, chat with them, provide excellent service, and always have what they're looking for.

Main Street draws artists

Artisans are among the retailers who are finding homes on Main Street. They are one reason for the rebirth of downtowns. Their businesses include art galleries, glass shops, pottery shops, and consignment art stores that sell everything from oil paintings to handmade one-of-a-kind clothing to quilts to furniture.

Why are these businesses settling on Main Street? Because the rents are affordable. Many downtown landlords purchased their properties at bargain-basement prices because of the deterioration that occurred in the last couple of decades, or they have owned the property for so long that they can make money on reduced rents.

I once worked with a gift shop in a small Iowa town. I was going through the owner's financial statement and didn't see a place for rent, so I asked what she was paying. She misunderstood me and said $4,200. I asked if this was her rent for the year, thinking that it couldn't really have been for a month (although downtown stores *can* pay that in rent). She said, "Oh, no! That's what I bought the building for." This woman was making a fortune downtown, and the value of the property had skyrocketed because the downtown area had been almost empty when she bought the building but had since been revitalized.

You can expect the peak hours of a neighborhood business to be early in the morning. You want to catch people before they go to work. The second busiest time of the day is usually between 11 a.m. and 3 p.m. Although you probably won't be able to meet with friends for lunch, you can close for the day between 4:00 and 6:30 p.m. — a lot earlier than if you were located in a mall.

Roadside locations

Roadside locations are just that — locations alongside the road (but not Main Street) in freestanding buildings. Think Wal-Mart, McDonald's, and huge furniture stores. Stores with roadside locations are true destination stores — their customers have to make a special trip to shop there. Nearly all the big box retailers are set off by themselves, but plenty of smaller independent stores have opted to build in their own locations along a road.

If you choose a roadside location, you have to rely on your own ability to do business. You can set your own hours, and parking probably won't be an issue. Roadside locations work well as long as you are committed to an aggressive marketing and advertising campaign or you've been in business in another location with a loyal customer base.

If you're a new business, make sure that you have enough money to wait it out. To entice customers to travel to your roadside location, you have to change your customers' shopping patterns. You must provide a reason for them to make the trip.

Watch out for *urban sprawl:* the endless lines of roadside locations that tend to blur a town's identity, making every town and city start to look the same. Many municipalities are addressing this issue with new codes and restrictions. Before you sign any agreements, check with the offices of community development or economic development or even the chamber of commerce to see whether any zoning or regulation changes could affect your business.

Strip mall locations

Strip mall locations are very similar to neighborhood locations — they attract convenience- and service-focused businesses. The main difference is that strip malls may be slightly farther away from your customers' homes and workplaces. These malls are generally placed where they can serve a population of approximately 10,000 people living within 10 minutes, or preferably less. They range in size from 3 or 4 stores to as many as 20 to 30 stores. This type of center generally welcomes independents and owner-occupied businesses, many of which do exceptionally well in strip centers.

By moving into a strip mall location — or any planned shopping center, for that matter — you have to give up some of your independence. Locating in a shopping center involves a lease, and with every lease come rules to live by, such as your business hours, the type of store sign you can use, the kinds of window displays you can create, and even the type of sales promotions you can do.

Although the existence of these rules sounds like a negative, the rules are absolutely necessary. They exist so that all the merchants in the center can do more business. At the neighborhood level, the rules aren't too restrictive, but as the size of the strip center increases, developers become more demanding. And justifiably so. Can you imagine having 20 or 30 stores all doing their own thing? The rules are there for everyone's benefit.

Community center locations

Community shopping centers are mid-sized planned shopping centers. They're generally the first choice for everyday shopping. A supermarket is often located at one end, and a major discount store such as Target or T. J. Maxx is at the other end. In between are businesses such as hardware stores, apparel stores, and appliance stores — all the everyday stuff that shoppers need.

Most tenants in these community centers are national or regional chains and franchise groups, but many centers welcome independent retailers. These centers are generally 15 minutes away from a potential buying community of up to 90,000 people. The rules in these centers are very strict, but you wouldn't want to locate your business in a center that wasn't strict. These centers have at least a general manager, a maintenance department, and a security department.

Regional mall locations

These are the big malls that have it all, with 2 to 5 department stores (referred to as *anchor stores*) and more than 100 other retail stores. Most regional shopping areas probably draw customers from up to an hour's drive away, but 25 to 35 minutes is a more reasonable estimate. They're located in areas that have 100,000-plus customers.

Opening an independent storefront in a regional mall is extremely difficult. However, many larger malls like to attract independent merchants, maybe offering only a cart location at first and leaving open the possibility of moving to a smaller store location within the mall if the merchant is successful. Exceptions may be made if you're buying a franchise and the franchise operator helps you through the extensive legal and financial steps.

A store located in a good regional mall (and there aren't many that aren't good) gives up some independence for the sake of the mall. But this isn't a negative at all. A regional mall has a brand that it must maintain. Getting lazy about your standards in a mall can be very costly. You could be in violation of your lease and be asked to leave or forced out, and whatever investment you may have made in the property will be lost. Many stores have tried to fight this, and most have lost.

Locating in one of these centers is expensive, but regional malls deliver customers to your door. They also can supply you with detailed demographic information that tells you who's coming.

Shop till you drop — literally

The largest regional mall in America is the Mall of America in Bloomington, Minnesota, managed by Simon Properties, the premiere shopping center management and development firm in the world. The Mall of America is the largest shopping and entertainment complex in the United States, with 525 stores and more than 12,000 employees. This mall is so large and famous that its entertainment complex and amusement park competes with Disney World for visitors.

The story of Mashpee Commons

Mashpee Commons (in Cape Cod, Massachusetts) started on the path of a traditional strip center — 82,000 square feet with 26 convenience-oriented stores anchored by a 26,000-square-foot food store. However, the developers became intrigued with the concept of creating a traditional neighborhood development shopping area out of the existing space. They could create a viable retail and housing development while making a difference to the community. They sought the services of Andres Duany, international guru in this type of development. If you hear of a project he's involved with, you can be certain that opportunities for independent retailers are about to open up.

Two years ago, a PBS TV special featured Mashpee Commons as one of the four best downtowns in America. Mashpee Commons is more than just a downtown, however, because it's managed and run like a mall. For every national chain that leases, space management officials want four independent retailers.

Manager Melinda Gallant, who has been there for 13 years, explains, "It's not that one type of store is better or worse than another. They are all equally important to the mix and the charm of the center." Officials work hard to ensure that the merchants succeed. Their goal is to build a community that improves the quality of people's lives — customers and merchants alike.

Is it all about making money? No. If it were, the developers probably wouldn't have placed the post office in the middle of the development or taken the time to attract small independent retailers. The money will certainly follow, but in this instant-gratification world, it's nice to see developers with a conscience and a true sense of community service. Future plans at Mashpee Commons include the construction of the crown jewel in the development, a $10 million cultural center that will present concerts and other events, truly making Mashpee Commons the ultimate in multi-use development — a place to live, work, and enjoy life.

Specialty center locations

A specialty center is exactly what its name implies: a center that specializes in something. These centers are different either because of the merchandise they carry, the types of stores they house, or the physical characteristics of the space. They can either be high-end, with exclusive merchandise, or low-end, featuring discount prices.

Neotraditional community shopping center locations

Neotraditional communities are beginning to pop up across the United States. You may have heard about them — they represent a new trend in real estate development. These communities are designed so that residents can live, work, and shop within the limited area of their community.

Currently, there are very few centers like this, but I believe that this type of center will experience significant growth in the coming years. Neotraditional community shopping centers offer the perfect venue for new and independent retailers. They combine the old and the new to create a hybrid shopping area.

Opposed to building traditional strip centers, some innovative developers have opted to create shopping centers that look and feel like the old downtowns of the 1950s. The stores are a mix of interesting and diverse storefronts, all with deliberate architectural features that make them unique. All the stores have second floors that are either apartments or offices.

These neotraditional community shopping areas have movie theaters, grocery stores, and housing all within walking distance of each other. You can walk down the block to the grocery store, across the street to the post office, and around the corner to your office. The entire community is designed with the idea that residents won't need to use a car for everything — a progressive idea in this age of urban sprawl.

Rick's Random Rule #3: Do the right things, and the right things happen.

Matching Your Business with the Right Location

Putting the right store in the wrong location is a killer. A dry cleaner in the middle of a mall won't work because a dry cleaner is a convenience-based store that must offer customers fast in-and-out access. A produce store in a mall won't work either. Do you want to carry around a dozen oranges while you're looking for a dress? You need to understand where you fit in to better understand where you belong. Try to identify your kind of business and its special considerations in the following list:

- **Convenience stores:** These stores offer items that customers buy regularly without a lot of effort. All you do is take the money. They usually sell lower-priced items such as milk, bread, magazines, and newspapers. They need to be hassle free, with quick in-and-out access and parking spaces that turn over quickly.

- **Shopping stores:** The customers of these stores will likely shop other stores as well. Shopping stores sell higher-priced merchandise that customers don't buy regularly, such as suits, better dresses, and furniture. Shopping stores don't need to have a super-convenient location, but most opt for malls or centers with other stores around because their customers are active shoppers.

> ✔ **Specialty stores:** These stores offer merchandise that's so unique, customers will drive out of their way to get it. Although convenience is always beneficial, a specialty store doesn't have to pay top dollar for a convenient location. A gas station has to pay a premium for location or it's out of business. But a specialty store can be a little off the beaten path and not be hurt.

Looking at Locations from Every Angle

You know what kind of store you have or want. You know what types of locations are available to you. So how do you decide where to go? This is a huge decision, but the considerations can be divided into four fundamental types.

Personal considerations

Running a successful retail business can affect your personal life a great deal and, in many cases, can determine your happiness. When considering where to locate your business, keep the following factors in mind:

> ✔ **Distance to home:** How important is proximity to home to you? A close friend of mine bought an existing franchise shoe store. The sales were excellent, he was drawing a great salary, he took home a nice bonus at the end of every year, and he even had great employees. But after five years, he sold it because he was spending three hours a day in the car. He closed at 10 p.m. and didn't get home until 11:45. It was too much.

> ✔ **Lifestyle:** How important is your independence? Are you the type of person who can work with restrictions? In a shopping center location, you give up your independence for the sake of conformity and consistency. You must be open when management says — seven days a week, between 10 and 12 hours a day. You can't work all those hours yourself, but in the beginning, you'll want to work as many as possible because you made a big investment that needs all the nurturing it can get. In another location, you may be able to set your own hours and do things the way you want to do them, but you won't get the benefits that a shopping center location provides.

Business strategy considerations

Several factors affect whether your business will succeed in a certain location. When choosing where to locate your store, consider these factors:

- **Uniqueness:** You want to be the big fish in a small pond. If you're the only store of your type in the area, you'll stand out. If you have to advertise more, you have the potential to become a celebrity and stand out in your community.

- **Customers:** Make sure that the customers you want to attract live or work in the area.

- **Competition:** If established stores in the area sell the same or similar products as you, consider a different location. However, if you're a car dealer, you'd benefit from being on Auto Row, where the multitude of dealerships, although competitors, attracts car-buying customers to the location.

- **Fit:** Be sure that there is a need or want for your type of business in the area.

- **Traffic count:** How many people walk or drive by the location you're considering? How many of those people resemble your ideal customer? You can get all this information from the landlord, the local chamber of commerce, the economic development committee, or private consultants.

- **Visibility:** This is the most undervalued consideration of all. A highly visible location can act as free advertising — priceless.

- **Accessibility:** Make sure that your location is accessible. I once consulted with a pet shop that had a beautiful store in a prominent outdoor shopping center. The store had great visibility, fair rent, and good neighbors, but you had to climb eight stairs to get to the store, and the stairs were steep. Yes, it was handicapped accessible. The ramp design, however, made it seem like you had to walk a city block to get to the store, because the shopping center was built on a hill and this store had the worst slope. When the store eventually moved, it almost doubled its business.

- **Parking:** Have at least five parking spaces for every 1,000 feet of store space. Less than that and you'll have a parking problem.

Rick's Random Rule #74: Traffic counts are great, but be sure that the traffic being counted includes people who could become your customers.

Joan and Ed's Deli: Great business that got even better

Joan and Ed run one of the most successful Jewish delicatessen restaurants and gift shops in New England. For 17 years, they were located in Natick, Massachusetts, in New England's first mall, Shoppers World. They had a very nice business, their customers loved them, and Joan and Ed were happy. Then that dreadful day occurred when all the rumors were confirmed. The landlord had decided to tear down the 40-year-old mall and build two strip centers facing one another. The bottom line for Joan and Ed was that they had to move.

When your choices are limited, you do what you have to do. Across the street was a strip center of approximately 30-plus stores that had been built to catch the overflow traffic from the big Shoppers World. Although the location was close and the center was very viable, it didn't have the prestige that Shoppers World had. But across the street they moved, hoping to bring their customers with them and hoping that everything would work out. They knew they had a good following, but retailers never really know how loyal their customer base is.

The one thing they underestimated was the power of visibility. The new location was right on the main highway, and their store and sign became a beacon that brought people to their business. The deli became a bigger success than they ever expected. As Ed Sanderson told me, "The most important aspect in finding a location is visibility. If they can see you consistently, then it's half the battle. It's like running a big ad every day that doesn't cost you any extra. I know they say location, location, location, but I believe it should be visibility, visibility, visibility." Little did Joan and Ed think that losing their original location would be a blessing.

Compatibility considerations

Having good retail neighbors can make or break your business. When choosing a location for your business, determine whether your potential neighbors are drawing your type of customer. If another retailer can attract customers to your store, those customers are what I call free customers. For example, my store sold dressy dresses, and beside me was a shoe store that sold dressy shoes. I advertised and the shoe store worked off our traffic. That's the type of location you want.

Be sure that the stores that would be around you are businesses that your customers would feel comfortable around. For example, you don't want to locate a gift or dress shop near a tattoo parlor or motorcycle shop. Neither do you want a high-end store near a discount store. Some neighbor issues to consider include the following:

- ✔ **Smells:** Don't underestimate the problems that your next-door neighbor's smells can cause. Obviously, restaurants present the number one problem, but stores that import goods can cause problems, too. I know of a Middle Eastern variety store that opened beside an apparel store. One day, over 1,000 pounds of curry was delivered to the store. Employees in the apparel store were offended by the smell, and the merchandise absorbed the curry odor. The problem was that these two businesses shared the same heating and air conditioning unit. The odor was so strong that it actually put the apparel store out of business.

- ✔ **Noise:** If you're considering a location beside a music store or any store that sells merchandise for younger people, beware of the noise level. I once worked with a shoe store that moved in next to a bakery. Employees loved the bakery aroma, and it didn't harm their merchandise, but whenever the employees started to bake, they played loud rock 'n' roll to get themselves moving. Needless to say, the two businesses had to work to resolve this issue.

Financial considerations

You've probably heard the cliché "Spend what you can afford." But you also have to remember that cheap can be very expensive. Determining what location you can afford is complicated by the fact that you can't base your decision on how much money you have today, but rather on how much money the better or more expensive location will mean to you in the future.

When you make your sales projections and plans, ask yourself, "Will the better location bring enough additional business to justify the additional cost?" You also have to ask yourself, "What will happen to my store if I spend that extra amount on the prime location and I don't do the extra business?" You have to determine the degree of risk you're willing to take. Keep the following financial factors in mind as you consider where to locate your business:

- ✔ **Think long term.** Determine how much money you can afford to invest in your business until the location becomes successful. Balance prudence with risk, but choose a location that will be great for today, tomorrow, and everafter.

- ✔ **Appropriate your funds carefully.** Most businesses that fail generally fail because they misappropriated their capital. Don't spend too much on a location that doesn't justify the cost. You have only so much money to devote to your business, and if you spend it all on a great location and skimp on everything else, your business will probably fail.

You can reduce your financial risk with knowledge and information. What are other similar businesses spending for rent? What are other similar businesses doing in sales? A wonderful source for this kind of information is the book *Dollars & Cents of Shopping Centers,* which is published every year by the Urban Land Institute. You can order this book online at www.uli.org, by calling 800-321-5011, or by writing to ULI — the Urban Land Institute, 1025 Thomas Jefferson Street, NW, Washington, DC 20007.

Applying the 8-Point Retail Filter

As you're considering where to locate your business, look at each potential location through the 8-Point Retail Filter (introduced and explained in Chapter 1).

- ✓ **People:** Are enough of your type of customers and workers near the location?

- ✓ **Price:** Can the customers in the area afford your prices? Will they find your prices too inexpensive?

- ✓ **Promotion:** Does the local newspaper have a wide circulation? How strong is the local cable TV station? How expensive are its advertising rates? How many radio stations are in the location's marketing area? Powerful local media can make an average location great. You don't even need all three to be strong. Only one will do just fine.

- ✓ **Presentation:** Does the location offer windows for display, and does it have sufficient space for effective presentations?

- ✓ **Profitability:** Can you make money there, and how long will it take to do so?

- ✓ **Product:** Can the area support the type of products you want to carry?

- ✓ **Procedures:** How will the location affect the way you do business? Is it close to a bank? Is it in an area that opens later in the morning and stays open later at night?

- ✓ **Brand:** Would anything in the area prevent you from building your brand name in the location? For example, you wouldn't want to open a Smith's Sporting Goods store in an area where a Smith's Gun Shop already exists.

Coming to Terms with Your Landlord

Obviously, the ease with which you can come to an agreement with your landlord greatly depends on the type of landlord you have. The more professional the landlord, the easier it will be. Communication is essential. Coming to terms is a two-way street: Your landlord should provide certain information to you, and you must supply certain information to your landlord.

Obtaining information from your landlord

Think of your landlord (the developer in some cases) as a recruiter. His task is to convince you to locate your business in his space. He should offer you plenty of reasons not to go anywhere else. Here is some of the information you can expect from your landlord:

- A site plan or blueprints of the property and the space available
- A map of the marketing area with circles around the primary and secondary markets (where the customers come from)
- A list of other tenants
- A breakdown of tenants by merchandise categories
- A fact sheet about the center that may include the following information:
  - Facts about the developer
  - A list of other centers they own or manage
  - A general description of the property
  - The mission or vision of the property and the company
  - The history of the property
  - Expansion plans
  - Estimated expenses
- Reasons why your business would succeed at this location
- The names of surrounding cities or towns
- The number of households in those cities or towns and the average income of those households
- Age breakdowns of the people who live within a specified area — 1/2 mile, 1 mile, 5 miles, and so on
- The number of males and females within a specified area

- Population growth
- Trend information
- Any pertinent newspaper or magazine articles
- A referral list (rarely printed but regularly offered)

Some landlords and developers provide more information, but if they offer less, use the lack of information as a major negotiating tactic. If the landlord is telling you that the property is hot, he'd better show you figures that verify that fact. If he can't, let him know that you have to pay for studies to prove it. A landlord has no excuse not to have a nice package to present to a prospective tenant.

Providing the information your landlord expects from you

When you're selling your business to your landlord, your objective is to convince him that he needs you and your business. Just as you want and expect a good-looking package from your landlord, he wants an attractive package from you. Prepare a presentation folder with a copy of your logo on the cover.

Don't spend money to have folders printed; just have a color copy of your logo duplicated on self-stick paper and affix it to the front of the folder. It will look as professional as any preprinted presentation folder and will cost much less.

Include the following information in your folder:

- A complete business plan
- Articles and reports about your industry
- Space requirements and your plans for the space
- Pictures of merchandise
- Pictures of stores like yours
- Pictures of the principal (or owner; that's you!)
- Financial statements
- Funding commitments
- Anything else that will enhance your professional image

Many landlords of smaller properties only want to know what kind of business you want to open and whether you can afford the rent. That's okay, but make the folder anyway because doing so will put you in a much stronger negotiating position later. Represent the quality tenant.

Avoiding Potential Problems

Renting a location (or leasing one) for your business is more complicated than renting an apartment or car. Complying with the conditions of your lease can become a real burden or even worse if you're not completely aware of all of them from the start. Unforeseen expenses can be disastrous.

Recognizing your real expenses

When trying to settle on a location, it's important to understand what your actual financial obligations will be. These obligations vary significantly from location to location. One thing you must know is the difference between rent and occupancy costs. You may think that your rent is all your landlord expects from you. Wrong. The rent is just the beginning. Your total occupancy cost is the combined amount of all the fees involved with setting up business in a particular location.

Some old-fashioned landlords still charge one amount that may even include heat. God bless them. However, such people are the exception, not the rule. Please be aware that lease terms and conditions vary considerably. The following are some of the probable expenses you'll be responsible for — some are negotiable, and others are not.

Base rent

The amount of rent you agree to pay annually per square foot of space. This amount is divided by 12 months to calculate the rent you pay on a monthly basis. For example, if the rent is $10 per square foot and you rent 1,200 square feet of space, your annual base rent is $12,000, or $1,000 per month. The base rent ensures that the landlord receives a minimum amount in rent.

Percentage rent

The amount of extra rent you have to pay after you reach your *base sales* (what you're allowed to sell before you have to start paying a percentage). Landlords would really like to charge you a percentage of your total sales, but because sales figures are unpredictable, they charge a base rent (to make sure that they get a minimum) with a percentage rent on top. Think of percentage rent as the frosting on top of the base rent cake.

For example, the annual base rent on a property might be $18,000 per year. This is the minimum amount of rent that the landlord will receive. If the landlord wants a percentage rent rate of 6 percent, $18,000 actually represents 6 percent of the base sales of $300,000. ($18,000 divided by 6 percent equals $300,000.) The landlord looks at it differently than the tenant — he wants 6 percent of total sales but guarantees himself a minimum return. As soon as the store generates sales of over $300,000, the tenant has to pay 6 percent of every dollar received over and above the base rent.

You may be thinking, "That's not fair — the landlord doesn't lose!" You're right. This is pretty standard practice, however. Can it be negotiated? Yes, and it's done every day, but the conditions must be right.

Remember, everything is negotiable, but "the right condition" means "how much the landlord wants or needs you." For example, if you have a chain of 500 stores and a top credit rating with no downside risk to the landlord, and the landlord wants to put you in all his malls, your chances of making a standard practice disappear are pretty good. Conditions can be just as right if you're a new or expanding business or if you're unique or different. If your concept is special enough, your chances that a standard practice will disappear are also pretty good. If you sell novelty or gift items for dogs and cats, for example, that may be different enough. Your type of business may not be represented in the shopping area. Luggage stores, better men's shops, unique gift stores, and unique, locally owned restaurants are always hard to find.

If the landlord can attract a tenant that draws customers to the center, it may be worth passing on one store's overages to get overages from the other tenants on the extra business the new store will bring to the center. *Everything is negotiable.* Be able to recognize your strengths.

CAM charges

Common Area and Maintenance (CAM) charges cover the cost of cleaning and maintaining all the common areas that the tenants share. If you're in a mall, these areas include the fountain in the center, the main walkways inside the mall, the ceiling, the parking lot, the hallways, and the sidewalks. In addition to routine cleaning, you'll pay for jobs such as snow removal and resurfacing and line painting of the parking lots. The cost of oil, gas, and electricity in the common areas is also the tenants' responsibility. You pay based on the percentage of space you occupy.

When you sign your lease, the landlord can only estimate these costs — they're generally based on last year's charges. If you have a bad snow year or an exceptionally hot summer that raises electricity costs for air conditioning, be prepared to pay more.

Other expenses

- ✔ **Taxes:** Property taxes are paid in the same way as CAM charges — estimated from last year's figures. Again, if the taxes go up, you could be in store for a shock at the end of the year.

- ✔ **Security:** Many centers include security charges in the CAM charges, but many do not. Expect to pay your share.

- ✔ **Insurance:** Insurance fees cover the building itself or could be only for the common areas. Like security fees, they may be included in the CAM charges, but aren't necessarily.

- ✔ **Promotional costs and merchant dues:** These fees cover any costs that tenants incur collectively. They can include the following:

  - Events at the mall

  - Holiday decorations

  - Marketing costs

  - Advertising

  - Awards and award dinners

- ✔ **Miscellaneous expenses:** These fees can include *bad debt expenses* (when a landlord is not paid by a tenant, usually in the area of CAM charges), professional services, elevator/escalator maintenance, heating/cooling repair and replacement, and leasing fees. (Leasing fees to a landlord are like dealer prep to an automobile dealer: the extra charge that they try to slip past the unsuspecting lessee.)

- ✔ **Triple net lease:** In a triple net lease, your rent does not include three things: taxes, maintenance and repair, and insurance. I don't like this term because *maintenance* is too broad and could cover just about anything. Make sure to break down everything you're paying for. Doing so takes time, but it's worth it. Another reason I don't like this term is that *triple net* doesn't always cover the same issues.

Examining other issues before signing a lease

The following list comprises various ways to avoid getting burned by a bad lease agreement:

- ✔ Have realistic goals. You have to know what you can reasonably expect from any location.

- ✔ Understand everything in the lease. I advise you to have a lawyer check your lease and explain every detail until you can teach it. Choose an attorney with real estate experience.

✔ Realize that *everything* is negotiable. Not everyone at the center is paying the same amount. Either retailers leasing under better terms negotiated better, or the landlord really wanted them as tenants.

✔ Understand how disputes will be handled.

✔ Determine whether the percentage you pay for all the extras will increase if the center has vacancies.

✔ Think carefully about the term of your lease. Don't make it too short.

✔ Understand your options if the landlord doesn't maintain the property and you do some of the upkeep yourself.

✔ Be sure that if the major anchor leaves the center, you can leave, too.

✔ Establish whether you can transfer your lease to someone else if you sell the business.

✔ Find out whether you can sublet some of your space.

Everything is negotiable, and good locations provide win-win situations. Both the landlord and the tenant are in business to make money.

You can find a sample lease in the Legal Forms folder on the CD.

Chapter 7

Designing Stores That Work

Store designs vary greatly. But they all share a common goal: to increase business. An effective store design creates an atmosphere that draws customers into a retail space and keeps them there for as long as possible. The goal is to get customers to linger. The longer people are in your store, the more likely they are to buy something. Sounds like a no-brainer, right? But it doesn't happen automatically.

You have to create the look and feel of your store in a way that expresses and strengthens your brand. Then you have to direct the traffic strategically through your store, making sure that customers see as much merchandise as possible. You accomplish this by creating displays that draw attention, placing merchandise for maximum effect, and selecting fixtures that make your retail space as flexible as possible.

All elements of your store design work together to make your retail space a place where customers want to spend time and money. And to be sure I offer you the best possible advice in this chapter, I consulted with Brian Dyches, president of The Retail Resource Group, one of the top retail store design and implementation firms in the U.S.

Considering Your Image

Before you can start designing your store, you have to consider what type of image you want to create — think about what kind of store yours is and then plan its look and feel around that. Here are three basic elements to consider when planning the look of your store:

✔ **The price level of your merchandise:** Lower-end stores need to be clean, bright, and functional. That doesn't necessarily mean that your furnishings and fixtures need to be inexpensive; I simply recommend that you avoid pricey finishes or ornate designs. Upscale stores need to create a look and feel of luxury.

✔ **The level of service you plan to give your customers:** Stores that plan to be self-service need to invest in a lot of fixtures (tables, display racks, shelves, and so on) so that all merchandise is out for customers to help themselves. But if you plan to offer one-on-one service, think about having a computer, phones, and even a desk so that your sales staff has a convenient place from which to call and send notes and e-mails to customers.

✔ **The level of selection you plan to offer:** If you plan to carry a large inventory, you have to be creative in finding ways to display your merchandise effectively, and you need to invest in lots of fixtures.

The one thing that can put a business out of business faster than anything else is sending mixed messages. If a store tells me that it's the lowest-price outlet, it had better look like it's saving money on everything it does. On the other hand, exclusive stores need to look rich — finely appointed with beautiful fixtures and furnishings. As you plan your store design, remember that everything needs to stay in alignment — your merchandise, packaging, policies, and advertising must support the same message. And that message is your brand.

Establishing Your Store's Look and Feel

Your look is your brand. It is what people will associate with your store. What feelings do you want your customers to have in your store? What images do you want them to conjure when they think about your store? Loud, bright, and in your face? Soft, subdued, and refined? The look and feel you create for your store depends on the customer you want to attract and the merchandise you plan to carry.

To understand what effective store design is, it helps to identify what it *isn't*. Visit stores where you *wouldn't* normally shop and ask yourself, "Why not? What's preventing me from shopping here?" They may look too expensive, too cheap, or too intimidating. Become aware of the reasons for your aversion and then avoid them in your own store design.

The sound of music

Music has a powerful ability to create a mood and a brand association. I suggest that you have a first-class stereo system in your store and play only music that you can sell. Whatever you do, DO NOT PLAY THE RADIO. Playing copyrighted music in a commercial setting without paying royalties is against the law. Inspectors can show up at any time and insist that you either pay up or remove your stereo. But there's a silver lining in this — you have an opportunity to make money by selling CDs of the music that you play in your store. At every trade show, someone is always selling CDs for resale. At a recent show, I met a concert pianist who sold more CDs to be played and sold in retail stores than in music stores.

Choosing a theme

One way to establish a memorable look and feel for your store is to select a theme or style that suits the type of business you have. For example, Rainforest Cafe uses a jungle theme, Eddie Bauer chose a great outdoors theme, and Foot Locker's theme is sports.

Consider using a theme to establish the look and feel of your store if you think it's appropriate to your business. But don't force it. You can create your store's atmosphere in numerous other ways.

Picking a color scheme

One of the most powerful tools in creating a mood is color. Grays and burgundies are more subdued and traditional, hot colors are hipper, and yellows and reds are meant for kids. You can totally change the look of the store with color.

Before you decide on colors for your store, talk to different designers and professionals about the impact that different colors have and how they affect customers' moods and attitudes. Color selection is a science unto itself, with many experts with different points of view. But don't be intimidated by designers. The look and feel of your store must reflect *you* — what you stand for and what your customers expect from you. Do your homework here. The effort will be worth it.

Selecting treatments

Retailers old and new often have preconceived ideas about what wall, ceiling, floor, and lighting designs they want. Instead, approach your store's decorating elements with an open mind. You have so many treatments and finishes to choose from that it's to your advantage to at least look at what's available.

Treatments are important because they create a look and feel for who you are — your brand. Retailing is about detail and all the little things that create an experience. The treatments you choose should reflect your image in the eyes of your customers. It's not that they make it better or worse; they just help reinforce your image. This section introduces a few of your options.

When you're selecting treatments for your store, don't forget that you have to satisfy building codes — they'll dictate your selection of materials and the manner of installation.

Floor treatments

Floor coverings motivate shoppers in a very subtle way. For example, a hard surface at the entrance encourages people to walk faster and deeper into the store. Similarly, soft surfaces encourage people to slow down. The following are some of your flooring options:

- **Vinyl tile:** This is the most popular type of floor covering because of the cost and flexibility. Vinyl is rarely used in high-end retail stores. It is the first choice of big box retailers, though, and because of that, it projects a value-oriented image. It's relatively easy to care for, and even if you plan on using carpeting in your store, pathways of vinyl tile work well. You can coordinate different-colored tiles to create interesting patterns, such as borders of dark gray with an interior path of light gray. Doing so gives the vinyl a slightly richer look, but it's still vinyl.

- **Ceramic tile:** Ceramic tile — shiny, smooth, or textured — creates a subtle exotic feeling. It's suitable for higher-end merchandise and anytime you want to present merchandise in a classy way. A gourmet foods shop might choose ceramic tile, for example, but I wouldn't use it in a china shop. Ceramic tile is more expensive than vinyl, but the look it creates can be worth the difference. One disadvantage to ceramic tile is that it can crack and scratch. Be sure to buy additional tiles in preparation for this possibility. Also, you must be careful when moving merchandise on this surface.

- **Hardwood flooring:** Wood flooring can accommodate numerous design needs. You can choose from parquet, small strips, large planks, and a variety of colors and stains. Wood has many of the same qualities as ceramic tile: It adds richness, but there is a cost factor, and it scratches fairly easily.

- **Carpeting:** Again, a multitude of varieties is available. Getting two solid carpets and using one as a border is a great treatment. The other trick with carpet is to create cutout areas of carpet near the cash wrap and the area by the front door. These areas get the most usage. So if you can design an area that's cut out, when that section gets really dirty, just throw it away and have another inset put in. Another easy way to address high-traffic problems is to use carpet tiles.

  One of the major disadvantages to carpeting is that it wears out and therefore requires replacement sometimes as early as three years from installment. However, the upkeep is generally much less time-consuming than it is with your other options. Moving merchandise on carpeting is also much easier.

- **Linoleum:** Some linoleum is nice, and linoleum is a lot less expensive than any other type of flooring. But if you can afford wood, ceramic, or carpet, they're better choices — they hold up much better to the wear and tear of a commercial space.

Wall treatments

Wall treatments are important because they softly help set a mood that enhances the merchandise. This is not about having beautiful walls; it is about having walls that put the merchandise in the most favorable light and help customers focus on the merchandise.

Here are your choices in wall treatments:

- **Wallpaper:** You can find wallpaper in endless varieties of patterns, colors, and textures. You can also paint over wallpaper if you get tired of the original color after a few years.

- **Paint:** This treatment may not be exciting, but it works for many stores.

- **Faux finishes:** Consider procedures such as sponging, ragging, white-washing, and stenciling to add texture to your store's walls. For tips on doing faux finishes, see *Painting and Wallpapering For Dummies* by Gene and Katie Hamilton and Roy Barnhart (Hungry Minds, Inc.).

- **Wood paneling:** This wall treatment gives a rustic look.

- **Mirrored walls:** Mirrors can make a store look bigger than it is, and they're great for security reasons.

- **Wall systems:** These floor-to-ceiling panels can be popped out and changed with any type of finish you can think of. Many stores use the mirror and laminate varieties.

Finding a designer

You can turn to a number of sources to find a professional designer. Check with your landlord, who usually can recommend some of his favorites. Visual merchandising magazines also have plenty of ads for first-rate companies. If you worry that your job is too small for them to take on, ask them whether any staff members moonlight for smaller jobs. Companies that sell fixtures usually have people who work on smaller jobs. Contractors are another source; good ones can help you find the right designer for your store. Choose a designer who has previous experience in designing retail environments.

Ceiling treatments

We've come a long way from the days of the drop ceiling as the only way to go. Yes, it's an option, but ceiling treatments can provide their own special "wow." You can find recessed ceiling treatments with indirect lighting that can transform an ordinary store into a one-of-a-kind shop.

Lighting

Merchandise that's effectively lit has an increased perceived value, so lighting plays an important role in your overall store design. You can select from a tremendous range of lighting options, but you have to be careful. Although some of the new lighting systems are magnificent and highlight the merchandise perfectly, they can draw a lot of electric power. Make sure that your lighting choices are energy efficient.

In general, better-quality stores stay away from fluorescent lighting — especially the long tubes. They just don't have an upscale look. Unique indirect lighting effects are a powerful way to create a mood. Dimming lights don't create the dramatic effect they once did because dimming is much easier to accomplish today.

Designing Specific Sections of Your Store

Think of every area in your store as a piece of real estate. Just like the Monopoly game board, where some properties are worth more than others, the various sections of your store have different real estate values. The areas that most customers see have the greatest value. The first display as you walk into a store, for example, is equivalent to Park Place. The value of various sections of your store will change depending on the pathway you create to direct customer traffic through your store. Without a doubt, the sections along your established pathway deserve the most design attention.

Straight lines have become passé. Create nooks and crannies to encourage customers to explore. These small spaces also help you build up certain departments within your store. You can create nooks and crannies simply by building a V and putting it against a wall. The V can be made up of slat wall or any kind of wood that can be covered. Attach shelves to increase your display options.

Making a grand entrance

You'll never get customers into your store if the outside is uninviting. Store design starts from the street to create a total experience for shoppers. The outside of your store must reflect the inside. Don't forget to make sure that your section of the sidewalk (or mall) is the cleanest part of the shopping area.

Because you never get a second chance to make a good first impression, be sure that the very first display inside your store makes a good one. See Chapter 20 for tips on creating effective displays.

Some experts think that the closer you put merchandise to the door, the more your store will be perceived as low-end or budget. If yours is a better store, leave at least 60 to 80 square feet near the entry free of displays.

Perfecting your pathways

One way to encourage customers to linger is to create a long and winding road that leads through your store. The straighter the path, the faster customers will walk through. Of course, the opposite is also true. Always place your best-looking and most enticing items along this pathway. To create a proper path, keep in mind the following rules:

- ✔ Make your path circle to the right because most people naturally turn 45 degrees to the right when they enter a store.

- ✔ Make the floor covering along the path a different texture or look from the general flooring of your store. Doing so encourages customers to follow the path — the distinct flooring provides a visual clue.

- ✔ Wind the path around the store in a lightbulb-type design to guide customers through all sections of your store — down one side, around the back, and to the front again.

- ✔ Avoid straight lines. Curves create additional display locations and are more aesthetically pleasing.

✔ Position displays, merchandise, and/or signage so that it can easily be viewed face forward along the edge of the path. You want to entice customers to wander off the path to explore merchandise. If they have to walk around a fixture to read a sign, many customers won't bother.

✔ Place denser or taller racks behind your display racks to create visual depth. This design technique also maximizes the amount of merchandise visible to customers at all times.

Rick's Random Rule #33: Where the eyes go, the feet will follow.

Dressing up store windows

Your store window is the second most valuable section in your store. Spend the necessary time and resources to make it special. It often provides people with their first impression of your business and serves to strengthen (or weaken, if designed poorly) your brand. In fact, store windows are so important that I devote an entire chapter to them. Go directly to Chapter 19 for the scoop on creating effective store windows.

Setting up the cash wrap area

The cash wrap area is the nerve center of your store. It's where your customers check out, visit with employees, and ask questions. And at the end of their transactions, it's where you hand over to them a nicely packaged bundle (that reinforces your brand) to take home. The cash wrap area is generally a lively spot that draws customers to it for its function or for fun.

The proper placement of the cash wrap area is one of the most debated issues in store design. To help you decide where to place yours, you need to be aware of the possibilities. This list introduces various placement options:

✔ **To the right of the front door:** Because there is almost always someone working the cash register, this position makes it possible for your staff to greet customers as they enter the store. The checkout area is also usually the store's hub of activity, so if it's the first thing customers see, they'll get the impression that your store is busy. One disadvantage to this placement is that the right front corner of your store is valuable real estate. Why not position the cash wrap area in a location where customers wouldn't otherwise spend much time?

✔ **In the center of the store:** From the center, you can greet customers as they enter, thank them as they leave, and keep an eye of all areas of your store. One disadvantage to this central placement is that although you may be close to every section of the store, your back is always turned to half of it.

To catch a thief

You can't build your store around the fear of merchandise getting stolen — unfortunately, it's part of the price of doing business. However, you can minimize this risk by keeping your racks low. You don't want to have a high rack that blocks your view of any part of the store. Consider making the area with the least visibility the markdown wall or section, because theft from the markdown area won't hurt your bottom line as much as losing your better merchandise will. Keep your most expensive items as close to the cash wrap area as possible. And remember, the best way to reduce shoplifting is through eye contact.

✔ **On the side wall halfway down the length of the store:** This midpoint location puts you close enough to the front door to greet customers. The negative is that you're breaking up a beautiful wall that could be better used to display merchandise.

✔ **At the back of the store:** This position enables you to draw customers to the back of the store (which can be a difficult thing to do), and its proximity to the back room area makes it very convenient. However, you lose your greeting effect and increase the probability of shoplifting because watchful eyes are too far away from the front door.

✔ **In the left front of the store:** This location works, but even though you're close to the front of the store, you won't greet as many customers as you might think because most customers turn to the right when they enter.

Wherever you decide to place your cash wrap area, it should be between 8 and 10 feet long and 3 feet wide. Plenty of fixture companies sell premade cash wraps; however, having your contractor make one for you is usually more cost-effective. The best finishes to put on the front and sides of the cash wrap are the wallpaper or carpeting that you use in the store or accent paper. As for the countertops, laminate is the most common, the least expensive, and by far the easiest to work with. Some retailers use ceramic, wood, marble, or granite, but I don't know anyone who's totally happy with any of those surfaces because you need a smooth surface into which holes for electrical outlets can be drilled. Some of these other materials are also extremely heavy and are not easy to move.

Designating a markdown section

Everybody — upscale stores and discount stores alike — has markdowns, and everybody has to get rid of them. Most shoppers appreciate all the markdowns being put together in a section that they can explore themselves. Consider naming this section of your store to give people something to talk about, such as "The Last Call Wall." Mark down merchandise at least twice a month and add new merchandise regularly. Position this section in the least valuable part of your store, usually a back corner, because customers seek out the discounted merchandise and on the way, they'll be exposed to all your new merchandise.

Creating a waiting area

As a courtesy to your customers, try to provide a waiting area. Plenty of people shop with children or elderly family members (as well as friends who take longer to look at things than they do), and they appreciate having a place to sit down and relax. When designing this area, keep the following points in mind:

✔ Provide comfortable seating, but don't select chairs that are so low that people have trouble getting up from them. And never have them face a wall.

✔ Place this area near some activity, like your cash wrap area or a unique store feature if you have one, so that the person waiting doesn't get bored.

Although children's play areas enable mothers to shop in relative peace, I don't recommend that you have one in your store. If a child gets hurt, you're responsible, and undersupervised children can cause other customers to feel uncomfortable. Proceed with caution.

Selecting Display Fixtures

Whether you like the rustic look or prefer the sleek lines of minimalism, there's a fixture style for every taste. The fixtures you use in your store do a lot to determine the character of the space. Choose wisely.

You have many different types of standard racks and fixtures to choose from. The following is a list of the different types of fixtures:

✔ **Table:** This most basic of fixtures comes in many different sizes and varieties, from a small square to a large oblong.

✔ **Shelving:** There are two major varieties: wall shelving, which can be used to feature one item or as a place to stack many, such as all size 34 jeans; and floor shelving, or freestanding racks. Floor shelving comes in all sizes and varieties, from glass shelving to the type you find in supermarkets.

✔ **Cube:** Another type of freestanding shelving. It consists of stacked cubes that can be made of all different types of materials. The two most popular are glass and wire.

✔ **Four-way rack:** This fixture, used primarily in apparel stores, enables merchandise to be displayed and viewed from four different angles. This rack can hold a considerable amount of merchandise.

✔ **Waterfalls and straight arms:** These are brackets that fit onto a four-way, T-stand, or slat wall — either straight out, which features one piece of merchandise, or cascading down to feature multiple items.

✔ **T-stand:** T-stands come in two varieties. The first is a single, which enables you to display only one piece of merchandise. The other type enables you to display merchandise on both sides of the rack. T-stands come in different materials, but the most common is chrome metal.

✔ **Round rack:** A circular rack with varying diameters that can be adjusted for height. Round racks are used primarily in apparel and hold the most merchandise. They generally should be used for promotional items.

✔ **Rail rack:** A straight rack with two bars on either side, again used primarily in apparel.

✔ **Showcase:** This is used to display merchandise of higher value, such as jewelry. Many stores use showcases in conjunction with the cash wrap area for loss prevention, and there is usually someone at the cash wrap area to help the customer with the merchandise. Showcases come in all sizes and varieties, and many have inside lighting.

Showcases are necessary fixtures, but for better or worse, they create a barrier. Customers need to touch your merchandise. Showcases are also a constant pain to keep neat, organized, and clean. Whatever you do, keep your showcases down to a bare minimum. And please, if you buy showcases, make sure that they're uniform. Hand-me-down showcases that are a little bit of this and a little bit of that only cheapen the merchandise.

Select fixtures with flexibility in mind. You always want your store to look full. That doesn't mean that your level of inventory will always be the same; it won't be. You need to be able to arrange your fixtures so that every rack is at capacity. Half-empty racks and tables make your merchandise look picked over. As a result, customers may postpone their purchases, waiting for new merchandise.

Have tables to which you can add larger tops. Use a T-stand as opposed to a four-way rack. T-stands take up almost the same amount of space as four-ways, but you only need half as much merchandise to fill up a T-stand. And whenever practical, put your fixtures on casters so that you can move them around easily.

Plenty of used fixtures are on the market. Used-fixture companies generally sell fixtures for between 40 and 60 cents on the dollar. Also consider using antique furniture. Antique tables and chests of drawers have a charm of their own and offer unusual display possibilities.

After you explore all the options you have in creating a visually great store, this news may come as somewhat of a bombshell: The look of your store must change in five years. Sure, certain things can stay the same, but stores need to be updated every five years in order to stay with it. So never buy something hoping that it will last forever. You just need five good years.

Satisfying Landlords and Building Inspectors

Most landlords want to know what you're going to do to their property, but they're even more concerned about how your store design will fit in with the rest of the tenants. Most landlords have a set of guidelines for you to follow that are intended to keep the character of the shopping area intact. If you or your designer wants something that the landlord doesn't allow, keep in mind that there is always room for negotiation.

If you want something that's out of the norm, do two things:

- ✔ Make sure that your original plans look as professional as possible. Without that, you lose credibility.

- ✔ Clearly spell out the facts and the reasons why you want the change in a professional-looking document. This tactic doesn't always work, but it does improve your chances of getting what you want.

When you're changing or creating electrical or plumbing systems or tearing down or putting up walls or ceilings, your local building inspector's office must approve your plan. You'll need to pay a professional to prepare the plan. You can choose an architect, a store planner, an engineer, or even a draftsman who works for a construction company. The more professional your plan looks, the less hassle you'll receive from the people who have to approve it.

Be aware that electrical, plumbing, and fire inspectors and the building inspector must sign off before you can receive your occupancy permit. (See Chapter 10 for more on permits and regulations.) If your scheduled store opening is looming closer and you don't have your occupancy permit yet, hire extra workers to make sure that everything the inspector says must be done is done and done correctly. Plan a "soft opening" instead of a huge grand-opening celebration in case construction problems delay your opening day.

When you're drawing up your store design, keep the guidelines of the Americans with Disabilities Act in mind — your store has to be accessible to everyone.

Part III
The Details of Retail: Shufflin' Papers

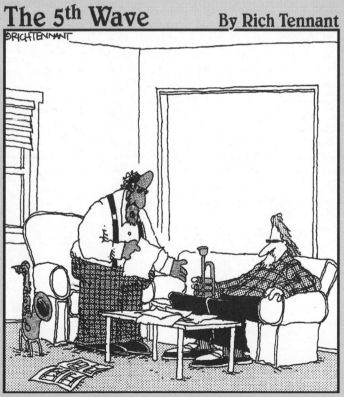

The 5th Wave   By Rich Tennant

"Here's my business plan for the Jazz Store. I think we should just fake the budget, improvise the marketing and make up the long range goals as we go along."

In this part . . .

*E*very business needs a plan and in this part you learn how to create a workable business plan that will become your blueprint for building a successful business — taking you from your initial financing stages all the way to an established business with valuable experience.

This part also focuses on helping you determine the legal structure of your business. It presents advantages and disadvantages of proprietorship and incorporation, as well as the many factors affected by your choice of business structure. You also learn about taxes, permits, and local requirements for going into business. This part is all about crossing every *t* and dotting every *i*.

Chapter 8

Creating and Working with a Business Plan

. . . .

In This Chapter

▶ Creating a business plan for bankers, landlords, investors, and you

▶ Presenting your business in the best possible light

▶ Explaining your operational plans

▶ Exploring the financial aspect of going into retail — what you need to know and show

▶ Defining your management style

. . . .

The purpose of a business plan is to serve as a guidepost — a document you can return to again and again to understand where you and your business have been and where you're going. It is *not* just a report that you prepare to obtain financing, establish credit, impress suppliers, or secure a location. Unfortunately, too many entrepreneurs think that these are the only uses for business plans.

I advise you to commit your thoughts to paper (or disk) in the form of a business plan. In doing so, you're more apt to cover all the steps involved in running a successful business and to consider all the relevant factors that you might miss if you simply rolled your thoughts around in your head.

Before You Begin

A business plan is *not* something that a consultant prepares and submits to you. That approach would be a waste of time. Yes, you can hire a consultant, but any good consultant will spend time with you, asking questions about *your* plans, *your* ideas, and *your* attitudes on different topics. For your business plan to be useful, it must reflect you — your personality, your goals, and your dreams.

The CD includes a tried-and-true exercise called the S.W.O.T. (strength, weakness, opportunity, and threat) exercise. You can find it in the Miscellaneous Forms folder and I recommend that you complete it before you begin to write your business plan. This exercise is designed to help you crystallize your thoughts, evaluate your abilities, and analyze your business goals, putting you in the right frame of mind to create a business plan.

There's no absolute right format for writing a business plan. Years ago, I was taught one way to write a business plan and thought for years that it was gospel. It always worked for me, but as I have gotten older and a bit wiser, I realize that there are other formats to follow. There *are* absolute elements in every business plan, though, including the following:

- ✔ Preview
- ✔ Description
- ✔ Marketing plan
- ✔ Financial plan
- ✔ Management plan
- ✔ Summary

The following sections look at each of these elements separately.

The Preview: Who Are You and What's This All About?

The preview is the first chance your business plan has to make a good impression, so take care in creating it. Your preview should consist of the following:

- ✔ Cover sheet
- ✔ Table of contents
- ✔ Executive summary

Crafting a cover sheet

Books have covers, and so do business plans. Your preview starts with a cover page. It doesn't have to look fancy, but it must look professional. Your cover page must include the following elements:

✔ **Title:** The title should say "Business Plan for . . ." You must use the words *Business Plan*. Don't try to disguise or change the title; very few people appreciate that attempt.

✔ **Name of your business:** Don't use "thinking of" to indicate that you haven't decided yet. By now, you should be sure.

✔ **Names of the principals:** Include the names of the owner(s) and any key employees who have an impact on the business, with brief descriptions of their backgrounds.

✔ **Your business address:** If you don't have an address yet, use your home address.

✔ **Contact information:** Include your phone and fax numbers, e-mail address, and Web site. Even if you're not in business yet, you can still have a one-page Web site, even if it's just a placeholder page indicating that it's the future home of your business.

Preparing a table of contents

A carefully organized table of contents helps readers find the information they're looking for. Few people read a business plan page by page. They skim it or simply go to the relevant sections. Your table of contents should list every section with its corresponding page number. Prepare this in outline form. Assign a number to each section and indicate each subsection by adding a period and a subsequent number. For example, subsection 2 of section 1 of the plan would be listed as 1.2 in the table of contents.

Writing an executive summary

The purpose of the executive summary (as opposed to the summary you place at the end of your business plan) is to cut to the chase. It's a courtesy you provide to anyone reading your business plan who doesn't have the time (or want to spend the time) to read through it page by page. Because the executive summary outlines your plan in a nutshell, just about everybody reads it. That's why it's such a crucial element in your business plan.

Your executive summary must address all the main sections of your overall business plan. Devote a few sentences to responding to the following questions:

✔ **Who am I, and what is this all about? (from your preview)** Describe yourself, your company, and your concept.

✔ **What's the nature of my business, what are my ideas, and why should anyone buy from me? (from your description)** Describe your business and ideas in greater detail. Who is the competition, and what makes you so special? What are your advantages?

✔ **How am I going to sell my merchandise? (from your marketing plan)** This is comprised of four parts: positioning, marketing, selling, and advertising your business. Explain your approach — self-service, full-service, discount, or regular price. Briefly describe your preferred method of reaching your customers. How are you going to market and advertise?

✔ **How much do I hope to make, spend, and need? (from your financial plan)** Explain that your business will cost X dollars to run, it will make X amount or lose X amount until when, and financing this business will take X amount of money. (All these questions are answered on the cash flow projection form introduced later in this chapter.)

✔ **How am I going to run my business? (from your management plan)** Establish who is going to run your business, why that person is qualified, and how your business will operate on a day-to-day basis.

✔ **Sum it all up. (from your summary)** Reiterate what you've already written and why your business idea is so great. Do this in no more than three sentences.

Present your ideas as succinctly as possible in your executive summary. Do your best to limit yourself to a page or two.

The Description: What's Your Business Idea and Why Should Anyone Buy from You?

The description section of your business plan is the place where you present all the wonderful things about your business idea, why it'll work, and how you're going to make it happen. This section includes an explanation of your business ideas, an analysis of the industry, and a description of your competition. Begin with a brief introduction of the information you're going to present in this description section.

Describing your business

After the introduction, describe your business, writing approximately a paragraph for each of the following questions (no, you don't have to write the questions themselves — just use them to guide the organization of your paragraphs):

- What business structure have you chosen — a corporation, partnership, or sole proprietorship? What type of business are you in? (State that yours is a retail business.)

- How long have you been a businessperson? Is your concept a new one? If so, describe it.

- What kind of customer do you want to attract?

- How many of your customer types are in your marketing area? Use industry and census data for information.

- What is your vision for the business?

- What is your mission statement, positioning statement, tag line, or slogan? Find the words that best describe who you are and what you represent in the marketplace. What things do you want your customers, employees, and investors to say and think about your business?

- Where do you plan to locate your business?

- What will your service and price levels be?

Describing your industry

Next, describe the industry that your business is in, such as gifts, apparel, hardware, or whatever. Craft your paragraphs in response to the following questions:

- Is the industry healthy?

- Is it growing? If so, why? (Don't merely state your opinion. Get facts to back up your statements. You can generally find this information in industry and trade publications. Quote the experts. Never use information you've heard from landlords, suppliers, sales reps, or friends. Use hard facts.)

- What are the negatives challenging your industry? Describe how they will affect you either positively or negatively.

Describing your competition

Next, comment on your competition, answering the following questions:

✔ Who are your competitors?

✔ How long have they been in business?

✔ How well are they doing, and what kind of plans do they have?

✔ What are their strengths and weaknesses? Explain how you plan to surpass your competitors' strengths and avoid the traps that make them weak.

Finally, write a concluding paragraph that sums up your description section. Include the high points — the things you want people to remember.

Your Marketing Plan: How Are You Going to Sell It?

This section of your business plan describes your marketing approach — self-service, full-service, discount, or regular price. It also describes your preferred method of reaching your customers. In other words, how are you going to market and advertise?

Like all the other sections of your business plan, your marketing plan needs a short introductory paragraph to provide readers with a quick glance at the information in it. Then you can launch into the heart of your marketing strategy. Organize your marketing plan into the following four elements:

✔ **Positioning:** How are you going to be perceived by your customers, your community, and the world? What are you going to do to influence this perception?

✔ **Marketing:** How are you going to find your customers, and how will you educate them about who you are, what you do, and what you can do for them? Are you going to place advertising, and if so, what kind? Will you use newspaper, radio, TV, direct mail, or the Internet? Are you going to hold seminars, host open houses, or use public relations vehicles?

✔ **Selling:** How will you entice your customers to buy your merchandise?

✔ **Advertising:** How will you tell the world about your wonderful business, outstanding merchandise, special events, and so on?

Positioning

In this part of your marketing plan, you explain your business's role in the eyes of consumers — a prestige resource, a low-cost volume retailer, or a convenience source, for example. Describe what your store will look like and the pricing methods you plan to use. If you're modeling your store after another store that you hold in high esteem, say so. If you plan for your business to be a specialty store or fill some retail niche, be sure to mention that, too. Finally, don't forget to include your store's signature line (also known as a positioning statement). See Chapter 2 to find out how to create one.

Marketing

Many people get confused about the difference between marketing and advertising. Marketing determines what your message is, who will receive it, and how you plan to communicate it. Advertising is just one part of this process.

In this section, repeat your positioning statement or signature line — what it means and who you're trying to reach with it. Discuss any public relations ideas you're considering. Are you going to hire a PR firm, and for what purposes? Why a professional and not internal? Be sure to describe any events such as festivals, contests, non-sale events, or sponsorships you're planning.

This is also the place to present a marketing calendar. Prepare a 12-month calendar listing all the advertising and promotional events you have planned. Explain each event on a separate page — its purpose and the steps you need to take to accomplish it.

Describe any unique services you plan to use to sell your merchandise. For example, perhaps you want to include a drive-thru window, be open 24/7, or use skywriting or banner ads on the Web to sell your product. You can also present your attitudes about price, item, or sale advertising and image or institutional advertising.

This section also needs a description of your ideal customer. Use the information you gather on your customer profile forms to do this and add an explanation of how you've used demographic data to help build your customer base.

Promise me something

I've asked for nothing from you to this point, but now I need a commitment. (I'm trying to make you feel guilty.) It's just three little things, really. Promise me that you'll do the following:

✔ Prepare your financial reports *with* your accountant. Don't just let your accountant handle them.

✔ Make a real effort to understand the full meaning and impact of the data in these reports.

✔ Refer to these financial reports regularly because they can serve as your budget. They can help you become your own consultant.

Selling

In this section, you describe the actual methods you plan to use to sell your merchandise. Discuss your selling strategies within the context of the following:

✔ **Retail:** A storefront with customers coming into the store.

✔ **Catalog:** Many retailers supplement their walk-in business by mailing catalogs directly to customers. State in your plan whether you have plans for this type of selling.

✔ **Online:** Web site commerce is becoming a necessity in retailing today. You must address the topic of online sales, which can increase the volume of your business, in this section of your plan.

✔ **Level of service:** Will salespeople wait on and sell to each customer, or will your business be self-service? If your merchandise is to be sold by salespeople, will they work on commission? How will they be trained?

✔ **Visuals:** Will your store have signage, and if so, will it be unique? An important trend in retailing is describing products with good signage. Mention your plans for signage in this section. Also describe the interior and exterior look that you plan for your store, including displays.

Advertising

First, discuss the size of your advertising budget — how much advertising you are planning and in what months you're planning to spend it. Then provide an annotated list of all your advertising options.

- ✔ **Newspapers:** Which newspapers circulate in your area, and which ones do you plan to advertise in? What type and size of ad are you planning?

- ✔ **Radio:** What stations reach your market area? What is the cost for advertising on these stations? What are your plans and why?

- ✔ **Television:** What cable and network TV stations are available to you? What does advertising on those stations cost? What are your plans and why? Discuss the use of media buyers or any other way of reducing costs here.

- ✔ **Magazines:** Are any consumer magazines affordable enough to advertise in? Many magazines have regional editions with more reasonable rates. If you intend to use your business plan to secure financing, national magazine advertising impresses some people.

- ✔ **Direct mail:** This category includes direct e-mail, too. Explain your strategies for this approach because direct marketing (also known as one-on-one marketing) is the most effective and economical form of advertising. Include your plans for database marketing, too.

- ✔ **Web advertising:** If you haven't previously described your Web presence, this is the time to do so. Include your opinions about banner and display advertising.

- ✔ **Co-op advertising from manufacturers:** Depending on the industry your business is in, co-op advertising may or may not be important to you. Regardless of whether it's important to your industry, you must mention co-op advertising in your report. Lenders want to see that you're wise about your spending and saving and that you're taking advantage of every opportunity.

Chapter 16 is devoted to advertising. Check out the information there for tons of tips on getting the biggest advertising bang for your buck.

Summary

Because this section is so long, highlighting your marketing plans is important. Pick out the important points from this part (one comment each on positioning, marketing, selling, and advertising) and present them in one paragraph.

Your Financial Plan: How Much Do You Plan to Make, Spend, and Need?

This part of your business plan shows the figures proving that if you do all the things you said you'll do, you'll be profitable.

It's natural for a business to take a few years to become profitable. The important issue for this part of your plan is to estimate when you think your business will become profitable and how you plan to repay your lenders.

This financial section of your business plan should include the following:

- ✔ Introduction
- ✔ Cash flow projection (also known as pro forma)
- ✔ Profit and loss statement (commonly referred to as a P&L)
- ✔ Balance sheet
- ✔ Risk analysis
- ✔ Summary

If there is one section of this business plan that you should keep with you always, it's your financial plan. Update it as often as is humanly possible!

Introduction

By now, you should understand the objective of an effective introduction. But if you still need a little clarification, look at the introduction as the opening remarks a lawyer makes to a jury in any good courtroom movie: "Ladies and gentlemen of the jury, the prosecution (or defense) will prove beyond a doubt blah blah blah." You want to prove beyond a doubt that your plan (specifically your financial plan) is the right way to go.

Rick's Random Rule #904: It doesn't matter how much you hate accounting. There's still some stuff you just gotta know.

Cash flow projection

Your cash flow projection (or pro forma) simply shows where your money is coming from, where it's going, and what's left over at the end of every month. This report comes in one of two basic versions: a detailed report or a summary.

Don't confuse a cash flow projection with a profit and loss statement. Cash flow is the actual money coming in and going out, whereas a P&L statement might reflect non-cash items, such as depreciation and cost of goods sold. They can be similar, but they're not the same.

✔ Detailed reports show exactly where all monies come from and list every expense category. They're critical for a new business because they enable you to evaluate your projections and to measure your actual expenses. Detailed reports are usually generated for a year.

✔ Summary reports are what the name implies — summaries. They just show revenues and expenses. You should generate a summary report annually for a minimum of five years because you need to show lenders when the money you're borrowing will be paid back and where you expect the business to be in five years. Lenders and landlords want to see business growth and how you envision it.

Some retailers prefer 18-month detailed reports because they show continuity from one year to the next. Additionally, some banks require detailed cash flow projections until a retailer's long-term loan is paid off. Banks often use the data to make recommendations that can help your business.

You can find samples of detailed, summary, and long-term cash flow projection charts in the Accounting Forms folder on the CD. Use them as models when you create your own.

Profit and loss statement

A profit and loss statement (P&L) is a summary of your financial activity over a period of time, generally one year. But it can cover any time frame you choose — a month or a quarter, for example. If you've been in business for a while, I suggest that when you prepare a profit and loss statement, you also include the figures from the preceding period for comparison. This additional information gives the people who read your business plan a little historical perspective.

I include a sample P&L in the Accounting Forms folder on the CD for your reference.

Balance sheet

You have to include a balance sheet in your financial plan because it shows how much of your business is your own (or your corporation's) and how much belongs to your lender. A balance sheet is especially important when you seek funding because potential investors want to know how invested you are in your business. They figure that the more you own, the more likely you're going to work hard to make it successful.

In the first day of Accounting 101, you learn the following equation:

Assets = Liabilities + Equity (Net Worth)

Assets are the things you own or your business resources. *Liabilities* are the monies you owe. *Equity* is what the business is worth. Just because an item is listed as an asset doesn't mean that you've paid for it. For example, your expensive computer cash register is an asset. The fact that you still owe $2,000 on it is a liability. On a balance sheet, you visually separate your assets (usually shown on the left of the chart) from your liabilities (usually on the right).

You can find a sample balance sheet in the Accounting Forms folder on the CD. It's nothing fancy, but it shows you what yours should look like.

Risks

In this section, you talk about what could go wrong with your plan. It's important to list the risks so that you're aware of challenges or problems that could occur. Landlords and bankers love to see a well-thought-out plan that thinks of everything — good and bad. After you've identified possible pitfalls, write a short paragraph explaining how you would respond to each scenario. Common risk scenarios include the following:

- You don't hit your sales goals. What will happen to your business?
- Expenses come in higher than projected. How will you adjust?
- You discover that you bought too much merchandise. What will you do?
- A natural disaster destroys your location. Are you covered with enough insurance? Would you reopen somewhere else?
- Your promotion doesn't work, and you've depleted your advertising and promotional budget. How would you handle that situation?
- You've bought the wrong merchandise for your customers. What do you do?
- You can't find good employees. What would you do until you found some?

You don't have to list pages and pages of these risks, but you do have to address some obvious ones. When you tell people about your new business idea, pay attention to the questions they ask you — the doubts they express. These are the issues you should address in your section on risks.

Summary

Pull all your financial plans together here and tell your readers what you want them to remember. It could be that your start-up costs are small or that your projections show significant cash earnings in a relatively short time. You may even add that you're willing to work longer hours and take less pay in order to build your business. Accentuate the positive, but keep it short and sweet.

Your Management Plan: How Are You Going to Run Your Business?

The operative word here is *you*. In your management plan, you state who you are, describe your background and experience, and explain what qualifies you to open a retail business. If you lack experience, offer a compelling argument for why you want to do this — and why you'll be successful.

If you already have some key employees, this is the time to list them and why they are key. What are their special skills? Maybe they worked for a competing store and truly understand the business of retail. Many businesses have been launched on the strengths of a key employee.

In your management plan, show that you have hired (or plan to hire) a credible (*in*credible) staff. Also include your planned association with consultants and experts. Here are a few possibilities:

- ✔ **Your accountant:** How long has the firm been in business? Who are the firm's other clients? What are its accomplishments? Some companies use large accounting firms simply for prestige.

- ✔ **A consultant:** I have been listed in business plans because of my 30+ years of experience, my writing, and my 500+ clients. Find a consultant who has a reputation that can lend credibility to your plan (in addition to advising you!).

- ✔ **A board of directors or advisers:** Ask prominent members of your business community to serve on your board. Bankers and well-known retired executives make great choices. Their names and resumes go a long way. You don't have to include their resumes, just brief descriptions of their backgrounds. See Chapter 9 for information about recruiting a board of directors.

Be sure to include family commitment. Does your spouse plan to be involved with your business? Will a parent be there if you can't get any help? This information goes a long way toward impressing those who'll be reading your business plan.

After you list all the members of your team, their special skills, and their qualifications, write a few paragraphs describing your management style and operational goal. For example, you want to run a fun, exciting, and upbeat business while maintaining high standards with a flexible management style. Or you plan to run a business that focuses on the customer experience. You can elaborate if you wish, but the shorter this section is, the better.

The Final Analysis: Summing It All Up

Make your final summary the summation of your summations. Each section of your business plan has a summary. Review them, pick out the key points from each, and compile them in a few paragraphs. Don't feel that you can't repeat. Repetition is important. Repetition is important.

A good business plan is the same as a good speech. Tell them what you're going to tell them, then tell them, and then tell them what you told them.

Use your creativity to customize your business plan for your needs, and make sure that your personality comes through in your writing. Check out *Business Plans For Dummies* by Paul Tiffany and Steven D. Peterson to find out more about creating effective business plans.

Don't panic! Help is on the Web

You can purchase software packages and even download free templates from the Web to help you organize your business plan. The software and templates accomplish the same things as a consultant — they walk you through a series of questions that, when answered, become your business plan. In fact, many consultants use the same software as a guide to writing their reports.

The Dell Small Business site, at `http://dellnetsmallbusiness.nbci.com`, maintains a listing of all the sites that offer a free service or guide to creating a powerful business plan. At the site, click on Business Basics. There, click on Business Plans.

The following are some of my favorite sites that offer assistance in writing a business plan:

- The American Express Small Business site and its section on business plans: `http://home3.americanexpress.com/smallbusiness//resources/starting/biz_plan/`

- Quicken's Small Business site: `www.quicken.com/small_business/`

- Business Plan Pro: `www.businessplanpro.com/`

- The Small Business Administration: `www.sbaonline.sba.gov/starting/businessplan.html`

Chapter 9

Choosing a Business Structure

*B*efore you can go into business, you must select a legal structure. The type of structure you choose can affect your liabilities, taxes, profits, and more. When considering a business structure, you have three basic choices: sole proprietorship, partnership, and incorporation. Each of these structures has its advantages and disadvantages. The information in this chapter is designed to help you determine which structure is best suited for your business.

You execute your selection with the help of your lawyer and your accountant. Most accountants and lawyers will work together to help you file the proper paperwork with the IRS and state agencies. The IRS Web site www.irs.gov contains useful information to help you with this process. Most states do as well, but a small mistake of forgetting something can cost you more than what you will pay to have professionals handle this task for you. Don't be penny wise and pound foolish.

You always have the right to change your business structure, and many people do.

Discovering the Advantages of a Sole Proprietorship

If you want to take the quick and easy route, consider a sole proprietorship. With this structure, the individual owner *is* the business. Establishing a sole proprietorship is easy because it involves fewer legal restrictions and it doesn't require government approval. It's also the cheapest structure to start.

In addition to the ease of forming a sole proprietorship, other benefits are as follows:

- ✔ You don't have to share profits with anyone — they're all yours.

- ✔ You're the only decision maker — no partners or boards to please or consult.

- ✔ It's very flexible. You can change the business's focus or purpose at will — no need for approvals from government, partners, or boards.

- ✔ You don't have to fill out intricate tax or legal forms.

- ✔ You can get your business up and running more quickly than with other structures.

- ✔ If you decide to terminate your business, all you have to do is close your doors.

Of course, where you find terrific advantages, you can almost always expect to find some disadvantages. The following list presents some of the negatives associated with a sole proprietorship:

- ✔ **Personal liability:** The biggest drawback to sole proprietorship is the unlimited liability, which means that if you're the sole owner of your business, you're also solely responsible for any liability. For example, if someone making a delivery for you got into an accident, you would be personally liable (responsible for paying all costs associated with the accident) after your insurance limits were exhausted.

  You can purchase supplemental insurance to protect you in the event of a catastrophic incident. However, remember that if someone wants to sue you for an amount that exceeds the limit of your insurance policy, you're still personally liable.

- ✔ **Personal credit rating:** If your business goes bad and you pay the bills late, your own personal credit rating is compromised.

- ✔ **Taxation:** All income from the business is taxed at a personal level.

- ✔ **Personal responsibility:** You're fully responsible for all business decisions — for better or worse. Of course, you can seek help, but as the cliché goes, "The buck stops here."

If you're considering whether to go this route, explore your insurance options, because purchasing additional insurance to cover the risks may turn out to be less expensive than incorporating your business, in which case you'll have to pay corporate taxes. I discuss the option of incorporation later in this chapter.

Rick's Random Rule #97: The only problem with being in business for yourself is that it's hard to criticize the boss.

Exploring the Benefits of Partnerships

A partnership is similar to a sole proprietorship. The difference is that in a partnership, two or more parties share the responsibility. They share in the decision making, the profits, and the liabilities.

Not all partnerships have to be 50-50 splits. You can have a partner who owns just 3 percent of your business. When a partner owns just a small percentage of a business, she's usually referred to as a *minority partner* because she can never have a majority vote. Although minority partners can voice differing opinions, the person holding 97 percent of the business (or whatever percentage the majority partner holds) can do whatever she pleases.

Another common partnership scenario is one in which someone receives a few percentage points of a business in exchange for lending money to that business. (Banks do not get involved in this practice.) If you need to borrow money from an individual but your business may be considered a high-risk investment, think about offering to throw in a small percentage of the business to make the deal seem sweeter.

Investors may be reluctant to accept this type of arrangement because, in addition to gaining a portion of your business profits, they also acquire an equal portion of your business's liabilities.

Business partners can range from the silent, inactive partner to the very active, involved type. Regardless of the degree of involvement, the real benefits to forming a partnership include the following:

✔ **They're easy to form.** Establishing a partnership is similar to setting up a sole proprietorship, except that you have to put two names rather than one on any legal documents, such as the lease.

✔ **You share the financial responsibilities.** This is one of the two major reasons why people go into a partnership. They may not have enough financial resources on their own, and a partner brings additional resources.

✔ **You can draw on the expertise of two people.** This is the second common reason why people form partnerships. If you're strong at sales and weak in accounting, for example, you can find a partner who has the opposite talents. This is the basis of a good partnership.

✔ **You have a source of moral support.** Some people just don't like to go it alone.

Here are some drawbacks to keep in mind if you're considering forming a partnership:

- ✔ **Possible conflict:** People don't always get along, and they can have disagreements. Here are some issues that may creep up:

  - • One partner isn't working as hard as the other.

  - • One partner isn't working to the other partner's standards.

  - • Both partners disagree over the spending or saving of money.

  - • The partners don't agree on the distribution of profits.

- ✔ **Unlimited liability to both partners:** As in a sole proprietorship, you both can purchase liability insurance, but your personal assets are still at risk.

- ✔ **Difficulty in obtaining bank loans:** Borrowing from banks, especially when you're first getting started, can be difficult because banks are looking for a proven track record. They want to work with businesses that have a good chance of success. They don't want to foreclose or take collateral. It's almost a vicious circle; you have to be successful before they want to lend you money, but you can't be successful unless someone lends you money. That's why there are many other options than going to a bank to borrow money.

- ✔ **Selling dilemmas:** What if one partner wants to sell his shares to someone the first partner can't stand?

Finding a *secret* or *silent partner* is another option. Secret partners aren't advertised as being partners of the company, but they invest money for a return on their investment and are not involved in the business's day-to-day operations. Secret partners get involved for many reasons, but the common denominator is the business's health and survival. The partner might be a family member who's trying to help out, a vendor who can sell the business's merchandise if the business succeeds, or a landlord who feels that a tenant will help the center, so he reduces the rent for a piece of the business.

You can also have a *nominal partner,* who is allowed to share your profits but isn't obligated to share your liabilities. You want to explore this kind of partnership only when you need to entice a high-profile individual to be a spokesperson for your company. For example, you may want to use a sports star to endorse your store.

To make a partnership work, creating a partnership agreement is important. In this agreement, you can spell out all the what-ifs and their remedies. The partnership agreement is a legally binding document that states the rules the parties will live by and the appropriate remedies if one or more of the parties doesn't abide by those rules. Partnership agreements are generally reviewed by all the parties' attorneys. They're necessary, not so much for when things go well, but for when things don't go as planned or one party tries to change the rules midstream. Sometimes things go so well that one party decides she wants more. Then it's time to renegotiate or make that party adhere to the agreement.

A partnership agreement prevents the situation in which one partner ends up with a partner for life who does nothing. An effective partnership agreement states clearly the roles and responsibilities of each partner. For example, one person may do all the sales work while the other person does all the book-keeping. But what happens if the bills aren't getting paid and you have to hire an accounts payable person? How does that affect your partnership? Don't forget to include a plan for what would happen if one of the partners dies.

The key clauses in any partnership agreement are how the partnership will end, how the parties will settle disagreements, and how the partnership can be terminated. Most partnership agreements have a section on terminations.

You can find a sample partnership agreement in the Legal Forms folder on the CD.

You don't *have* to consult with an attorney when preparing a partnership agreement. I strongly suggest that you do, however, because an attorney's advice early in the game can help you avoid costly legal problems later. I also recommend that you try to work out as many of the details as possible before you visit with an attorney to avoid extensive legal fees.

Rick's Random Rule #716: Only one type of partnership works — one in which both parties get a good deal.

Understanding Corporations

A corporation is a separate legal entity — separate from you personally, that is. This means that a corporation has the ability to enter into agreements, sign contracts, and sign leases, and only the corporation is responsible for the outcome. All liabilities and risks belong to the corporation. Officers and shareholders can come and go, but the incorporated business can continue forever.

There are numerous advantages to forming a corporation. Here are a couple of the most significant:

✔ The corporation protects you from personal liability. It serves as a great separation between your own individual assets and liabilities and those of your business.

> ✔ Transferring ownership by selling, buying, or issuing stock is relatively easy. Also, an incorporated business isn't affected if the owner dies.

The disadvantages of forming a corporation include the following:

> ✔ You have to plow through a lot more paperwork than if you were setting up a sole proprietorship or partnership. You have to register your corporation on a state level.
>
> ✔ Setting up a corporation is more expensive than setting up a sole proprietorship or partnership because first you must form the legal entity of the corporation and then you must register that corporation as a legal entity.
>
> ✔ You really should consult an attorney. Doing so adds an additional (and potentially costly) step to the process. Although business starter kits and even Web sites can help you form your own corporation (some for as cheap as $300), you still need an attorney to at least review your work.
>
> ✔ Taxes on a corporation are generally higher than those on a sole proprietorship or partnership.
>
> ✔ Corporations often suffer the *double taxation penalty.* If your corporation makes profits, it has to pay a tax on those profits. After the taxes have been paid, the corporation can pay a dividend to its stockholders (assuming that you're the only stockholder, that would be you), and then you must pay income tax on the dividend income that you receive. Your corporation's profits are taxed twice!

Rick's Random Rule #56: You don't have to be big to form a corporation; skinny people form them, too.

If you decide to incorporate your business, you still have a couple of options to consider. (I told you that this is a little more complicated than setting up a sole proprietorship or partnership.) Two types of corporations are designed specifically for smaller businesses:

> ✔ Subchapter S corporations
> ✔ Limited Liability Corporations (LLCs)

Subchapter S corporations

The Subchapter S corporation is limited to companies with fewer than 75 shareholders. The major difference between a Subchapter S corporation and a regular corporation (referred to as a C corporation) is that an S corporation avoids the double taxation penalty (see the earlier section on corporations for an explanation of this penalty). Income from an S corporation is taxed only once as personal income and not as corporate profits.

Do it right!

Nothing is more frustrating than setting up a business the wrong way, not realizing the different types of corporations. I once had a client who set up as a regular corporation rather than as a Subchapter S corporation. He invested $50,000 of his own money to get his company up and running. The company closed after three years, and instead of being able to write off the losses against normal income tax, the losses were treated as a capital loss, which can be deducted only at the rate of $3,000 per year. If he had set up his company as a Subchapter S corporation, he would have been able to deduct the entire $50,000 as regular income, saving him a substantial amount of money.

The real benefit to an S corporation is for a small-business owner who may experience some financial losses at the beginning. These losses can be passed on to the owner as tax losses to offset personal income.

Limited liability corporations

The newest type of corporation is the LLC, or limited liability corporation. It was established in the U.S. tax code in 1988, and since then, all 50 states have adopted this type of corporation. The LLC has all the protective benefits of a regular corporation but works almost the same as a partnership.

The way I look at it, the LLC is to partnerships what the Subchapter S is to sole proprietorships. The LLC protects the partners against liability but passes tax income and losses to the individual investor, partner, or shareholder. I'm sure some lawyers would vehemently argue that there are more differences, and I'm sure there are. That's why I recommend that you consult with your own attorney before opting for either Subchapter S or LLC.

Working with a Board of Directors

Whether you decide to set up your business as a sole proprietorship, a partnership, or a corporation, you need a board of directors to advise you on many things, from negotiating a lease to reviewing financial statements. This group of advisers is made up of individuals (generally no more than five) who, with their various areas of expertise, can guide your company through good times and bad. (See Chapter 8 for more on the benefits of having a board.) Having a prominent board of directors whose members are respected in your industry adds credibility to your business.

Every board member should have a term of between one and three years — one year for new members to try them out and two or three years for everyone else.

Selecting board members

The best people for your board are business owners or executives who have been in situations similar to yours and who understand the needs of your business. If your business is new, you want someone who has succeeded in starting and running a business. You probably want an advertising expert as well as a financial whiz. You would also benefit from having an insurance expert on your board. Some businesses like to include a banker, but not necessarily their own banker. However, if the only banker you can get is your own, that's okay.

A close friend of mine owns three different companies and employs three different accounting firms. One representative from each of those firms always serves on his boards, but they never serve on the board that they're doing accounting work for. He firmly believes that he gets better information that way.

Why would these people agree to help you? Here are the three basic reasons why individuals are willing to serve on boards of directors:

✔ Serving on a board is prestigious and enhances people's credentials.

✔ Membership on a board presents networking opportunities. Many a deal that has nothing to do with the board meeting business has been made between board members after a board meeting. But the business's board meeting brought them together.

✔ Participating on a board is interesting — it's fun to be part of.

Resist the temptation to recruit board members simply because they have high-profile jobs, such as bank vice presidents or insurance company executives. Although such individuals do offer some prestige to your business, they are *not* entrepreneurs. They don't take risks. They're also used to going to meetings and have mastered the skill of agreeing with everyone just to facilitate the meeting's early adjournment. Try to attract members who will become your advocates.

Compensating your board members

There are no hard-and-fast rules as to compensation for board members. When your business is new, you may find that many people are willing to serve for nothing. As your business becomes stronger, a stipend of between $100 and $300 per meeting is usually appropriate. You can also offer discounts to board members as if they were employees of your business.

Try to pay as soon as you can. This added incentive makes people a little more obliged to come.

Running a board meeting

I recommend that you conduct a board meeting either annually or semi-annually. And do it over lunch or dinner. How do these meetings work? Either the president of the company or the chairman of the board of directors runs the meeting. (In most small businesses, they are one and the same.) The typical agenda is as follows:

- ✔ A report of the state of the business (how the business is doing). Board members review the financial information and respond to the figures.

- ✔ A presentation and discussion of the marketing plan for the year.

- ✔ An open discussion and review of various individual issues.

The board functions as the Supreme Court of your business, rendering opinions on the issues of the day. The issues might include the following:

- ✔ Who to hire and what they'll do

- ✔ Whether the business is asking too much or too little of the new employee

- ✔ Advertising or promotional strategies

- ✔ Whether to consider expansion

- ✔ Analysis of the business's financial strength and how to improve the financial picture

Many times, board members never reach a conclusion; it's up to the business owner to do that. The board is just there to offer suggestions to guide the owner's decisions. However, in reality, a good, cohesive board with a sense of camaraderie can come up with a strong, workable solution.

Plan for each meeting to take between three and four hours max, and allow plenty of time for discussion. To keep your board happy, always start and end your meetings on time.

Chapter 10

Keeping Public Officials Happy: Permits and Registrations

· ·

In This Chapter

▶ Knowing which permits and licenses you need

▶ Identifying local, state, and federal tax regulations and responsibilities

▶ Making sure that all your ducks are in a row

· ·

Although this chapter isn't the longest in this book, the information it contains can save you the biggest headaches (or cause the biggest problems if you ignore it) you might encounter in business. This chapter introduces you to the painstaking efforts of filling out retail-related forms and dealing with government bureaucrats — work that you have to do.

One advantage to going into business today is that local, state, and federal government agencies have really been trying to simplify and streamline the process. They haven't necessarily succeeded, but they're attempting to make forms more user-friendly. The attitudes of the people at the government agencies haven't improved, either, but things are getting better. Now, at least, you have places to go and people to ask for help. The best place is still the Web. Every local and state government, and even the IRS (www.irs.gov), has a Web site that can save you countless hours on the telephone.

Retail businesses need so many registrations, licenses, and permits that it's easy to forget what they're all for. Basically, they're there to protect the public and also to raise funds for the municipality.

> ✔ Registrations make the public aware of who's involved with the business and what type of business it is.
>
> ✔ Licenses protect the public from unskilled workers. For example, they guarantee that a licensed pharmacist fills your prescription at the drugstore.
>
> ✔ Permits protect the public from buildings or businesses that may be unsafe by regulating construction, thereby ensuring safety.

Be prepared to pay the fees for this protection they provide. Some are a little high, but most are nominal.

Getting the Necessary Papers: Registrations, Licenses, and Permits

The required registrations, licenses, and permits vary significantly from community to community — listing all the possibilities here would be impossible. However, in this section, I present the most common requirements that are used throughout the United States.

Most government agencies want their forms and procedures followed according to the letter of the law. They frown on people who want to take shortcuts or try to change the laws that they're required to enforce. You're *not* going to hear people say, "That's close enough." Yes, you'll deal with some bureaucrats and laws that seem silly, but in many cases, you'll have to go through this only once.

Business certificate (also known as a business license)

This form states the name of your business, the type of business, and its location. Maintaining these permits is usually a function of local government.

Contact your town clerk's office to apply for a business certificate. Some cities and towns require you to fill out a separate form if your business has an assumed or fictitious name, such as John Smith Company, DBA Quick Stop Umbrellas. The DBA stands for "doing business as." Most towns include the DBA name on the same form; however, some towns actually have a separate form you have to fill out to get your official DBA certificate. The fee for this certificate varies, but it's usually nominal.

Zoning permit

This permit is the product of another local ordinance. Failure to obtain a zoning permit has crippled many businesses that weren't aware of the zoning laws in their location. If you're opening your store in an established shopping area, you probably won't need a zoning permit. However, be aware that many

The sympathy card

I once received a call from a frantic woman who needed help. She had been in business for 18 years, paid her bills on time, was very active in her community, and had never used a consultant before. She owned a greeting card store that sold custom invitations. Her business was doing fine, but she had an opportunity to buy a beautiful old Victorian home on the edge of the downtown area. She wanted to live upstairs and have her business downstairs. So far, so good. She actually bought the home, moved in, and started to renovate the downstairs. But one day, a customer told her that her house was the first house within the borders of the residentially zoned area. She asked me what to do. I explained to her the concept of zoning laws and referred her to an attorney.

A few years later, I ran into that woman again, and she told me the rest of the story. She did eventually open the store in her home, but getting the clearance to do so took a little over three years, countless public hearings, and over $30,000 worth of legal fees. She said she felt so stupid that she had never thought to ask about the zoning before she bought the house.

This woman was not the first and will certainly not be the last retailer affected by zoning laws. Be careful!

communities pass zoning laws for the express purpose of keeping certain types of businesses (usually the controversial ones) away from their residents. For example, if a convenience store wants to carry X-rated magazines and a zoning ordinance prohibits the sale of pornography in that area, the store could be in violation, receive a fine, or be closed down.

More commonly, zoning ordinances are in place to preserve the charm and character of communities. You have to be careful not to open your store in an area that's not commercially zoned. A quaint street with beautiful older homes may seem like a terrific location for a boutique or florist; that street, however, may very likely be zoned residential. If you find such a location, make sure that the zoning can be changed before you proceed.

Zoning laws are usually in place for bars, restaurants, music stores, and any other type of business that a town or city council may find objectionable. In one town where I worked, there was an ordinance against lingerie shops on Main Street. Be sure to check.

Sign permit

This is my favorite type of regulation. Most cities and towns have sign codes and sign commissions that regulate the commercial use of signs. The regulations cover about anything you can think of: the size of the sign, the material it's made of, the colors, the distance it overhangs onto the sidewalk, how the sign will be lit, and the kinds of signs that can appear inside a store's window and even on the door. These commissions can even mandate that you clearly post your store's street number.

Many towns have banned neon signage altogether, regardless of the design, due to its association with bars and tattoo parlors. The problem is that everyone has different tastes, and some of these commissions are comprised of older folks whose aesthetic judgment may not be as modern as yours. As one commissioner described it, "Neon is the sign of devil's work."

Check with the town clerk's office or a building department office. In one of those two places, someone should be able to direct you to the party who can tell you about the sign regulations in your community and how to apply for a sign permit.

Police or fire department permits

Many people aren't aware that police and fire departments issue permits, which generally are related to alarm systems. Every town has an ordinance that each business is allowed a certain number of false alarm calls in the course of a year. After that, the town charges a fee to the business for responding to false alarms. To avoid many of those problems, towns are requiring stores to have their alarms certified by either the fire or police department or both before they recognize that it is an official alarm. The question is, what if you don't tell them? Nothing, as long as the alarm doesn't go off. If it does go off, however, the police or fire department will respond, and you'll get a notice of a healthy fine in the mail the next day.

The fire department is also involved in wiring inspections that are part of the occupancy certificate, which I cover later in this section. Your alarm company will be aware of the local ordinances.

Building permit

To do almost any kind of construction, remodeling, or renovation for old or new properties, you must apply for and receive a building permit. Every town has a building department and inspectors (or their equivalent), and before construction begins, an inspector has to approve your building plans. Building permits cost money, and they may be expensive, depending on what you're doing and where you're located.

Of all the departments in government I've worked with, I like this department the best because most inspectors were once independent contractors and understand a businessperson's needs. You can ask your building department to recommend reputable contractors. They'll rarely give you this information due to conflict of interest, but they may let you know which ones to avoid.

Sign paints negative picture of laws

In my hometown, the owner of an art studio taught art classes on the second floor above some stores. He had been in the town for more than ten years when he put up a small neon sign in his window saying "Art Classes." That's all. The sign was great — colorful, tasteful, and very creative. The sign was no more than 36 inches by 20 inches. He never applied for a permit because it wasn't an outdoor sign; it was just a sign in his window on the second floor.

The city council insisted that he take the sign down. He thought the council was kidding and ignored the council's warnings. The issue was brought before the city council numerous times and was debated on cable TV for the whole community to watch. The art studio owner never hired an attorney — he represented

himself every time. This little sign created such a controversy that the story made front-page news on at least five separate occasions over a three-year period. The owner finally won, but he had to appeal to the state. Of course, his business skyrocketed because of all the favorable press he received.

This story is significant because every town has different, and in many cases strange, laws pertaining to signage. In our town, there was a law against any type of neon sign. If you used neon, you were in violation of the sign code. Our town fathers associated neon with sleazy, sinister places and alcoholic beverages. (Oh, I forgot to mention that our town was dry.) Obviously, our town fathers wouldn't have been very popular in Las Vegas, but every municipality is different.

Your contractor will apply for the permit and work with the inspectors until they receive an occupancy agreement. Understand that the inspector is there to protect you from shoddy contractor workmanship. Don't be afraid to check with the inspector as to how your contractor is doing if you feel you have to. We have a tendency to side with contractors and sympathize with them about what the building inspector made them do. In most cases, though, they make them do certain things because of the town's building codes.

You do need permits signed off indicating that the work was done, but your contractor will handle that task. Every trade must be signed off, such as plumbers, electricians, wiring, alarm, fire prevention equipment, and general construction. When all the permits have been signed off, you receive certificate of occupancy from the head building inspector (see the following section).

Be careful of contractors who want to cut corners or don't want to apply for permits, telling you that they aren't necessary. Don't believe them.

Certificate of occupancy

A certificate of occupancy is a document saying that the work has been approved by all the inspectors, the building permit has been completed, and you're allowed to open. This document is more important than you think because your liability insurance is not in effect without this certificate. If a customer falls in your store and sues you and you don't have a certificate of occupancy, you're liable. Don't open your store without this certificate!

Minimum wage poster

Many states require you to post the minimum wage chart (which the state and federal governments will send to you) and other state regulations on a common bulletin board that all employees can view. If the sign is not posted, the state department of labor can levy a fine. I've never heard of anyone being fined for this infraction, but of course, I've never heard of anyone being fined for ripping those "Do Not Remove" tags off of pillows either.

State minimum wages can differ from the federal minimum. They can't be lower, but they can be higher. The reason is that some states have higher costs of living, and their minimum wages reflect that.

Health and safety permits

If you're planning to sell food, drugs, tobacco, firearms, gasoline, or any product that can be harmful or dangerous, you need a health permit. Vendors in many states aren't allowed to sell to you until you have the proper permits. Many cities and towns also have laws pertaining to locally enforced health codes. So the first place to go to find out about permits is the town hall — look for an office called "Permits."

Fortunately, towns today are quickly putting up Web sites that simplify the process. Look for the FAQ (frequently asked questions) section. The state will also have a site that will be helpful.

After you apply for and receive your permit, you receive all the information you will ever need, with a phone number to call for questions. The safety part is not so much of a permit but an awareness of the Occupational Safety and Health Administration (OSHA) and the safety laws governing your business. If you have an unannounced spot inspection and officials find that you're in violation of any safety laws, you can be fined.

Specialized retail licenses

Industry-specific stores, such as those that sell alcohol, tobacco, firearms, prescription drugs, lottery tickets, and any type of hazardous waste, need specialized retail licenses. Certain professionals — barbers, hairdressers, manicurists, and pawn shop owners, for example — also need licenses to operate their businesses. Check with your industry association to find out its requirements.

Taking the Necessary Actions

The list of all the things you have to do when setting up your business goes on. Don't get discouraged or bogged down. Just take it one step at a time, and all the necessary components will start to fall into place. Remember, if you forget one of these, it could take you longer to correct. So, as the saying goes, "A stitch in time saves nine."

Getting workers' compensation insurance

Most states require employers to carry workers' compensation insurance. This coverage isn't as expensive in the retail industry as it is in other industries, such as construction, but it can still be a major expense.

Although you're required by law to have workers' compensation insurance, please realize that it's in your own best interest to have it. You're responsible for your employees' safety — if any employee were to file a workers' comp claim and you weren't covered by workers' comp insurance, you could kiss your business goodbye. People can stay on workers' compensation for years, and if you add in your liability for their medical bills, the amount it could cost you is staggering.

The good news is that many state retail associations have instituted a self-funded workers' compensation trust. It's similar to regular workers' compensation insurance, but it's much cheaper — in many cases, almost half the price. You generally save 20 to 25 percent up front and receive dividends if the trust doesn't have to pay out many claims. It takes about three years for the real savings to kick in, but check with your state retail association for details. It's worth the wait!

Avoiding "honest" mistakes

During my second year of business, I successfully completed tough negotiations on a ten-year lease, which called for an increase in rent in the fifth year. My mother, who was a crafty businesswoman, insisted that I record the lease, which I did immediately. I forgot about it until three years later, when I received a rent increase from the landlord. He included a copy of the page in the lease, but he saved the wrong lease. I knew this because the one he sent us was the original, before we started to negotiate. I called him up and told him about the error. He was very pleasant but disagreed, saying that he remembered an increase after year three. I remembered that I had the lease recorded and got a copy of the recorded lease. He had no argument after that.

Recording your lease

Recording your lease entails taking your signed lease to the clerk of courts or the registry of deeds and having it recorded in a public record in the same way your home mortgage is recorded. Many landlords don't allow this because their tenants would be able to find out what the other tenants are paying. Retailers do it nonetheless. Recording your lease means that if anything were to happen to the copies of your lease, they could always be found in a public place.

Again, every state is different, but many states record only leases that are for seven years or more, and today most leases are for five years. Always record a lease when you're dealing with a single building owner — his record keeping may be a little slipshod.

Contacting credit reporting agencies

Credit reporting agencies are not government agencies, but sometimes you may think they are. Credit reporting agencies keep track of your creditworthiness. The largest is Dun & Bradstreet, but each industry has a favorite credit reporting service. These firms are as important as government agencies because of the importance of credit today. During your first year in business, you will be establishing credit and will probably have to pay for things up front or COD (cash on delivery). Some people may extend a small limit of credit to you, however.

Check with your vendors as to which credit reporting agency services your industry and send the agency a letter introducing yourself, a copy of your business plan, and a form from your bank confirming that you have received financing or have sufficient funds in the bank. If you're smart, you'll contact the credit reporting agency before it contacts you, and you'll score points. If you follow my advice here, you'll thank me later.

Staying Informed about Important Issues

Ignorance is not bliss. Forget about a tax and it will cost you. That's why it's important to stay informed of the latest rules and changes in any of the areas that affect your business. The areas discussed in this section can serve as a starting point.

Taxes: Different kinds from different areas

Governments need taxes to support themselves, so you know how essential they are. It's important to remember why government makes you jump through hoops because there will be times when you will question how and why some laws were ever passed. Get your scissors ready, because here comes the red tape.

Dealing with the feds

Your dealings with the federal government will mainly concern taxes. However, certain types of retail stores deal more extensively with federal regulations and their governing agencies. For example, if you plan to sell alcohol, tobacco, or firearms, you'll need to work with the Bureau of Alcohol, Tobacco, and Firearms.

When it comes to taxes, though, the federal government will be with you as long as you're in business — and maybe even after. Make sure to consult your accountant on all tax-related issues.

Before your accountant contacts the IRS to receive your federal tax number, you have to determine whether you even need one. (Have your accountant contact the IRS and state and municipalities — that's generally part of the job that accountants do.) You must determine what type of company you are: sole proprietor, partnership, C corporation, S corporation, or a limited liability corporation, as explained in Chapter 9. You need to know that because different types of companies require different tax forms; for example, a sole proprietorship uses the owner's social security number.

If you plan to hire employees, you must apply for an Employer Identification Number (EIN). This form is called the SS-4, and it's available from your local IRS office or Social Security Office, or by calling 1-800-TAX-FORM. Your accountant can also obtain a copy for you.

Publication #583, *Starting a Business and Keeping Records,* is an IRS publication that you *must* get from the IRS because it explains every federal tax that you should be aware of. It also mentions possible state taxes, but because every state is different, the usefulness of this state information is limited. You can request a copy of this free report (that's the least the government can do, right?) by calling 1-800-TAX-FORM, sending a fax to 703-368-9694, or going online to www.irs.gov and then clicking on "Forms and Publications." (You just have to type *583* to download the report.) Your accountant should have it, but get a copy for yourself. It's easy to read and covers everything you'll ever need.

For your convenience, I include an excerpt from IRS publication #583, *Starting a Business and Keeping Records,* in the Accounting Forms folder on the CD. But you should still check with the IRS for updates.

Many small businesses get into trouble because they don't pay the federal and state withholding tax deposit. This money is deducted from an employee's paycheck, and the business is responsible for depositing it with the IRS or the state revenue department when it's due. (Due dates vary with the size of the deposit.) Some businesses don't set this money aside and end up paying it late. *Don't* do that! Penalties and late charges can be astronomical and have taken some businesses years to pay off in installments.

Remembering state taxes

Each state has its own set of taxes. Although all states are different, here are some types of state taxes you're likely to encounter no matter where you are:

- ✔ State income tax
- ✔ State excise tax
- ✔ Unemployment insurance tax
- ✔ Sales tax (but in some states, certain things are exempt)

If your state has a sales tax, register with your state's sales tax office to receive a sales tax resellers certificate. This document is important because it enables you to buy merchandise from manufacturers or distributors and not pay them a sales tax.

To find more about your individual state's requirements, check with your state department of revenue and, of course, your accountant. Most state agencies do have Web sites, but some of them are a little confusing, although others are excellent. The easiest way to access your state department of revenue is through the Web site www.startupbiz.com/.

Never let your tax payments slide. They don't go away . . . ever.

Americans with Disabilities Act (ADA)

The Americans with Disabilities Act (ADA) gives civil rights protection to individuals with disabilities. It guarantees equal opportunity for individuals with disabilities in public accommodations, employment, transportation, state and local government services, and telecommunications.

The ADA ensures that public facilities are accessible to all people, regardless of their physical challenges. Most business facilities that have been built in the last ten years are in accordance with the ADA, but many older buildings need to be brought up to current standards. This is the law of the land, and although real estate salespeople may tell you that you won't have to do anything to comply, don't believe them. Find out for yourself. Besides, it's the right thing to do.

Public accommodation is only one aspect of the ADA. It also stipulates that you can't deny employment to a qualified applicant based on disability of any kind.

Covering All Your Bases

Covering every permit and tax regulation for every state and municipality in this book is impossible. The important thing for you to remember is to be proactive. The following is a list of resources that can help you make sure you satisfy all requirements specific to your type of business. Seek out these resources and comply with all regulations. Believe me, doing so is worth the initial hassle.

- ✔ **Chamber of commerce:** Just about every town has one or is involved in a regional chamber. Asking questions about local laws, permits, registrations, and taxes can serve as a good time to get acquainted and see what other services the chamber offers. Most chambers today have networking sessions that are very helpful.

- ✔ **Trade associations:** Some industries have very strong associations, while others are weak. For example, the photo industry and jewelers have very strong associations (PMA, Photo Marketing Association, and JA, Jewelers of America), but apparel and gift associations are either weak or nonexistent. The reason is that they have strong trade show operators that in many cases serve in a similar capacity to an association. They have dedicated staff and offer educational programs. They may not always know the answer, but they usually know someone who does.

✔ **Trade publications:** Every industry has a publication that can be a wonderful source of information. To find the best publication in your industry, ask your sales reps and other retailers which publication they read.

✔ **Tax collector's office:** If you want to be sure about local taxes, ask your local tax collector what taxes a business of your type has to pay. I would rather have my accountant handle this part of the business.

✔ **Town clerk's office or planning board:** Sometimes a town clerk knows everything that's happening regarding permits and local regulations. Sometimes the clerk at the planning board is the source of this information. Either way, they're good people to know.

✔ **Insurance agent:** A good insurance agent is a valuable person to have on your team. Not only can she protect you in case of a disaster, but she's always aware of those quirky little laws that require surety bonds or special insurance. A good insurance agent knows everyone in town and where to go to get things done. Most agents are involved in many civic groups and usually know all the local politicians. (I don't know whether that's good or bad.) The bottom line is that a good insurance agent is usually two phone calls away from anything you might need to know.

At the beginning of this chapter, I say that getting all the paperwork done wouldn't be too bad. But it can be if you wait until the last minute to get it done. Work with your accountant or tax professional. Consider using a payroll service because it will pay your taxes for you electronically (using *your* money, not its own!). The fees payroll services charge are much lower than those a bookkeeper would charge. The two largest payroll service companies are Paychex (www.paychex.com) and ADP (www.adp.com). They can even handle a retirement program when you're ready.

Part IV
Running Your Business

The 5th Wave By Rich Tennant

"Don't worry Mr. Brennen. The 'OPEN' sign is on the door. I can see it from here."

In this part . . .

You have your location, your plan, your vendor contacts. Now it's time to focus on the day to day stuff. In this part you learn how to set up your store's procedures so your business can run smoothly, to plan your buying, including how to pay for and receive the merchandise, to work with salespeople, to find and maintain a fantastic staff, and to keep your business out of trouble. Sounds like a lot, doesn't it! Well, retailing isn't easy, but it sure is a lot of fun!

Chapter 11

Creating Your Internal Systems: The Day-to-Day Stuff

Friendly hellos, thank-yous, and good-byes are important to good customer service. But they're not the only things that matter. If you have good customer service but don't have a system in place for handling all the necessary retail functions, the result can be the same as ignoring a customer: lost business. It's the difference between being busy and being productive. One of the things that many retailers forget to do is to document the procedures for all the little things that help a business run smoothly — opening and closing the store, receiving merchandise, restocking, and so on.

Although my philosophy is that customers always come first, I acknowledge that tasks have to be performed. The smoother you can make your back room functions, the more time you'll have to focus your efforts on your customers. Nothing is more aggravating than going into a store where everyone is so focused on the operations of the store that they don't have time for a customer. That's why creating systems and procedures that all employees know and understand is in your best interest. Doing so eliminates wasted time so that everyone can be as productive as possible.

Rick's Random Rule #47: Having happy customers in a slightly messy store is much better than having unhappy customers in a neat store.

Creating a Procedure Binder

A procedure binder documents the way you do things. It serves as a manual for *your store*. I suggest that you buy a three-ring binder and divide it into the following main categories:

- ✔ Merchandise functions
- ✔ Operational functions
- ✔ Marketing and promotional functions
- ✔ Safety and security functions
- ✔ Personnel functions

Then create subcategories within each section that explain the following:

- ✔ **Who** should do it
- ✔ **What** has to be done
- ✔ **When** it should be done
- ✔ **Where** it should be done
- ✔ **Why** it has to be done
- ✔ **How** it should be done

At first, you may want to create pages in your binder with just these major categories. You can add subcategories that you think may apply. As you establish procedures for the various functions of your store, type them up and keep them in this binder for reference. I recommend that you review all your procedures and print them on an annual basis.

This binder will become the basis for training of your new employees. It also will become your central collection spot for instructions on how different functions should be performed in your store. Keep it in the most accessible spot in your store and make it available to all employees.

Rick's Random Rule #68: The customer always comes first. Operations come second. But the goal is to focus your operations on the customer.

The procedure binder is not etched in stone. Procedures may change as the business and you evolve, and you should constantly work to refine them.

Identifying Your Internal Procedures

All the internal procedures you create should outline who needs to do what — when, where, why, and how. I use these question words throughout this section to help you identify the elements you need to include in your various procedures. Look at these procedures from various points of view — that of the person who is performing the function, the owner, and the customer.

Creating procedures for merchandise functions

The procedure that covers your merchandise functions should start with your initial plans to buy your merchandise and end when the merchandise is finally sold. I break down the merchandising functions to make it easy for you to design a procedure that includes everything related to merchandising. Use your responses to the question words to help formulate your merchandising procedure.

Buying your merchandise

One of the most complex processes in the retail business is the buying process. That's why I dedicate an entire chapter (Chapter 12) to the creation of a buying plan. Having an established procedure in place makes this process as smooth as possible.

Who? To run a successful store, you need the input of everyone who works there. Ask your employees what customers ask for when they call. Also find out where you lose sales because you don't have the merchandise in stock. Find out what you could sell more of if you had more of it.

What? Selecting merchandise that can be sold profitably and delivered in a timely manner.

When? Decide in advance the times you're setting aside to buy. If you're shopping trade shows, the show's schedule will determine your buying times. If you're working with salespeople in your store, call them and set up an appointment.

Where? Make a list of the places you can do your buying. This list can include in-store, trade shows, and permanent showrooms. Decide where you want the buying to occur.

Why? You want to select the finest merchandise at the most competitive prices so that you can provide fantastic merchandise to your customers.

How? This is the actual buying procedure. See Chapter 12 for step-by-step information on getting the goods.

Receiving the merchandise

Who? Will everyone be trained in this function, or will you assign one or two people?

What? Everything that comes into the store.

When? This depends on the delivery services; however, sometimes you can request delivery times.

Where? On the selling floor or in the back room? (Receiving merchandise on the selling floor is messy, but it creates excitement and excitement makes sales. Ignore this advice if you're in the restaurant business — receiving a side of beef at the front door won't generate extra sales.)

Why? Because you need the goods. You must also be able to account for the receiving in case of dispute from a vendor.

How? Determine how you will record the merchandise received and deduct it from what's on order. Create a receiving log that gives you all the key information. This log should include the following:

- Name of the vendor
- Name of the shipper (UPS, FedEx, and so on)
- Date of receipt
- Merchandise received
- Dollar amount
- Invoice number

You can find a sample receiving form in the Daily Operation Forms folder .

Pricing and ticketing the merchandise

Who? Will one or two people be assigned, or will everybody be trained to do this job? Who will determine the prices charged? Will you use a formula, or will you evaluate each piece of merchandise separately?

What? Creating price tags and putting them on the merchandise.

When? Do you ticket as soon as the merchandise comes in, save it for a slow time, or do it first thing in the morning?

Where? On the selling floor? In the back room?

Why? Because customers want to see merchandise with price tags on it and to receive the maximum markup that you can sell the merchandise for and still sell it as quickly as possible.

How? List each step that's required to either hand-ticket, machine-ticket, or computer-generate a ticket. Also, you must determine whether you're going to list a suggested retail price and your price, or just one price.

I include a sample price tag in the Daily Operation Forms folder on the CD.

Putting the merchandise on the sales floor

Who? Give this job to the employees who have a natural flair for placement. Some employees (the ones who don't have the flair) can unintentionally hide your great buys.

What? Placing the merchandise and informing all employees of the new merchandise.

When? Some stores will leave the merchandise in the back room until it is ticketed and properly prepared to be placed on the selling floor. Other stores put the unticketed merchandise out in a new arrival area (generally near the cash wrap) and prepare it for sale in view of the customers..

Where? Either provide a diagram of what merchandise goes where or meet with your employees to discuss this matter. You also have to decide what merchandise to feature or put on display. Sometimes you may want to feature merchandise that has been there for a couple of weeks since an emphasis on these items may increase their sales potential.

Why? Because placement of the merchandise can determine how fast it sells. Merchandise placement is a critical issue.

How? This part of the procedure should cover the issues of what goes where and even when something gets moved. Expect to change this part of the procedure as often as you change the layout of your store. The most important step is making sure that everyone is aware of the location of the new merchandise.

Processing special orders

Who? I strongly recommend assigning one person to this task because you can prevent needless confusion that way. However, you should always have a backup person, fully trained and prepared, to cover vacation and sick days.

What? When someone wants to order something that's not currently in your inventory.

When? Some people do all special orders first thing in the morning, while other stores believe that you should take care of them while the customer is in front of you. Your industry practices will determine the best time. Ask your vendors when they prefer them.

Where? Close to the computer and the phone.

Why? In some industries, special orders and layaways can represent 75 percent of the business. The higher the price of the merchandise, the more special orders play an important part of the business.

How? Taking special orders involves more than just calling your vendors. You must create a receipt for both you and the customer. (I made up a third copy that I filed under the vendor's name. If I called a vendor about something, I could check all my outstanding orders.)

Check out the special ordering section in the Daily Operation Forms folder on the CD.

Handling reorders

Who? The buyer or the person in charge of special orders.

What? Order again something that you have carried and has performed well.

When? After reviewing your sales report and your buying plans. It can also occur after customer and/or employee requests.

Where? Store office.

Why? A reorder should be a proven winner, something that you know will sell.

How? A purchase order must be written for this item so that you have some way of tracking what's on order. Once the reorder is written, treat it the same as any other order.

You can find a sample purchase order form in the Buying Forms folder on the CD.

Reticketing your merchandise

Who? Whoever does your ticketing should do your reticketing.

What? Reticketing is necessary when tickets fall off merchandise, or something is returned and needs to be reticketed. You also may need to reticket if you marked merchandise down for a sale event and then must reinstate the original price.

When? ASAP.

Where? Usually you reticket on the selling floor so that you keep the merchandise in the customers' sight.

Why? Old tickets, ripped tickets, and missing tickets are the sign of a poorly run or unprofessional store.

How? Most electronic systems allow you to make a duplicate ticket. This step depends on your particular system. Whatever you do, make sure that the new ticket has the same information as the original ticket.

Restocking your merchandise

Who? Everyone who works in the store should be involved in restocking.

What? Putting things back on the selling floor

When? ASAP.

Where? The selling floor.

Why? To put the merchandise back to work. The longer it's off the floor, the more money it costs you because you're offering your customers less of a choice and eliminating a possible sale.

How? Make it a policy to replenish the merchandise on your selling floor before you go home each evening or first thing each morning. Without some type of policy or procedure, restocking can slide.

Marking down merchandise

Who? The owner or manager.

What? This is the physical action of reducing the price of the merchandise.

When? Any time you want to reduce the price — at the end of a season, for a sale event, as an adjustment when a customer is dissatisfied (like a care token) or an especially good customer who deserves a discount.

Where? On the selling floor or in the back room.

Why? Reducing the price makes the merchandise sell faster. Lower-priced items also appeal to a wider variety of people.

How? This depends on the purpose of the markdown. Technically, you mark down merchandise by drawing a red line through the selling price and establishing a new lower price. Then you record those markdowns in a markdown book. Better yet, attach separate sale tags.

Establishing procedures for operational functions

This is the one section that if ignored creates more problems, aggravation, poor morale, and customer dissatisfaction than any other aspect of your business. Yet, if done properly, no one will even notice. And that's what you want!

Opening the store

Who? Whoever is responsible for opening.

What? Opening the store involves a series of steps that someone must take in the morning in order to be ready for customers.

When? On time or a little early.

Why? When you have a snowstorm and there's 2 feet of snow in front of your door, you'll ask yourself the question "why?" again — unless you're selling shovels, that is.

How? The steps here might go something like this:

1. Shut off the alarm.

2. Lock the door behind you until all the lights are on and the store is ready.

3. Make sure that the selling floor is restocked.

4. Make sure that the store is clean (vacuum, clean the glass, and so on).

5. Check the displays.

6. Put money in the cash register (if you put it in a safe at night).

7. Reconcile sales from the day before. (Make the cash balances.)

8. Check to make sure that the credit card machines are ready for the day's business.

9. Unlock the door.

After you create a procedure for opening the store, have it printed and laminated. Or you can use pads of paper printed with the procedure as a check-off sheet every day.

Closing the store

Who? Anyone authorized and anyone who will be with the authorized person.

What? The steps to close down for the night.

When? Always on time, not a minute early or late.

Why? Because you're tired and want to go home.

How? Here are the questions to ask yourself to determine the steps involved in closing your store:

• What happens to the cash and checks in the register?

• Do any doors need additional locking? (Some stores have a back door that gets an additional double lock at closing.)

- Are the doors locked at exactly closing time, leaving customers in the store to be let out by employees? This is a common practice.

- Is the deposit done at night, and if it is, who goes to the bank and with whom?

- Should the store be cleaned and vacuumed?

- How late should employees stay to close up, and how many employees should stay?

- Are there any racks or fixtures to be moved? Many hardware stores put goods on the sidewalk during the day, so someone needs to be responsible for moving them inside at closing time.

Accounting for cash

Who? Whoever is authorized. The less hands involved, the better.

What? The system you use to assure that cash, checks, and charges are properly accounted for. The cash procedure can be incorporated in the store opening procedure, but many stores make it a separate task with instructions. Accounting for cash also includes making sure that the store has what is referred to as a bank of money — enough extra cash on hand so that you can make change.

When? At closing, opening, and anytime the drawer contains a significant amount of cash that should be taken out of the register and put into a safe.

Where? Out of the view of the general public. If you count your cash in the morning before the store opens, however, then you can do this at the cash counter.

Why? Sloppy cash management leads to missing money, less profits, and the risk of putting employees in both tempting and uncomfortable positions.

How? Establish rules and procedures to determine the maximum amount of cash that should be in the register. Decide at what point cash should be reduced and placed in a safe or secure place. When should deposits be made — morning, afternoon, or after closing?

The amount of cash in change (dollar bills, quarters, dimes, nickels, and pennies) in the in-store "bank" must be established. Most stores have between $100 and $200 in a safe for change. Money from the register buys change from the in-store "bank." That money must be replenished so that change is always available.

Create a form to record and reconcile the day's business. Many stores use a daily sales envelope with the form printed on the outside.

Check the CD for a sample daily sales envelope. You can find it in the Accounting Forms folder.

Dealing with the alarm

Who? All employees should be aware of the alarm systems, but only authorized individuals should know the codes to activate or deactivate the system.

What? The system that notifies the police of burglaries, break-ins, or robberies.

When? Sure, you activate it when you close and deactivate when you open, but when should you push the panic button? Some people believe that you shouldn't set off the alarm when a robber is in the store, while others believe you should trip the alarm at the first threat of danger. People can easily misinterpret some behaviors or noises as potential dangers, but a common argument is that it's better to be safe than sorry.

Where? Alarm systems today cover every part of a building — doors, windows, and the selling floor. Employees must know where the panic button is and how it works.

Why? Because crime is something that is always a possibility.

How? Print the code and give it to authorized employees. The code must be changed regularly. When you give the employees the new code, collect the old instruction sheets to prevent confusion. Post the location of the panic button system, review the system twice a year, and included information about it in new employee training.

Processing sales

Who? Any employee who has anything to do with the process.

What? The way sales are rung in or recorded in the register.

When? Hopefully often — as much as possible.

Where? From anywhere a customer says, "I'll take it."

Why? So you can pay your bills and go on vacation.

How? Does the salesperson just tell the customer to go to the checkout counter, or does she walk the customer there? Does the salesperson ring in the sale, or does a cashier do it? Every system is different, and the steps, which should be on laminated paper, must be clear, short, and followed faithfully.

You can find sample sales slips, credit slips, layaway forms, and "on hold" forms in the Daily Operation Forms folder on the CD.

Processing credit card purchases

Who? Anyone who processes a sale, opens or closes the store, or reconciles the charge sales.

What? Establishing a system to accept credit cards and selecting a credit card processor.

When? Anytime.

Where? Wherever your system is, or where the telephone to call your processor is.

Why? Because you must take credit cards, and special challenges always arise (especially when a card is declined).

How? Everyone should know which credit cards are accepted, and signs with that information should be posted at the door and near the cash register. Every credit card processing company will send you step-by-step instructions for processing cards.

Part of your training must be on how to handle a declined credit card. Simply say, "That one didn't work; do you have another?" Everybody has multiple cards today. If you treat declined customers like criminals, they'll never return to your store.

You must also have a procedure in the unlikely event that the credit card processor instructs you to keep the card because it is stolen. This situation can be scary because you probably do have a criminal in front of you. Tell the customer that someone reported the card stolen, and advise him to call the card company as soon as he gets home, giving him the benefit of the doubt. If you feel you're in danger, give the card back and call the police.

If you don't know where to go to find the best rates for credit card processing — or even to find a processor — check with your state retail association or the National Retail Federation (www.nrf.com). Both organizations offer programs and recommendations.

Accepting checks

Who? Anyone responsible for processing sales.

What? Accepting checks.

When? As many times as you can.

Where? At the cash counter.

Why? Because checks are a common way for people to pay.

How? Ask yourself these questions:

- Do you accept checks? From out-of-state people?

- What proof of identity do you want? Photo ID? Driver's license number and state?

- Does a clerk need an approval from a supervisor if a check is over a certain dollar amount?

- Do you use an outside check processing company, such as Telecheck? What are its procedures?

Processing returns

Who? Decide exactly who will be responsible for this function — the owner, the manager, and/or the salesperson at the cash wrap area. Is an approval required? Most stores empower their sales personnel to handle this procedure.

What? Accepting returned merchandise.

When? All the time.

Where? At the cash counter.

Why? Because it's an accepted procedure.

How? Decide what information you're going to require. A sales receipt? The charge card used? Will you give the money back in cash? (It costs you the credit card processing fee if you do.) Do you inspect the merchandise? If so, what do you look for? Above all, make sure you check your procedure with your state's attorney general's office Consumer Affair Division to verify that you are within the established parameters. You also want to make sure that you keep your policy consistent with all customers — treat your worst customer as well as your best.

I put a sample return authorization form and a sample return policy on the CD. You can find them in the Daily Operation Forms folder.

Rick's Random Rule #121: When customers return goods to you, it's a sign of their confidence in your store and another opportunity to sell them something.

Taking cash readings

Who? The owner or any authorized person.

What? Looking at the sales of the day.

When? Establish regular reading periods. Taking readings every hour is good because it can help you plan your sales help.

Where? The register or computer terminal.

Why? To see how the store is doing.

How? Every system is different, but when a reading is taken, decide where it should be recorded and do so every time. You should have a permanent log of readings.

Analyzing inventory and sales

Who? The owner, manager, and/or buyers.

What? The process of reviewing your inventory levels and your sales figures for the purpose of buying merchandise, determining hot and cold sellers, deciding what to mark down, and spotting trends.

Creating a "beat yesterday book"

Create a "beat yesterday book" in which you document the sales of the day. There are many ways to do this and a variety of books you can use, but the key idea is to have a book in which you can religiously enter your daily sales. This type of documentation enables you to store all your sales records in one place and keep the information year after year. Doing this helps you spot trends and gives you quick information on how your business is doing. Record your net sales (sales less refunds) for the day and compare this figure with last year's figure for the same day or compare it with your sales plan.

When? Once a week is perfect, but every other week is fine.

Where? This is an office function that may require an occasional visit to the selling floor to look for merchandise or review the placement.

Why? Your inventory is your single biggest investment. In many cases, it's what defines you. The flow of merchandise in and out of your inventory determines your success. What you buy and what you sell are two of the most important reports you can generate and review.

How? Look at your inventory level in dollars (as opposed to a unit count) and then look at sales, what merchandise you have received, and what is on order. Make sure that you have enough inventory to generate the sales you're projecting. The more times you turn your merchandise over, the more money you can make.

Managing the flow of supplies

Who? Whoever will be buying supplies.

What? Establishing a system for ordering supplies, including packaging, materials for display, register tape, and so on.

When? Three times a year when you're new, and then twice a year.

Where? This is a back room function.

Why? So you never run out of what you need.

How? Create a permanent file that tracks supply usage. Track your usage so you can prevent the aggravation of running out.

Presenting the merchandise

Who? Assign someone, who could be the owner or the most talented person you have, to be in charge of displaying the merchandise. In a planning meeting, however, anyone's input is helpful.

What? Your presentation of the merchandise, including the windows.

When? New displays every month create just enough change to make the most boring store exciting. Planning meetings should take place once or twice a year.

Where? Make the most of every spot where you can tastefully display your merchandise.

Why? Customers tend to buy what's featured. Displays put your merchandise in the most favorable position for sale.

How? Have a planning session, create a schedule, and then execute your plan. If it isn't planned, it doesn't get done.

Creating store rules and regulations

Who? The business owner should do this.

What? These policies are designed for employees, vendors, and customers.

When? At almost any time.

Why? A business needs to know its boundaries — what is acceptable behavior, and what isn't.

How? Developing these rules and policies is an ongoing project. I suggest that you shop at other stores to see what store policies similar businesses have. In your research, look for policies that cover such topics as refunds, receipt of damaged goods, and accepting return merchandise that was purchased by a customer over a year ago.

You can find a sample employee handbook, time card, vacation schedule tracker, and work schedules in the Daily Operation folder on the CD.

Developing procedures for sales and marketing functions

Sales and marketing are the engines that make the retail business move. Planning how they are going to work is critical to the success of your business. Take time to answer all the questions that follow in order to devise a set of procedures that will work for you.

Planning your marketing calendar

Who? All interested parties in the store.

What? This is the planning process to determine sale, non-sale, and PR advertising and promotion schedule.

When? Once a year, with constant review.

Where? Anyplace that's quiet so you won't experience any interruptions.

Why? To know what you're going to be doing, to make sure that you're going to do it, to make sure that you're buying merchandise around the promotions you're planning, and to budget the necessary funding.

How? You need a calendar, a pencil with a good eraser, and perhaps *Chase's Calendar of Events* (a book full of promotional ideas that's available in the reference section of your library). Discuss month by month, week by week, the events that will be happening in your store. Once the event has been determined, select a date to begin planning, such as planning in July for the after-Christmas sale. Event planning needs to start well in advance because that's generally when the merchandise is purchased. You must balance sale events with non-sale or public relations events. Once you have created a calendar, plan the dates that you must start executing the steps of the plan.

You can find samples of a visual display calendar and visual display prop inventory in the Daily Operation Forms folder on the CD.

Setting up your selling system

Who? Everyone in the store. No one should be excluded.

What? This is the way you want your employees to conduct themselves on the selling floor for maximum selling performance.

When? All the time.

Where? The selling floor.

Why? Selling is what retailing is all about!

How? Develop your own way of selling to your customers. This can range from complete self-service to the ultimate in personalized service. Whatever it is, document how to approach, question, and bond with a customer. Also explain how the original sale should be closed and how add-on items should be suggested. See Chapter 19 for tips on how to do these things.

Creating procedures for safety and security functions: shoplifting and employee theft

Unfortunately, shoplifting and employee theft are part of retailing all retailers deal with. But you can't merchandise or design your store from a security point of view or everything would be behind the counters (or behind bars) or in showcases. Still, you need to be aware of and prepared for these security issues.

Who? It affects everyone in the store, however, the buck stops with the store manager and the owner.

What? The stealing of merchandise from your store.

When? All the time.

Where? On the selling floor, but unfortunately it can also occur in the back room.

Why? To protect yourself and your store.

How? Each store must create its own set of policies pertaining to theft. Does the employee confront the customer? Does the employee press a silent alarm? Or does your shopping area have a security service? See Chapter 14 for information on how to handle shoplifters.

In relation to employee theft, some stores require that all pocketbooks and personal belongings be stored in very visible places, and some even have a policy covering inspection. The smaller the store, the smaller the problem — but the problem of theft can exist anywhere.

Make sure that you check with your state's Attorney General's office for information on laws pertaining to shoplifting, employee theft, and search of customer and employee belongings. Know the laws before you accuse. Every state is different.

Designing procedures for personnel functions

The information in this section is to help you manage your employees and to addresses the issues that are most important to them — employment policies and benefits. If you should grow to have multiple employees, you can take this section and convert it into an employee handbook.

Setting up your employment policies

Who? Obviously this covers everyone, but there must be a person assigned to be the keeper of the records and policies of the business. Construct your policies with input from the owner, manager, professional consultants, and your rank and file employees.

What? Include policies that deal with compensation, attendance, tardiness, calling in sick, job description, reasons for dismissal, and minimum levels of acceptable performance.

Where? This should be printed and handed to the employee upon hiring, and it also doesn't hurt to have one posted.

Why? So that employees are treated fairly and decisions aren't made in the heat of the moment.

When? As soon as you have employees.

How? By meeting with the key people involved with creating the policies, discussing the issues, and then distributing the written policies to each employee.

Dealing with employee benefits

Who? Everyone in the store is affected, but either the owner/manager or bookkeeper/office manager administers this function.

What? Address the issues of compensation, performance reviews, raises, sick days, paid ho/lidays, insurance, vacations (paid and unpaid), time off (paid and unpaid), pension plans, store discounts, education, and any other type of benefit that would apply to your industry.

Where? This should be printed and handed to all employees upon hiring, and it also doesn't hurt to have one posted.

Why? So that employees are treated fairly and decisions aren't made in the heat of the moment.

When? As soon as you have employees.

How? By meeting with the key people involved with creating the policies, discussing the issues, and then distributing the written policies to each employee.

The story of Elizabeth, the good-natured but intelligent failure

Elizabeth owned an accessory store in the Midwest. She sold expensive handbags, costume jewelry, scarves, pins, and novelty items. Her concept was wonderful, her sales were good, her presentation was breathtaking, but unfortunately, the store was forced to close because of a lack of rules and policies.

The most obvious problem was that her store didn't have regular hours of operation. It was supposed to keep regular hours, but sometimes the store manager slept late and didn't open the store until 11:00 or 11:30 a.m. This was a problem because other employees arrived at 8:45 a.m. They were so used to waiting for the store to open that they would meet at the coffee shop across the street and wait until the manager or Elizabeth arrived to open. Elizabeth was such a nice person that she always paid them for working the hours the store *should* have been open. The employees never complained because they were well paid. They received three weeks of paid vacation and a total of 12 paid holidays and personal days — even though the store really couldn't afford that.

Another problem was that the store seemed to have different prices for different people, and if somebody bought a lot of merchandise, the employees always threw something in for free.

This was the first store where I observed, during a sale, four salespeople waiting in line to ring in and package their own personal purchases while lots of customers were waiting for help. The employees always took their 40 percent discount in front of customers.

Although Elizabeth had a wonderful talent for selecting and displaying merchandise, her store eventually went into bankruptcy because of the lack of rules and policies.

Chapter 12

Getting the Goods: Controlling Your Buying

*W*hen will one more stroke ruin the painting? When will one more ingredient spoil the soup? When will one more item ruin your mix of merchandise? Each and every piece of merchandise is important to the success of a retail store. If you have too much merchandise, it'll stay in your store longer than it should, and your store will be crowded. You'll eventually have to mark it down, reducing your profits. You also risk boring your customers if they come into your store and see the same merchandise over and over again. On the other hand, if you have too little merchandise, your store will look empty, and no one wants to come to a store with empty shelves.

The goal of this chapter is to show you how to buy merchandise, negotiate the best price, price your merchandise for maximum profits, and finally recognize when enough is enough. In this chapter I present buying strategies in the context of buying from a rep at a trade show, but you can use these strategies when you're buying from anyone — anywhere. See Chapter 5 for some ideas on other merchandise sources.

Visiting a Trade Show for Your First Buy

Your first buying experience should probably be at a trade show — a good place to start because trade shows present so many different choices of lines to buy. A trade show can be local, regional, national, or even international, but they all generally consist of a group of salespeople trying to sell merchandise.

Trade shows are where all the players come together. Each manufacturer has a booth, which is what the individual showrooms are called. Manufacturers' reps attend to show multiple lines in their booths. Importers are there, and depending on the industry, you find distributors and wholesalers, too. Buying offices and buying groups generally don't have booths, but many of them have their own trade shows.

The general public is not allowed at trade shows. Once you have established your business, you're permanently in the trade show database, but to establish yourself as a buyer, you must show proof. Proof can be a business card, federal tax ID number, or any other legal document, such as a sales tax form or a reseller's certificate or paperwork from your town clerk that shows you have registered as a business. They may also want pay stubs for the staff people who accompany the buyers.

Spend your first day at a trade show just looking around. Absorb information — who's selling what and for how much. Yes, you'll get tired, but keep on walking. Don't buy anything or stop at any booth yet. Take a few notes about places where you must stop later. See who's busy. Remember that knowledge is power.

The biggest asset you can have when you buy merchandise for your store is your knowledge of the marketplace. Knowing what's available for sale in a category is a valuable negotiating tool. When you can tell vendors the price of their competitor's merchandise or what products the competition is offering, they'll stop and listen to you. You become a respected buyer.

Sales reps and manufacturers confirm that the biggest stores don't always get the best deals and the best merchandise — great buyers do. And a great buyer is a great negotiator, and a great negotiator is a great salesperson. When you buy merchandise from vendors, you're also selling them an opportunity to present their merchandise in your store. Buying is more than just looking at a piece of merchandise and saying, "I love it and I'll take it." Of course, you'll experience such moments, but buy merchandise only when you see a real advantage or opportunity.

Never buy without a buying plan or a budget showing you what you can spend for the various categories or departments in your store. Make a list of vendors you want to see as well and, if possible, make appointments.

Dealing with Sales Reps

On the second day of a trade show, you're ready to start to work with a few salespeople. Visit their booth or showroom and introduce yourself and your store. Never ever try to act as if you know more than you do or give an impression that you're a big buyer, someone who places big orders. Doing so will not impress the salesperson. Every business has a credit limit. Being humble works when you're trying to develop professional relationships.

Being humble is good, but don't overdo it so that a sales rep will take advantage of you. They'll try to *load you up* — sell you too much merchandise from a single resource. They try to convince you to buy more by telling you that everyone buys like that. Or they may tell you that you have to carry that many numbers, models, or styles (call it what you like) for the line to have an impact in your store. Those sales pitches have worked for years — but not to the retailers' advantage!

Gathering information

Here are some perfectly acceptable questions to ask a salesperson:

What other stores do well with your line? You have a right to know. In addition, those become good stores for you to shop.

Who else do you sell to in my area? You don't want to carry the same thing as a close competitor. Try to avoid that type of line. Plenty of different lines of merchandise are out there.

Can I work on an extra markup? Technically, a sales rep can't answer that question because it's construed as price fixing. But no one said you can't ask. Most reps will let you know whether you face competition in your area or whether the merchandise has a high perceived value, and they may suggest that you give it a try. Do some stores work on extra markup? Maybe so, but just because others do it doesn't make it right. Just as when a sales rep tells you that everybody is buying it, does that mean you should? I don't think so.

What kind of order minimums do you have? This question is important because many companies refuse to open an account if the dollar amount of the order is too small. If the amount of merchandise that you want to order doesn't meet the minimum, try this: Either leave the order and ask the salesperson to try, or take it with you and send it to the company yourself with a nice letter explaining you want to try out the merchandise and hopefully can place a bigger order next season. These approaches do work.

Are minimums strictly enforced for a new store? When sales reps talk about minimums, you can ask this question. They might be willing to make an exception for a new store, but don't count on it.

Do you have any promotional or off-price merchandise I can buy to help me maintain a good markup with your merchandise? Start practicing saying that because you should always ask that question *every time* you work with any salesperson. If you don't ask, you don't get. Remember that not all the merchandise the sales rep has will be sold at regular price. Because of that, you have the right to try to offset the markdowns you will have to take.

Is this merchandise reorderable? Many times, once you buy merchandise, you can never get any more. The manufacturer made his allotment and then moved on to something else. This question is especially good to ask if you have a customer who wants to special order some merchandise from you. Is the merchandise that I reorder available at the same or a lower price? You can at least ask — you have nothing to lose. Some people do ask and have been very successful at getting a lower price. However, I've received a reduced price only a few times.

Do you have any color photos you could give me (at no charge) so that I can use them in my advertising? Most companies have pictures and would love for you to use them.

Do you offer any co-op advertising money? A manufacturer sometimes gives retailers a percentage of the money that they spend on merchandise to advertise their product. This offer isn't worth it for a small store — too much paperwork for what you get.

Do you offer any classes, tapes, a Web site, or literature on how to sell your merchandise better? Not many manufacturers do, but some are unbelievably helpful. In some industries, manufacturers send good accounts to weekend retreats.

What do I need to do to get a little better price? Try this question to get the price reduced. There are many other approaches you can try. They don't always work, but at least try. You never know when you might get lucky.

Do you offer an extra 5 percent if I leave my order with you now? This is a brand-new tactic that some manufacturers in the bridal industry have experimented with. If it's good for a manufacturer, why not try it? The salespeople may laugh at you, but what if they don't?

If I buy something and it just isn't selling, can you swap things over for me? This is always a tricky question. My experience is that a quality manufacturer will always help you out if you have a good working relationship with the company and don't try to take advantage of it. If the sales rep gives you a hassle from the outset about that question, be careful of the company you're about to do business with.

Do you have a private label program? A private label program means that a manufacturer will put your store label on its merchandise for a reduced price if you buy in quantity. Be aware of this option, but wait till you're ready to buy those quantities.

When do your prices break in the season? Most manufacturers reduce the price of their lines after certain time periods. Find out what they are so maybe you can have the first pick of reduced-price merchandise.

When will the goods be delivered? You need to know when the merchandise will be in your store and what delivery date you should put on the order. After that date, the merchandise will automatically be canceled. What good is Christmas merchandise if it shows up January 10? Delivery dates are critical, and the manufacturer must know when you will no longer accept the merchandise.

Can you show me your newest (or most popular) merchandise? There are two major groups of customers: sheep who want to buy the most popular, and trailblazers who want to be the first on the block. Ask a sales rep to highlight the best things in the line.

What are the terms of payment? Terms of payment refers to the timeframe of when the manufacturer or seller wants to receive payment. Examples include "net 30," which means that you must pay for the merchandise in full in 30 days. Another example is 2/10 net 30. This translates to receiving a 2 percent discount if you pay the invoice in 10 days. Otherwise, you will receive no discount and must pay in 30 days. For years, the apparel industry used the term of 8/10 EOM, which meant that you would receive an 8 percent discount if you paid for the merchandise within 10 days from the end of the month.

Can I get dating? This means that you can ask for extra days to pay the invoice if the manufacturer gives you credit. It's called dating because it's as if the merchandise was shipped at a later date. Normal terms might be +30, which means you have an extra 30 days to pay the invoice. Longer dating is sometimes available with holiday merchandise — as much as several months. Don't be afraid to ask.

An old retail expression says, "You can't sell from an empty wagon." Sales reps love to use that line to get you to buy more. The job of sales reps is to sell merchandise. It doesn't matter whether they're independent reps or they work directly for the manufacturer. They want you to try their merchandise in the hopes that it will sell in your store. Sales reps use different approaches to entice you to buy, but you're likely to hear two of those approaches over and over again:

- **"I have a HOT line!"** This means the line is popular. Reps may follow up with the line, "It's blowing out of the stores" or "They can't keep them in the store." Many times it's true, but sometimes reps rely on this old hackneyed line because it works. The saying is based on the age-old concept of greed. Everyone wants to get in on the action. You be the judge of whether the line or item is that hot.

✔ **"Everybody's buying it!"** Reps use this line as if to say, you're one of the few stores that don't carry the line — what's wrong with you? Stop and think about something: If everybody is carrying it, then why would you want it? Price would be the only difference between you and all the other stores with the item (except for your store's wonderful setting and service), and the players who win in a price war are the consumer and the manufacturer.

Some manufacturers are right for some retailers and not right for others. Some prefer to do business with 50 small stores rather than one chain store. The reasons for that are simple. A big retailer can demand extra discounts, allowances, return privileges, shipping accommodations, and even ad and markdown money. A small store simply wants goods that will sell. Plus a manufacturer who loses a big account could go out of business. If the manufacturer loses only a small account, the world won't come to an end.

Buying is all about power — either real or perceived. When you're buying merchandise for your store, remember that it's your money and you can spend it anywhere you like. But you also need to realize that there's no reason to have an attitude of being all-powerful. You're better off with humble confidence. I liked to say, "I'm a small store. I try to be a loyal account and pay my bills. I just want merchandise that sells. I don't want to be your biggest account." Humility goes a long way — you want the reps to like and respect you.

Asking for deals

If you want something, you have to ask for it, right? This section is designed to help you get the most merchandise for your money. You can ask for certain things that'll make you "in the know" and help you to talk the talk with sales reps. Even as a small store, you can request some special considerations. Ask every sales rep you work with for a few things, including the following:

✔ **Off-price merchandise:** This is merchandise that the manufacturer is willing to mark down to get rid of it. Sometimes the manufacturer has only a few pieces left — perfect for a small store. But if you don't ask, the rep will rarely ever offer it to you. Because sales reps usually make only half of their normal commission on off-price merchandise, they'd rather sell you the new merchandise. Most manufacturers will tell you they don't have any, and that's okay. You don't need much to sweeten your mix. You can sell off-price merchandise at regular price or use it as a promotion and still make your normal markup.

✔ **Promotional goods:** This is merchandise that the manufacturer makes specifically to be sold at a reduced price. Most manufacturers generally have something, but again you must ask.

✔ **Dating:** These extended terms allow you to delay your payment for the merchandise. Terms such as *plus 30 days* mean that you have 30 extra days to pay. The goal is to be able to sell the merchandise before you have to pay for it. Getting special terms when you're just starting out is hard because you'll have either limited credit or no credit at all until you have a chance to establish some. But once you've established yourself as a legitimate account, you can ask for dating.

✔ **Trunk shows or demo days:** They go by different names, but these events occur at your store and give the sales rep a chance to spend an afternoon showing samples of his entire line to your customers and to take special orders. You can collect the deposits from your customers, and the manufacturer ships the goods to you presold. You have to advertise the event, but sometimes you can promote it by just calling your best customers or the ones who you know will like that line.

✔ **Advertising money:** Be cautious about asking for advertising money because the ads that manufacturers want you to run are all about promoting their product — not about your store. You always want to promote your store first.

✔ **Photographs:** Pictures are more important than ad money. Manufacturers spend big money having their merchandise professionally photographed. You can use these pictures in your advertising and on your Web site. You can mention the manufacturer's name, but you generally don't have any restrictions on how you use the photographs.

These are just some of the things you, as a small store, can ask a sales rep for. And remember, you'll have a lot better luck getting what you ask for if you've created a rapport with him first.

Never insult a sales rep's merchandise. You can simply say that it's not for you. Remember that sales reps have to look at their lines all day long for an entire season. After all, somebody must have liked the item; otherwise why would someone have put it in the line in the first place? Think about this: Before you even got a chance to see it, the line probably passed through four or five approvals. (Sometimes you wonder how.) The line you may be insulting is the line that's putting bread on the table for the sales reps. If you insult the line, you'll never get a concession from the sales rep.

Leaving paper

Leaving paper is the practice (some would say controversial practice) of leaving an order with the sales rep when you view their line. Let me explain both sides of the controversy.

Many retail experts believe that you should first look at a line, take notes, even take pictures if the reps allow you to (some reps are afraid you'll show the pictures to their competition), compare all the merchandise you've seen, and then go back later to place orders for the stuff you actually want to buy. The sales reps don't like this practice because they want to get your order on the spot. They don't want to have to track you down to get your order, and they worry that you may change your mind and not place one, or that you may reduce the size of your order.

Both views are understandable, but I tend to take a middle-of-the-road approach. I believe that if you want to take notes as you review a line and then come back later, you should let the sales rep know when you plan to place your order — then stick with your promise. Remember that good reps can be very valuable allies, so you don't want to aggravate them unnecessarily. Another approach is to leave an order for the items you're absolutely positive about and then think about the others. But still let reps know when they can anticipate your order. But whatever you do, before you ever leave an order, make sure that you have enough money in your budget to spend! (I show how to do this later in this chapter.)

Don't rush your buying. Take your time at the shows. Network with other buyers. Ask them what's hot. Spend the time to shop, buy, and then place your orders. Remember the brand you're trying to create. Make sure that the merchandise fits in. I can't repeat it enough. This is the time to test, test, test. Don't buy too much of any line.

Placing an Order

Understand the terms *deep and narrow* and *shallow and wide*. They refer to two different styles of buying. When a store buys deep and narrow, that means they don't carry a lot of styles, but they have them in depth (in every color or size). The store may have 500 to 1,000 pairs of just that one style number. That's a deep and narrow selection. Shallow and wide selections may be appropriate for a gift store that buys 12 style numbers from a manufacturer but the total order was only 18 pieces. They bought 2 each of 6 items and 1 each of another 6 items. That's shallow and wide. At the beginning, lean a little more toward shallow and wide. You may just stay there. Many stores are successful that way.

Everyone has different approaches or styles to the actual buying process. Here are a couple that have worked for me:

✔ Let the rep show you his entire line. Select what you like and then ask the rep whether you've made any mistakes. Ask whether there are any style or model numbers you should eliminate or numbers, models, or styles that you should add. Give the rep a chance to give his opinion. Ordering merchandise should be a partnership, but you don't have to agree with the rep's opinion — you still make the final decision. But at least you're respecting his knowledge of the line.

✔ Make sure that the merchandise appeals to the widest audience possible. First understand that I was an apparel buyer when I devised this approach; however, you can apply this formula to almost any type of store. Before you ever buy anything, it should meet the following criteria:

- Not too old: Consider whether younger customers would be attracted to the item. You don't want them to say, "That's something my grandmother would like."

- Not too young: Consider whether the item would appeal to an older customer. Make sure it isn't too hip or extreme.

- Not too cheap: You want to make sure that better customers might buy it because it looks good and they could save a little money without compromising quality.

- Not too expensive: The budget buyer wouldn't mind trading up a little for the item and would look at the item as a good value.

You want to buy the middle-of-the-road merchandise (but not the mediocre!) that has the widest audience. Also, because casual lifestyles have become popular, you might add two more criteria: not too formal and not too casual.

Use your own order forms or purchase orders. Doing so will save you money and time. A few more advantages include

✔ You'll have a better feel for how much you're buying. Companies often have forms that confuse the buyer. Before you know it, you're spending more than you wanted to spend.

✔ Your buying terms, not the manufacturer's terms, are listed on the purchase order. Every manufacturer is different, and you just don't have enough time to realize what you're signing when you submit your order on a manufacturer's forms.

For example, your order form may state that you'll pay all invoices 30 days from the date you receive the merchandise. The manufacturer's form may say 30 days from the invoice date. But what if you receive the merchandise 2 weeks after the invoice date? That means you have only 2 weeks to sell the merchandise before you must pay the invoice. This type of schedule is not uncommon.

✔ Your own order forms will fit in your files better and will be easier to work with.

What makes a great buyer?

Great buyers understand that buying is an art, a science, and a selling game which, when played carefully, can build a business and make a lot of money. Great buyers understand that they want to get as much for their money as possible so they can give their customers the most for *their* money. Great buyers realize that buying is selling what they have — their assets, their advantages, their strengths — to the vendors to get what they want. They believe that having a manufacturer's merchandise in their store is an asset. They know that new businesses and great retailers are the lifeblood of any industry. They know that their store's advertising featuring the manufacturer's merchandise is an advantage to the manufacturer. Also, having a database of customers who like to buy a manufacturer's product is an asset to the manufacturer. Great buyers can use all these elements as leverage to get the best deals from manufacturers.

You can find a sample purchase order form in the Buying Forms folder on the CD.

The last issue you face when placing an order is how to pay for the merchandise. How are you going to establish credit? Which credit reporting agencies should you contact, and what information should you send them? Are you going to pay with a credit card, a check, or C.O.D. (cash on delivery — you pay for the merchandise when it arrives), or will you establish credit with the vendors?

I prefer to pay everything with a credit card because it allows you 30 days to pay your bill and many offer frequent flyer points. The next best way to pay for your merchandise is to open an account with the vendor. Again, you usually have 30 days to pay the invoice. You always want to be able to pay for the merchandise after you have had some time to sell it.

But if you don't have a credit card with a sufficient limit and you can't open an account, you will have to pay C.O.D. This is the least desirable method of payment because you lose the 30 days and if you have a problem with the merchandise you are at the mercy of the vendors to stand behind what they are selling. With most vendors it is not a problem but some vendors can make adjustments difficult.

Pricing Your Merchandise

Good merchants should strive to always have fair and competitive prices, but they still must work to have the highest possible markup. Too many retailers look for ways to lower their prices rather than ways to increase their margins. That's why so many small stores go out of business. They focus on the wrong issues. People pay extra money in the right situations. For example, they may pay more for brands, convenience, packaging, status, hard-to-find merchandise, and another 100 or so factors.

Too many retailers make the mistake of believing there's a set formula to pricing merchandise. Historically, the practice of *keystoning* (which means you just double the cost you paid for the merchandise) has been the rule. Keystoning is a term that has been around for many years. I don't know the origin, it's just one of those crazy terms that has stuck. Some stores use a formula called *Keystone Plus,* which means doubling the price and then adding $1, $2, $3, or even $5 more to the doubling.

My opinion is simple: keystone is dead! You're the merchant, so you determine what you can sell the item for profitably. It's against the law for a manufacturer to dictate the sales price of an item. In other words, it's illegal for manufacturers to tell you what the "suggested retail price" should be. That prohibition is part of the Sherman Antitrust Act. Manufacturers can choose not to do business with you because of various reasons, but they *cannot* dictate what price you must sell the merchandise for.

Consider the factors in the following list — rather than a formula — and you'll always get the maximum markup available. But remember one vital rule: You need to be willing to mark down or adjust your prices if you've made an error.

Here are some things to consider as you determine the prices of your merchandise:

- ✔ **Competition:** If the item is popular and many stores carry it, then you'll likely have to price it at the prevailing rate. But if you're the only one in your area selling the item, you may be able to take an additional markup.

- ✔ **Perceived value:** Does the item look expensive or cheap? If people say to you, "Is that all it costs? What's wrong with it?" you priced it too low.

- ✔ **Brand value:** Does the brand warrant a prestige price level? Always consider the complete value of the item, including the value of the brand.

- ✔ **Merchandise category:** You can make the greatest buy in the world, but if it's more than your customer is willing to pay for something in that category, what good is it? I once got a great deal on a famous designer's blouses that normally sold for $200 to $300. I was able to buy them to sell in my store for $79.98. It was a super deal, and I was very lucky to get it. The only problem was that no one cared. The $79.98 price was more than my customers were willing to spend for a blouse. When I finally marked them down to $49.98, they sold. Know what your customers are willing to pay for various merchandise categories.

✔ **Store setting:** What does your store look like? Does it have the ambiance of a luxury store or the look and feel of a warehouse? The way the store looks can and will determine the price you can get for your merchandise.

✔ **Merchandise look:** What does the merchandise look like when it comes into the store? Sometimes the sales rep's sample looks better than the merchandise that arrives in your store, and sometimes the merchandise can look a lot better than the samples. Wait till you actually receive the merchandise and can take a look at it before you decide what to price it.

✔ **Employee opinion:** Ask your employees (and even your customers!) what price you should sell your merchandise for. Do a mini market survey. Never tell them what you paid for it — just ask what they think you should sell it for. You'll do much better than you think. Besides, both customers and employees will appreciate the fact that you asked.

✔ **Market value:** Although you should always consider what you paid for your merchandise, the most important thing to keep in mind when you're pricing it to sell in your store is what the market will bear. Think about this — do you think Bill Gates is selling his Windows software package based on doubling his cost? I doubt it. I'm sure that Microsoft calculates the highest possible selling price it can get for the product in order to sell the most it can. Microsoft even gives away some free software to make sure that it's the dominant resource in the marketplace. The company takes its markup when it can and takes less when it has to.

The difference between what you pay for merchandise and what you can sell it for is called your *margin*. As competition grows, margins are reduced. Try to buy and sell items that have good margins. Sure, you can sell things for any price, but if there's no margin, why bother?

Rick's Random Rule #423: Three are three ways to make money in the retail business:

✔ Sell a lot of merchandise with small markups.

✔ Sell fewer products with very good markups.

✔ Sell a lot of merchandise with very high margins. Bingo! This is how you get rich.

Managing Your Buying

You're about to begin the most difficult and crucial part of retailing — controlling the amount of merchandise in your store at any given time. Managing this is difficult for the following reasons:

✔ **Temptation:** You see so much merchandise that you want to buy — beautifully decorated showrooms filled with attractive merchandise, polished sales reps with smooth presentations . . . who could resist? Showrooms seem to call out your name to seduce you into buying from them.

✔ **Timing:** It's hard to know exactly when merchandise you order will actually arrive in your store. You may write an order that the manufacturer has three months to deliver. But what if the manufacturer sends you all the merchandise the next day? Or what if the manufacturer ships you everything on the last day of the three months? These are the problems you must contend with.

✔ **Paperwork:** Stocking your store with fabulous merchandise takes time — it requires a lot of paperwork and planning. You probably decided to become a retailer because you love selling, shopping, or interacting with customers — probably not because you love to do paperwork.

You may wonder why you wouldn't be able to sell all your merchandise, if everything you buy looks good? That would be nice, but retailing doesn't work like that. This section is designed to help you measure how much you can actually buy — responsibly.

Traditionally, the retail industry has embraced a system (it's really a formula) called open to buy to help retailers keep track of their inventory so they can know how much they can spend on new merchandise. The expression *open to buy* represents the dollar amount available in your budget to purchase new merchandise.

Reviewing the open to buy system

I want to briefly explain a traditional open to buy system for those retailing traditionalists who believe that the wheel has already been invented and there's no need to change it. The purpose of an open to buy system is to tell you exactly how much merchandise you must purchase to satisfy the amount of inventory you have budgeted for a specified period, usually one month. Here's how to reach that goal:

Presume that for the month of March you want to have a $50,000 inventory at the retail selling price. The items that affect that are the following:

Planned BOM (beginning of month) inventory for March	$50,000
Plus planned sales (what you plan to do in February)	+ $18,000
Plus planned markdowns (for February)	+ $2,000
Minus planned receiving (merchandise to come in February)	– $15,000

Minus on order (how much you already have on order)	– $5,000
Minus BOM inventory (for February)	–$40,000
Open to buy	$10,000

The system works, but there are two basic problems with it:

✔ It's very time consuming.

✔ It doesn't take into account your ability to pay for the merchandise.

To give you a better idea of how this would work in a real-life situation (although I made it up for this book), see Figure 12-1.

SIX-MONTH MERCHANDISE PLAN

CLASS/DEPARTMENT/CATEGORY: _____ YEAR: _____

		Feb.	March	April	May	June	July	Season
MONTH SALES	Last year $	30,000	30,000	35,000	40,000	45,000	45,000	225,000
	Plan $	33,000	33,000	40,000	45,000	50,000	50,000	251,000
	This year $							
STOCK/SALES	Last year	4	4	4	3.5	3	3	3.58
	Plan	3.5	3.5	3.5	3.1	2.7	2.7	3.17
	This year							
BOM INV	Last year $	120,000	120,000	140,000	140,000	135,000	135,000	
	Plan $	115,500	115,500	140,000	139,500	135,000	135,000	
	This year							
MARKDOWNS	Last year $	3000	3000	3500	4000	4500	4500	
	Last year %	10	10	10	10	10	10	
	Plan $	3300	3300	4000	4500	5000	5000	
	Plan %	10	10	10	10	10	10	
	This year $							
	This year %							
STOCK PURCHASES	Last year	33,300	53,000	38,500	43,500	49,500	4,000	221,800
	Open to receive	36,300	60,800	43,500	45,000	55,000		240,600
	On order	6300	10,800	3500	0	0	0	20,600
	Open to buy	30,000	50,000	40,000	45,000	45,000		210,000

FORMULA TO CALCULATE PLANNED OPEN TO RECEIVE

| **Planned BOM (Beginning of Month) Inventory for Next Month** |
| **Plus +   Planned Sales of Current Month** |
| **Plus +   Planned Mark Downs of Current Month** |
| **Less -   Planned BOM of Current Month** |
| **Equals = Planned Receiving for the Current Month** |

Figure 12-1:
Sample
six-month
merchandise
plan.

You can find a blank six-month merchandise plan to use with your own store's numbers in the Buying Forms folder on the CD.

The open to buy system is a horribly complicated calculation that was originally designed by large-store retailers that had people whose only function was to work on such a system. This doesn't sound like you, does it? With everything you have to do to start and run your business, operating with an open to buy system is just way too time consuming.

Introducing the open to thrive system

But because retailers need *some* method for maintaining their inventories and planning purchases, I devised the Open to Thrive system — it's easy to understand, simple to use, and effective enough to keep on using. But before you get started, there are a couple retail concepts you need to be familiar with:

✔ **Turnover:** This is the calculation of how many times you sell and replenish the merchandise in your store during the course of a year. You can figure out your turnover rate by dividing your annual sales figure by your average inventory (at retail prices) for the year. For example, if your annual sales are $300,000 and your average inventory is $150,000, then your store turns its merchandise over two times a year. The more times you can turn over your merchandise, the better. Here's why:

• You'll have less old merchandise.

• You'll have more opportunities to buy. This can lead to better buys and being more current with your offerings.

• You'll have less money tied up in your inventory.

✔ **Stock-to-sales ratio:** This simple ratio divides your sales for a given month into the amount of merchandise that was in your store at the beginning of that month. In other words, how much inventory does it take to sell X amount? Obviously, the less inventory it takes, the better, because then you can spend less money on inventory. Stock-to-sales is related to turnover in that it tells you how well you're managing your inventory.

Ideally, you want your stock-to-sales ratio to be about 3:1 because it means that you have a three-month supply of inventory — you can change your inventory with the seasons. It also means that you're maintaining a strong inventory level, yet new merchandise is coming in all the time.

Open to thrive: In the beginning . . .

Mastering the concept of planning my open to buy system took me a long time. Sure, I understood what I had to do, and I did it. But it took some time before I felt qualified to teach an open to buy system to other retailers. I'll never forget what happened when I did my first seminar on open to buy. It was in Nashville, Tennessee, for a group of owners of specialty stores. I had practiced my material, prepared great examples, and even had a dozen oranges I was going to use for props. I took my time and explained everything well, but at the end of the seminar, there seemed to be more questions than answers. The audience didn't get it, and that bothered me.

Because open to buy is one of the most requested seminar topics at trade shows and other places where retailers gather, I started attending other speakers' seminars on the topic. I observed that the same thing happened to

them that happened to me. The audiences just didn't understand the open to buy system. At first I thought it was because the speakers who talked about *open to buy* were always selling products or services to make open to buy easier. I thought maybe they tried to confuse the audience on purpose, but I really don't think so. The concept is hard to understand.

So I designed the open to thrive system — a system that is so simple and so dumb, and works so unbelievably well, I wish I had thought of it 20 years earlier. I created a workbook and two audiotapes that I sell for $60, but I share the concept for free to everyone. Please understand one thing, though. The traditional open to buy system does everything right, but it doesn't work for many retailers because they simply don't understand it. *Open to thrive works for everybody*.

The open to thrive system takes less than a hour to first start your planning and then only about ten minutes a day and an additional hour a month to review. It helps you control your expenses and makes sure that you're profitable. I haven't received any criticism on the concept — only raves from around the globe on its simplicity. As one retailer described it to me, "It's as necessary as training wheels on a bike — you don't need them, but they work well and help you get from point A to point B."

The open to thrive system, as I present it here, is targeted for industries that work on a markup of approximately 50 percent or better. If you're in an industry with smaller markups, the open to thrive system still works; you'll just have to change the percentages. This system also assumes that new merchandise is what generally sells well — customers want to see what's new, not what's old.

The open to thrive system answers the age old question, "How much inventory can and should I have? It will also tell you if your expenses are in line. It works with actual invoiced costs, not retail selling dollars or mark down totals. This eliminates the chances for error. If you follow the open to thrive system, you will always know if you actually have money available to buy more inventory.

Open to thrive is based on a very simple rule called the *40-55-5 Rule,* which means that

- ✔ 40 percent of the money you made on sales will go toward expenses. It can be less but never more.

- ✔ 55 percent of the money you made on sales will go toward new merchandise.

- ✔ 5 percent of the money you made on sales will become your Positive Cash Flow (PCF). Technically, you can't call this profit, but that's really what it is. (Just don't tell my accountant!)

Open to thrive does *not* focus on your current level of merchandise, although I recommend that you take an inventory before you begin to make sure your stock-to-sales ratio is between 3:1 or 4:1. If your inventory is larger, start promoting goods to get rid of them, unless you're at the beginning of a season such as Christmas. If your inventory is smaller or if you have a new store, estimate what your sales will be in the first month and have three times that inventory (at retail) on hand — that's your starting point.

You can find all the forms mentioned in the following sections in the Buying Forms folder on the CD. Just click on "Open to Thrive."

Planning your purchases

You actually keep track of your monthly figures on a spreadsheet called the *planned monthly worksheet.* This is the planning stage that I promised would take less than an hour. Take a look at it as you go through the following steps:

1. **Guesstimate what your sales are going to be for each month of the year and place these figures on the planned monthly worksheet.**

   That was the tough part — now the rest is easy!

2. **Multiply those guesstimated figures by 55% to find out how much merchandise you can bring into your store and when.**

3. **Multiply those same monthly guesstimated sales figures by 40% to find out what your expenses should be (or at least the amount of money to budget for them) and write those in.**

4. **Multiply the monthly sales figures (the guesstimated ones again) by 5% to find out your PCF.**

   Your planning is almost done.

5. **Total your planned figures for the quarter and write those on the proper place on the form. Then total the quarters and place the number on the bottom grand total line.**

   Your planning is now done for the year.

Keeping a daily record

Now it's time for the 10-minute-a-day part. All you have to do is record all of your sales, then record all of the invoices you receive for that day in either the expense or merchandise column depending on the category they are in. For example, on the first day of the month, you receive an electric bill and two invoices for merchandise. You record the electric bill in the expenses column and the total of the merchandise invoices in the merchandise column. Just follow the steps below. It's as easy as it sounds.

Record your daily expenses on the *daily worksheet*. The steps in this process are a cinch.

1. **Total the expenses and write them in the column and line that indicate the day and the place for expenses.**

2. **Do the same thing for merchandise received.**

3. **Do the same thing for sales generated.**

   That's it!

Merchandise sometimes comes in without an invoice. I suggest waiting for an invoice to come in before recording it. Some things, such as your rent, don't have invoices, however. In that case, record the amount when an invoice would normally have been created, such as the first of the month for the rent.

You really need to faithfully record these daily expenses because you'll need to compile this information about expenses, merchandise, and sales at the end of the month. The better your daily records, the easier it will be to do the end-of-the-month work.

Monitoring your orders

The other thing you do is write down the totals of the orders you placed during the month. Record this information on the *on order sheet*. You can find a copy of this in the Buying Forms folder on the CD, too.

Be sure to record the information according to the date of completion. For example, if you wrote an order that will be in your store by the end of March, record that total on the on order sheet as a March order. Calculate the total for each month.

Putting it all together

Finally, you need to get a monthly total of the business you actually did. Record this information on the *actual monthly worksheet*.

At the end of every month, simply transfer the totals from the daily worksheet to the actual monthly worksheet. You can see how you're doing on the system by comparing your planned monthly worksheet to your actual monthly worksheet.

At times, you're going to overbuy — most buyers do. They fall in love with merchandise, and they just have to have it. That's okay. Here's my message: buy whatever you like, but make sure that, at the end of the quarter, you can balance your expense and merchandise received numbers to come as close as possible to the 40-55-5 rule. If you're off, you'll know what actions you need to take to correct the situation to be in better shape for the next quarter. That's it. That's the whole open to thrive system. It allows you to become your own consultant.

I once consulted with a mom and pop store. Mom and Pop argued about the fact that if *one* of the two didn't overbuy, the business would be in great shape. I applied the open to thrive system to their situation and discovered that the buying was in great shape but the expenses were out of whack. Mom's buying was consistently between 51 and 56 percent of sales — definitely not a problem. But Pop had leased an expensive car, and the business paid for this. In addition, all of their travel went though the business. This brought their expenses to over 50 percent of sales, which was definitely higher than the planned 40 percent. The real problem was identified — the expenses were just too high. Use the open to thrive system to analyze your own business in this way.

Chapter 13

Finding, Hiring, and Keeping a Great Staff

*O*ne of the biggest challenges in retailing today is hiring qualified people to work for you. There are just too many jobs for the number of applicants. Some companies are having problems expanding because of a lack of qualified personnel. As one McDonald's franchisee told me, "The burger business is great, but the people business stinks."

Strangely enough, some stores *aren't* having problems attracting and retaining employees. I first discovered this while working with the Massachusetts Retailers Association on an awards program. We started asking these lucky businesses what they were doing to attract and keep their employees. We found out that one reason why the winners are winners is that they know how to treat their employees in a manner that makes them want to stay.

Many people are quick to point out that one reason retailers have a problem attracting employees is that other industries pay more money. Yes, they do, but I believe that money isn't the only motivator.

Retailers should ask themselves the following three questions about staffing. (Unfortunately, few do.)

🖛 What attracts new employees to your business?

🖛 Why do your best employees stay with you?

🖛 Why do your employees leave?

When I ask employees, "Why do you stay where you're working?" the response is overwhelmingly "My boss cares about me." This explains why major retail chains can have two stores in similar areas but one has a terrible employment problem and the other has no problem at all. It is the *power of one:* One person on top who cares can change the culture of a company. Make sure that your business is one that cares about its employees.

Retaining Employees Requires Specific Strategies

You must adopt particular attitudes, mind-sets, or management strategies to be successful at retaining qualified people. Here are some things to keep in mind:

- ✔ **An opening always exists for someone good.** Good people always justify their pay, and they also raise the bar for all employees. Good people are too hard to find; you can't pass them up because you're "fully staffed."

- ✔ **You're always in recruiting mode.** Always be on the lookout for good people, and let all your friends know it, too!

- ✔ **All your existing employees must know the two preceding rules.** Everyone involved with your store must know that you're on a quest for excellence. Consequently, your employees feel better about themselves, and they know that they have to keep producing.

- ✔ **Understand the power of the "What have you done for me lately?" philosophy.** This works both ways. Don't wait a year to do something special for your employees. They appreciate recognition for their hard work. Also let them know how owners appreciate extra effort from their staff.

- ✔ **Understand that a little turnover is healthy.** Sometimes employers go overboard trying to keep employees. Employers love to pride themselves on not having any turnover, but sometimes parting company is the best move for both parties.

- ✔ **List the assets of your business that would attract prospective employees.** Everyone is different here. Make a list of reasons why great people would want to work for you, such as the possibility of working part-time or job sharing, the opportunity to work in an exciting environment with great people, employee discounts, and so on. Consider making a small tri-fold brochure that boasts of these benefits. You can give it to prospective employees.

Things job applicants want today

Today's job applicant wants *everything*, because everyone knows someone who knows someone who got everything. Either that or they read the help wanted section and saw all the bonuses and incentives that companies are offering and are positive that they deserve these perks as well. Besides, who's kidding who? Everyone knows that staffing and employment are the toughest obstacles retailers face. So why not want it all?

Before you give the store away, start with the ideas listed here:

✔ **Above-average pay:** If you offer minimum wage or low wages, applicants get the message that that's all you think they're worth or that you don't value your employees very much. Remember that most applicants could make more money collecting trash, working the third shift somewhere, or cleaning houses, but they would rather work in your store.

✔ **Good working conditions:** Employees want to work in clean and up-to-date places. That shouldn't be a problem because every customer wants that as well, and your store has a great atmosphere, right?

✔ **A place where they can be proud to work:** No one wants to hear, "Oh (gasp), you work there?!" Working at Nordstrom, Tiffany & Co., or even the Gap carries some prestige. My son was a ball boy for the Boston Celtics. You bet he was proud of that job. He mopped floors, got on his hands and knees to clean sweat off the court, and picked up dirty, smelly towels. The job wasn't glamorous, but he was proud of the company and surroundings.

✔ **Respect for their opinions:** Respecting your employees' opinions makes them feel part of your business team — it makes them feel important. Let your employees know that you value their views.

✔ **Appreciation for their work:** Nothing is worse than trying really hard on a task and making sure to do everything just right, only to have your boss not even mention what you did or acknowledge your efforts. What's the sense of even trying? Failing to acknowledge employees' efforts can sour their feelings for your business. That's how you lose good employees, and that's how employees with good attitudes become cynical.

✔ **An opportunity to enjoy their work and have some fun:** Fun has become an integral part of any workplace environment and helps reduce employee turnover. People who like their work may stay in a job even though they could make more money somewhere else. When you humorize, you humanize, and that makes a nice work environment.

✔ **A job close to home:** Many prospective employees are willing to work for less money if the job is convenient. With traffic and congestion, the cost of gasoline, and the wear and tear on your car and your nerves, is it worth it to travel? Most people don't think so. People compromise many issues (including money) for the sake of convenience.

Finding Super People

Your chances of finding great employees by running an ad in the help wanted section of the newspaper are slim. Such a strategy fills only 17 percent of the jobs available. Besides, the best people aren't always looking for work. Most people will change jobs for the right situation, but they're not necessarily out there looking.

Great people don't respond to boring signs, either. I don't know about you, but a store that puts a sign that says just "Help Wanted" is not the type of place where I would want to work. Be creative. If you want to have a sign in your window, make it interesting and fun — you're selling! Use your sales ability to attract employees with your signage. Try something like this:

> Mary left. We are all going to miss Mary.
> That leaves us with a job and a place in our hearts to fill.
> If you're anything like Mary, come in. We'll treat you like family.
> (If you didn't know Mary, come in anyway and we'll tell you all about her.)

Yes, it's a lot of words, but I would much rather put that sign in my window than the traditional "Help Wanted" poster. You may not attract more people (although I suspect that you will), but you just may attract someone who wasn't actively looking for a job. This section presents various avenues you can explore to find and attract super employees.

Referrals

The majority of jobs are filled via the following types of referrals:

- **Employee referrals:** These are great because these employees like the store so much that they want their friends to work there as well.

- **Paid employee referrals:** These referrals offer incentives to your employees to refer people to the store. Generally, the referrals have to work from one to six months before the bonus is paid. The bonus is anywhere from $50 to $500. This technique works because in reality you're paying your employees to be recruiters.

- **Customer referrals:** Retailers often overlook this type of referral, probably because they're embarrassed to tell their customers that they need help. The owner of the convenience store near me admitted to me that he had a real problem attracting help. I never knew that he had this problem. He refused to put signs in the windows and was too proud to ask for referrals. After I helped him write a clever flier that he handed only to customers he knew, he was able to fill his open positions.

Community networking

Use every opportunity to let others know that your business is always on the lookout for good people. Network at civic events. Work with senior citizens organizations, many of which have job postings in newsletters and at meeting places. Participate in your town's welcome services, which generally send welcome packages to new residents — you can include a flier. You can also stick a recruitment flier in your local merchants' Val Packs or coupon mailings.

Also contact community agencies or government and religious groups that help people find work. Start by contacting the religious leaders of local churches. Most churches are very aware of members who may be down on their luck. Many of these people may have just lost a job or a loved one and need a job desperately. Then contact your state's unemployment office and find out what state-sponsored programs are available. The state office also will be aware of any companies that have recently laid people off.

Lastly, contact your city or town offices for local programming, which can include senior citizens groups.

Job listings

List your job openings on various Internet job-search services. Many times, using these services is free, and this venue is getting more popular all the time. Monster.com is a great Web site, for example.

Many shopping areas and city governments post job listings for community businesses on their Web sites. List your openings there as well. For that matter, don't forget to list your openings on your own Web site!

If you're looking for student employees, consider placing an ad in area high school publications. These ads don't cost much, and a few retailers have discovered student publications as a good source of help.

If you take out a newspaper ad, try to place it in the lifestyle or sports section. Those locations may be more expensive than the classified section, but they're more effective because people who aren't necessarily looking for work will see your ad.

Job fairs

Job fairs are becoming a popular vehicle for finding employees. Service clubs and local chambers of commerce generally sponsor these fairs. Prisons have started holding job fairs of their own. Yes, you read that correctly. Many prisons conduct job fairs to help inmates find jobs prior to their release. Many prisoners are convicted of victimless crimes and, with adequate rehabilitation, turn out to be wonderful employees.

You may be eligible for financial benefits if you hire higher-risk people. Check with your accountant about work opportunity tax credits, earned income credits, and other credits.

Cause marketing

Every retail business should be involved with a cause or charity. It's the right thing to do. It gets you involved with your community and introduces you to people whom you might not otherwise meet.

The Woman's Industrial Union runs a retail store in Boston. This organization was created to help women support themselves and their families through education about business and related topics and as an outlet to sell merchandise that these women produce. It's a well-run organization and a first-class retailer. The store is located in a wonderful shopping area of Boston. It has an interesting problem, however — so many volunteers want to work there that it's hard to give them all hours.

The point is, the more you give, the more you get back. People want to be involved with companies that care. Be that type of company, but do it for the right reasons. Don't expect anything in return.

Government programs

Several good government programs can help you find employees. The local unemployment office is the most obvious, but many cities and states offer welfare-to-work programs, Job Corps centers, and one-stop career centers. The Department of Labor even has a helpful Web site at www.doleta.gov.

Know how to steal from other companies. No, not in a bad way — in a way that's both ethical and good for business. This is how it works: When you're shopping in a store and receive good service from an employee, hand the employee your business card on which you've preprinted on the back the following lines:

> Thanks for the great service you gave me. My company is always looking for outstanding people like you. If you ever think of changing jobs, give us a call. If not, best of luck and thanks again.

Chances are that this employee is very happy with his job, and that's fine. But you just delivered a compliment. You made him feel good about himself. That's a wonderful thing. Don't you think he's going to tell his friends and family that someone came in and told him what a nice job he did? At the least, you'll have made someone's day and created some positive word-of-mouth advertising. And if he's not looking for a job, he may know someone who *is* looking and pass along your card.

Interviewing for Fun and Profit

To find the right employee, you have to know what you're looking for. You need to consider what's important to you and your store and what's important to the applicant. You're looking for a good fit. I believe that the most important quality in a retail job candidate is the ability to communicate.

Ask questions during the interview that give the applicant the chance to demonstrate her personalities, experience, and expertise. (See the section "Questions to ask" for suggestions.) Listen carefully to her responses and see whether you can identify traits that would make the applicant a super employee.

You can find stock application forms at a stationery store, but what you need to know may be a little different from what the forms offer. So I've devised an application form specifically suited to retailers and have placed it in the Employment Forms folder on the CD.

Questions to ask

To gain a pretty deep understanding of your applicants (and to be better able to measure their suitability to your business), ask the following questions:

- **What did you like best about your last job?** If the applicant says "lunch" or "paid sick days," you're in trouble.

- **What did you like least about your last job?** This probing question can help you pick up negative attitudes and find out more about the individual.

- **Why did you accept your last job?** If the applicant says, "My mother wanted me out of the house," be careful. Seriously, this question is important because some of the reasons the applicant took his last job may be the same reasons he accepts his next job. Listen carefully.

- **What is the most important element to you in a job?** You want to find the thing that excites the interviewee.

✔ **What are the most important features to you in a supervisor?** The answer to this question can provide valuable information because you can use it if you hire this person. It can help you understand what your staff wants.

✔ **Where would you like to be in two years?** Someone may trip on this one and tell you that she's planning a move to Florida in two months. If you're hiring seasonal help, that response may not hurt the candidate's chances, but if you're looking for a long-term relationship, that answer is not acceptable. You're looking for someone who says, "Right here, making more money with more responsibility."

✔ **What are your goals?** This is a trick question because very few people can answer it. I believe real intelligence is knowing what to say when you don't know what to say. See how the applicant handles the question. Notice his facial expressions and body language, and be quiet and listen. The applicant may take 30 seconds or so to reply, but wait it out.

✔ **Could you describe your ideal job if you were to work here?** This is my favorite question because you want people to stay with you a long time, and the applicant may if you use her answer to create an ideal job situation. You want people to feel that they're working in their ideal jobs.

I routinely asked this question in interviews so that I could try to accommodate employees' requests. People often told me that they would like to work three days a week with customers and not work any weekends or nights. I told them I couldn't grant that wish immediately but would work as hard as I could to give them their ideal situation in time. I meant it and worked hard to fulfill their needs.

In addition to the preceding questions, I recommend using the following two lines, which I believe are the two most important things you can say during an interview:

✔ **Tell me about that.** Get the applicant talking. The interview isn't about you; it's about the applicant. You'll have plenty of time to describe the job. Whenever the applicant makes a statement, ask him to tell you more about it. This technique will help you keep your mouth shut and the applicant's open, and that's what you want.

✔ **Which means what?** When the applicant says something that you don't quite understand, just ask, "Which means what?" Keep asking, and you'll eventually get to the real meaning.

Traits to look for

Think about the personal attributes that are important to you. Ask applicants a question or two that pertains to some of these attributes. Rate applicants' responses on a scale of 1 to 5. The following is a list of attributes that are commonly valuable to retailers:

- Attitude
- Sales skills
- People skills
- Common sense
- Communication skills
- Motivation level
- Product knowledge
- Promotability
- Leadership

If you rate employees on a scale of 1 to 5, don't be afraid to hire the 5s just because they make you feel inferior. You need great employees to make your business grow; weak ones will drag you down.

Rick's Random Rule #67: Hire attitude; train skills.

Dealing with Generations X and Y

I am a baby boomer. Loyalty is more important to me than to my kids. They were brought up in a time of corporate mergers and acquisitions, layoffs, and foreign imports — companies are not loyal to their employees these days. So why should Generations X and Y be loyal to companies? They realize that to make more money, you have to change jobs. My friends and I wanted to work at our jobs for a lifetime. Today, it isn't uncommon for people to change jobs after two to four years.

Employees today want information that's going to affect their lives. They want to learn as much as they can and move on. They want responsibility, but many times baby boomers are afraid to give it to them because younger employees may have earrings, tattoos, or pierced body parts. Retailers must look past those body decorations because they themselves might have chosen those things if they'd been brought up in a later generation.

Understand that their loyalty must be earned, and Generations X and Y are loyal to themselves first. They will stay with you as long as they're learning, growing, and being challenged. Having said all that, understand that I have been generalizing, which can be dangerous. Everyone is different, but all people have one thing in common: They want to feel important. It's just that some people want to feel important in different ways. It's your responsibility to discover what those ways are.

Keeping Your Employees — Especially the Good Ones

After you've taken the time and trouble to find and hire terrific employees, you want to hang onto them! This section presents strategies designed to help you create a working environment that makes your staff want to stay. I also give you tips for building relationships with your people so that everyone benefits.

Creating a great work environment

Paying attention to just a few employment concepts can make the difference between providing your employees with a fun and satisfying work experience and dooming them to oppressive and dreaded toil. Consider some of the following strategies — your staff will be glad you did!

Have brainstorming sessions

When you're looking for innovations or solutions, solicit your staff's input. When your employees participate in this process, they feel valued and connected to your business. The benefit to you is that they become more invested in your business. Remember that your employees are good sounding boards and can be a terrific source for new ideas.

Conduct training

With training, employees can become skilled, efficient, dependable, and even enthusiastic. The more you train, the better off you are.

Training must be an ongoing process. Offer one-to-one training, send your employees to seminars and trade shows, invite them to sit in on teleconferences. I conduct three training sessions a week that are filled with retail employees.

Make it fun

For the good of your store, accept that having fun on the job is very important these days. Making the workplace fun can be as simple as posting a joke of the day on a white board in the back room. A joke (as long as it doesn't poke fun at any racial, ethnic, gender, or religious group) puts a smile on everyone's face.

Treat employees as individuals

To be a good employer, you need to treat people differently. Although standardization and homogenization guide almost everything we do, everyone is different. That means that different people are motivated by different things. Some people are motivated by the amount of money they're paid, and others by the merchandise you carry. A successful manager knows the right buttons to push with every individual employee.

A great basketball coach once said, "I will treat every player differently, but when we are on the court, we will play as a team." Remember that policies can be standardized, but motivation can't be. Care about your people as individuals. Acknowledge (and even appreciate) their differences, and they'll care about you.

Establish boundaries

Employees want to know how far they can go in different situations. They want to know what's considered good and what's considered bad behavior. Many times, employees make mistakes because they didn't know that they were making a mistake. Establish workable, consistent standards.

Create task lists

Daily, weekly, and monthly task lists are among the best tools that retailers can use. These lists itemize nonselling tasks that employees can work on when they're not busy with customers. You can post these lists at the cash counter. Prioritize your task lists in order of importance so that everyone knows what to do when things are slow.

Even more important is that creating and posting task lists takes the guesswork out of what it takes to please the owner or manager. You are clearly stating your goals and expectations without having to remind, nag, or play games. Task lists have another benefit, too: When employees complete the tasks on the list, they feel a sense of accomplishment. Employees just want to know where they stand. Specifying what you expect them to do (in addition to selling) makes for better and much happier employees.

If you're going to create task lists, be sure to check them! The fastest way to damage employee morale is to ignore the task list once it's in place. Such neglect communicates that you don't care what your employees do. Be sure to notice and express your appreciation when an employee takes the initiative to complete one of these tasks rather than sitting around waiting for customers.

Be an effective manager

Today, the role of a manager or supervisor is to be a mentor, coach, or adviser. The dictator style of management is dead! Motivation by fear just doesn't work anymore — it may get a job done today, but you'll be looking for new employees tomorrow.

Keep in mind that the person on top doesn't have to know all the answers. Let your staff know this, too. Today, most retailers employ many bright people who work part-time. You're smart if you can tap into their knowledge and experience.

Ask your employees how they would handle a situation. Many businesses are starting to employ a concept that's referred to as "ownership from inception." A manager or supervisor describes a situation or problem to her team. For example, maybe the store needs to find more employees who fit in, and the manager wants ideas on how to attract and hire them. Let the employees brainstorm the problem and help develop a plan. Chances are, they'll make it work because it's their plan. In situations like this, employees give 110 percent because they own the plan.

Assign a mentor

Every employee should have one person to lean on, to go to with questions, and to guide him through the awkward moments of a new workplace. As much as an owner strives to be a mentor, it's difficult for the owner to have a truly open relationship because the owner has the ability to hire and fire. Choose mentors who have experience and positive attitudes.

Avoid petty rules

Nothing turns employees off more than rules that don't make sense. Review your policies regularly and ask yourself why you have each rule, how could it be modified, and whether it should be eliminated. Get rid of any that don't have solid reasoning behind them.

Making your employees love ya

Maybe you think, "I don't care if my employees like me or not, as long as they respect me." My response to that is simple: You want to be respected *and* liked. You can respect someone and not like her, but it's hard to like someone and not respect her. You want your employees to work hard for you and go the extra mile, and they will if they truly like you.

The following is a list of proven techniques that will not only keep your employees but also motivate them to go that extra mile.

Praise them

"Good thoughts not delivered mean squat." Those words come from business author Ken Blanchard. The important thing to remember is that actions praised are actions repeated. Everyone loves praise, recognition, and, most important of all, appreciation. You can deliver these to your employees in a variety of ways, including the following:

- **Face-to-face personal praise:** If someone does a good job, tell him! This is the simplest technique of all.

- **A personal note:** Write just a short three- or four-sentence note praising a specific action — like a thank-you note. Send it to your employee's home, especially if you're trying to get a spouse on your side.

- ✔ **An official letter:** Letters are especially valuable to high school and college-age employees because they can use them when they apply to college or for future employment. Gain a reputation for being a source for great letters. Doing so goes a long way — you'll have a line of student applicants the next time you have a job opening.

- ✔ **Public praise:** Praise a great employee for a job well done at a meeting. But be careful not to upset anyone or pit one employee against another. Make sure that you're not using the star employee as an example that says to everyone else, "She can do it. What's wrong with the rest of you?" No one likes that approach.

- ✔ **Bulletin-board note:** Write a note and post it on the store bulletin board. But be cautious here, too, because this action can have the same negative ramifications as praise at a meeting if you don't word it well.

Whatever method you choose, offer praise immediately when it is deserved! If you wait too long, your praise is worthless. Try to do it within 24 hours of the employee's exemplary action, but never wait longer than the next pay period.

Reward them

Giving your employees a little something extra for doing an exceptional job never hurts. Unfortunately, too many businesspeople have made bonuses something that employees expect. *Please don't give bonuses!* No one looks at them as bonuses; employees look at them as a right. If you ever have a bad year and are unable to give bonuses, your staff will be upset. The battle cry could become, "I did a good job, so why should I suffer?"

My advice is not to give a regular anything. But do offer something, sometimes. Rewards don't have to be big; they just have to be thoughtful.

Make all your employees feel like they are the most important people in the world. If you do that, you'll never again have a problem attracting or retaining employees.

Learning a Lesson When Employees Leave

The exit interview is one of the most powerful tools a manager has because it's the first time in your relationship with your employee that you're considered true equals. The employee or almost ex-employee can be a valuable source of information about you and your business, and the exit interview is the time to unmask that information. If you have a disgruntled employee, you'll get an earful, but remember, *you can learn something from everyone.* Use the criticism you hear in a constructive way to improve your business.

Exit interview helps catch thief

During a seminar I once did for gas station franchise dealers, I talked about exit interviews. I got a call about a week after the program from a man who couldn't thank me enough for the information. It turned out that one of his key employees quit just a few days before the seminar. This person's departure bothered him because he liked him and was very fond of his work. The owner decided to do an exit interview. As he explained, it wasn't easy, and he had to pry some of the information out, but when he did, he learned the real reason that this employee was leaving.

The employee left because he had observed the manager stealing money — actually taking money out of the register and putting it in his pocket. He was afraid that he would get blamed and felt it would be better if he left before anything really happened. The owner assured him that his name would never be mentioned and couldn't thank him enough. Within two days, the manager was caught on videotape stealing money. The owner fired the corrupt manager, and the employee who had given his notice decided to stay and eventually became the manager. All these events occurred because of an exit interview. That is an extreme case, but why not take advantage of this valuable tool?

Chapter 14

The What-Ifs: Your Legal and Financial Responsibilities

This is the chapter of what-ifs, which is a nice way of saying that it covers many of the possible challenges, problems, awkward moments, disasters, near disasters, and anything else that might happen on your road to retail success. You can't say, "It'll never happen to me" because something always happens — you can count on it. In this chapter, I address many unsettling scenarios, focusing mostly on situations that could get you into financial or legal trouble.

Finding Out about Insurance

Going to your insurance agent can be like going to the supermarket — there are so many different types of products from which to choose. Going into business is a risk, so you don't want to invest your money, time, and energy without protection from a catastrophic incident. But other risks are involved, too. The following list introduces some common types of insurance that you may need in order to protect yourself and your business from ill fortune:

- ✔ **Automobile insurance:** Covers company cars and non-owner vehicles and hired cars.

- ✔ **Boiler and machinery insurance:** Generally covers the boiler, air conditioning unit, and any other major type of equipment. Many policies will cover all electrical and mechanical systems, and some even cover computers, phone systems, copy machines, and computerized cash registers. Because insurance policies vary greatly, use this list as a guide to possible coverages or options.

- ✔ **EDP (Electronic Data Processing) insurance:** Covers anything to do with your computers.

- ✔ **Employment practices insurance:** Covers wrongful terminations, discrimination, and sexual harassment.

- ✔ **Liability insurance:** Usually sold in a comprehensive business package referred to as a *business owner's policy* (BOP). It covers your furnishings, property, inventory, robbery (when you lose money, not merchandise), employee dishonesty, and damage from catastrophic incidents, such as tornadoes, hurricanes, severe storms, and fire (you'll need a separate policy for flooding). Insurance against shoplifting is very expensive and generally is more expensive than the cost of the stolen merchandise.

- ✔ **Excess liability insurance:** Also known as an umbrella policy. This extends the financial limits of your existing policy.

- ✔ **Workers' compensation insurance:** Covers employee accidents at work and is a mandated coverage in many states.

In addition to the insurance that you need to protect your business, you also have to provide employee benefits. These benefits usually include the following types of insurance:

- ✔ Dental
- ✔ Disability
- ✔ Health
- ✔ Life
- ✔ Long-term care

In the paragraphs that follow, I present some common questions (and their answers) concerning insurance.

How do I know I can trust my insurance agent to be working in my best interest? Always interview three insurance agents before selecting the one you feel most comfortable with. Compare not only the prices, but also the reputations of the insurance companies they represent. How fast do they pay claims?

Insurance plans are available within my industry. Should I use them instead of my agent? Sometimes insurance companies associated with industries do very well. They may know your industry but they do not know you or your community. The best advice is to compare both quotes.

What if an employee falls in my store? Workers' compensation insurance (you better have this) covers the medical expenses and wages that are due to the employee. Because every state is different, check with your insurance agent regarding the limits of liability.

Will my insurance rates be affected if an employee files a workers' compensation claim? The answer varies by state and policy, but as in any insurance, the more times an incident occurs, the higher the rate. Insurance companies really watch out for multiple claims for each policy. In other words, if you have six smaller nuisance claims, as opposed to one claim regardless of the size, red flags and rates will be raised.

What if I get a phone call from an insurance company that says that it can save me almost 50 percent on workers' comp if I belong to a state retail association? Is this legit? Yes, programs sponsored by state retail associations can save you significant amounts of money on this type of insurance. State retail associations create self-funded trusts for their members only that can save retailers a lot of money. Depending on the claim experience of the trust, this determines the amount of proceeds returned to the policy owners. Always check with your state retail association before sending anyone a check. And yes, membership in the association is required.

What happens if an employee has a car accident while she's making a delivery for me? If she's driving a company car, your store automobile insurance covers the damages. However, if she's using her own car, you need a separate type of insurance called *non-owned and hired car insurance.*

What if a customer falls in my store — what insurance covers that? Your business owners policy covers customer injury. You can buy an extra million dollars of coverage with an umbrella policy. These umbrella policies are relatively inexpensive to purchase because they go into effect only after your basic coverage has been exceeded.

What if a piece of the ceiling falls on my merchandise? Clean it up. Chances are, your deductible on your insurance policy won't cover the claim. So fix it yourself as fast as possible.

What if it falls on a customer? You are or at least should be covered, but try to have the customer sit down and regain his composure. See whether the customer needs medical attention and call an ambulance if necessary. Customers generally collect on cases such as these and usually get more than they deserve. So be careful of everything you say or do. Never say, "I've been meaning to fix that for the last six months." Such a comment means you're admitting negligence. Your lawyer will have a heart attack if you make statements like that.

What happens if a product I sold injures someone? This is called a product liability case, and you and the manufacturer will get named as defendants in a lawsuit. Your basic business insurance policy covers most of this, but you may want to double-check to make sure. The customer will sue everyone involved but really wants to go after the person with the deepest pockets — usually the manufacturer.

Rick's Random Rule #79: Whatever you think is going to go wrong usually doesn't. But whatever you think is going to run smoothly often doesn't either.

If I just buy enough for $50,000 worth of inventory but I really have $100,000 worth, would an umbrella policy kick in and save me a lot of money? No. The umbrella policy requires you to have your inventories and fixtures fully covered. Ask your insurance agent about a co-insurance clause. This states that if you insure your inventory for $50,000 but you really have a $100,000 inventory, you're insured for only 50 percent of the inventory. In the event of a major loss, you would be paid only 50 percent of the amount insured, or $25,000. Many insurance companies have eliminated the practice of co-insurance clauses. However, it is something to watch out for.

If my store is seasonal and my inventory peaks in October, November, and December, should I insure for the highest inventory? No. Most BOP policies have provisions for ordering peak insurance coverage which means that your policy allows for higher coverages during certain busy months. This coverage does not necessarily cost any more because the insurance company averages the coverage for the entire year.

If I have a loss of $25,000 due to a bad storm, do I get all that money right away? Before you start counting your money, most of the policies discussed so far have deductibles that can vary a great deal. The lower the deductible, the higher the price of the policy (the premium). When you're trying to decide what size of deductible you should have, ask yourself how much money you could stand to lose without really getting hurt financially. Deductibles of $5,000 are common. Because you're responsible for the first $5,000 of loss, the insurance company doesn't have to bother with small claims, so the rates are cheaper. Face it — you could handle a $5,000 loss. It wouldn't be easy, but most businesses could. However, a $25,000 loss would be out of the question.

What if I suffer a catastrophic loss that puts me out of business for three months? Am I covered at all? Probably yes, but make sure that your policy has a business interruption clause and find out how much money would be paid in the event of such an occurrence.

What if I catch my bookkeeper stealing money? Am I covered? Most BOP insurance plans cover not only employee theft but robberies as well, even if money is stolen when you're transporting it to the bank.

What if merchandise is missing and I'm pretty sure it has been shoplifted? Unfortunately, losing merchandise to shoplifting is not covered, and unless it is a specific incident that has been reported to the police, you're unlikely to collect. Insurance companies rarely pay claims on what they call "mysterious disappearances."

If I own the building as well as the business, will one insurance policy do?
No. These are two separate entities, but you don't need to cover the same things twice.

What if my air conditioning unit breaks? Am I covered? That depends. First, check your lease to find out whether you or the landlord is the responsible party. Every lease is different. That's why it's important to completely understand your lease — who does what. Not just because you should know, but because if you're responsible, you need to get boiler and machinery insurance to cover the unit.

What if I have a fire in my office area and I lose all the data on my computers that will take weeks to reenter. Will my insurance cover the time to reenter? Probably not. However, EDP insurance may offer some protection. Ask your agent about this type of coverage. But the best insurance you can have is backing up your system every day and keeping the backed-up data someplace else.

Will I be covered if my roof starts to leak? Maybe. If you have a small leak that is a constant drip, you probably won't be covered, but if you have an "incident" such as a windstorm, hurricane, or any delightful natural disaster, you probably will be. However, flood insurance is separate. The Federal Emergency Management Agency (FEMA) sponsors the National Flood Insurance Program. Every insurance agent will have information concerning this program. Find out whether your business is located in a designated flood zone.

Should I offer insurance as a benefit to my employees? Traditionally health insurance has been a standard in the industry, but the times are changing. Health insurance is very expensive today. If you want to offer benefits for your employees, I recommend the "cafeteria benefit plan." This means that you as the employer offer each employee $1 per hour for each hour worked for benefits. Employees can use the entire amount for health insurance, but many times they are covered under a spouse's health plan. Instead, they may want a dental plan or even long-term care insurance. They may just want to take that money. The advantage to doing it that way is that it's fair for everyone.

Rick's Random Rule #43: It's okay to ask dumb questions of your accountant, lawyer, and insurance agent. If you don't ask, you'll never know. And if they make you feel stupid, you're dealing with the wrong person.

Getting Legal Advice

A lawyer is one of the key players on your team of professionals. Everything today seems to have legal ramifications. It's your attorney's job to make sure that everything you sign or have a policy for is legal and will help you to avoid problems.

What should I look for when I'm hiring a lawyer? After you shake hands, you still have all your fingers. (Only kidding.) Yes, I was joking, but the sad truth is everyone has a lawyer story and that can be a problem because people are reaching the point that they're afraid to call their attorney. So before you make a decision on an attorney, interview a few of them. Make sure that the chemistry is right between you. If it isn't right before the battle, it will only get worse during a battle.

Ask about fees. If an attorney is going to charge you for every little phone call or bit of advice, don't use him. You won't call because you don't want to pay a fee.

What do I need an attorney for? The most common time to consult an attorney is when you're trying to establish the structure of your business. Do you want to be a corporation and, if so, what type, Subchapter S, LLC, or a C corporation? Or do you want to be a partnership or sole proprietorship?

What if my lawyer and accountant disagree on how the company should be formed? Who should I listen to? Your lawyer and accountant should get along. Otherwise, you'll be paying fees for their arguments. In this situation, you must determine which one you like the best and dump the other. Then replace that one with someone who gets along with the one who you've kept. Remember that you'll use your accountant 100 times more than you'll use your lawyer. So as to which one is the most important, the accountant has the edge.

What's the biggest mistake retailers make with attorneys? Underutilization. Retailers are often afraid to call their attorney to simply check to make sure that they're doing the right thing. People get into trouble because of ignorance of laws, not just intentionally breaking the law. If you're going to have an attorney, use her. But make sure that she isn't the type who starts her stopwatch as soon as she answers the phone.

Rick's Random Rule #56: Never trust a lawyer or accountant whose fees are odd numbers with cents in them. That means they're charging you for things that you don't want to be charged for, such as photocopies, parking meter expenses, telephone expense, and so on.

Avoiding Financial Troubles

Your accounting procedures are only as good as the people who are doing them. Be sure to associate yourself with a thorough, accurate, honest, and responsive accountant (and bookkeeper) who can explain your financial reports in laymen's terms. You must be able to communicate with your accountant without feeling stupid or intimidated.

How do I know if I have a bad accountant? He doesn't return calls in a timely manner. You get notices from the IRS and state agencies about errors in calculations. You're constantly applying for extensions on deadlines. But the top reasons are that the work looks sloppy and you can't relate to him.

What do I do if I discover a big mistake in my tax return? Contact your accountant immediately and have him submit an amended return. Mistakes can cost you fees and penalties, but the sooner you realize a mistake, the better and cheaper it will be for all. Uncle Sam will forgive you, but you still have to pay a penalty.

What happens if I skip a tax deposit? It's the same answer as the preceding question. You have to pay a late fee and penalties.

What if I'm always late making my tax deposit? Get a payroll service. It's inexpensive, and the money it will save you, providing that you're using its tax pay services, over the year on just the one or two-day late tax deposits pay for themselves.

What if I have a problem with balancing my inventory and using an open to buy system? Can my accountant help me? No. That is not what an accountant does. This work is as foreign to them as it is to you and maybe even more so.

What do businesses do or not do that cause them to get into financial trouble? The most common are the following:

- ✔ They give their accountant wrong numbers (either intentionally or unintentionally), thus creating inaccurate financial statements and a picture that does not reflect the truth.

- ✔ The retailer has no understanding of the financial statements.

- ✔ They never do any year-end planning.

- ✔ They sometimes spend money that should be used to pay taxes.

- ✔ They don't know the difference between a cash flow statement and a profit and loss statement.

- ✔ They give one person the authority to count the cash, write the checks, and balance the checkbook. The temptation is too great, and this person takes off with the money. This occurrence is called the good technician syndrome — the plumber knows how to plumb but lets someone else take care of the money. People like this get wiped out. It happens to rock stars, athletes, and retailers as well.

- ✔ Businesses are undercapitalized. They don't have enough money to get through the first few years.

What if the only way I'm able to pay my bills on time is with constant borrowing of short-term money? What do I need to do? If you're profitable, this situation is telling you that your business is undercapitalized and you probably need to put more money into the business or convert your short-term loans into a long term note. And of course, keep an eye on your expenses and level of inventory. If you're not profitable, this means that you're keeping the business alive with borrowed money. Take a hard look at your expenses.

Rick's Random Rule #30: Never be afraid to question a fee. It's your money.

What should I say if I get a call from an IRS agent? Nothing. You'll probably be nervous for no apparent reason and feel stupid because you don't have an answer. Refer the agent to your accountant. They talk the same language. Let them work out what they need. Generally the IRS calls when it has a question about the accountant's work.

What if the store is really busy and my accountant says that I'm very profitable, but I still don't have any money and I struggle to pay my bills on time? This could mean one of two things or both. The first thing is that you're increasing the size of your inventory and therefore offering your customers a larger selection. This situation puts a strain on your cash flow. Or it could mean that your debts are too big. Your financial statement may look strong, but your loans are draining too much cash out of the business to pay back the loans. Here are ways to remedy both situations:

- ✔ Be careful of your level of inventory.
- ✔ Reconsider refinancing your business to stretch out the payments to make it easier to pay your bills.

What if I get involved with a barter exchange? Is there a downside risk? Barter can work if in fact you can barter your merchandise for goods or services that you would buy for the store anyway, such as magazine ads that you would normally place. Barter doesn't work when you end up getting things that you normally wouldn't buy, such as vacations. Another consideration is the tax liability, which you should discuss with your own accountant.

Exploring Security Issues

Due to increased competition for both customers and employees, today's retail environment presents security situations that are more challenging than ever before. Many retailers don't have longevity with their employees and it's becoming easier and easier to shoplift. In order to deal with these issues effectively, you need to be prepared.

What do I do if I suspect that someone's shoplifting? Watch the person carefully and have your employees be on the lookout. If you think that someone may have taken something, try to contact security (if you're in a mall that has security) or call the police. You can detain that person and ask for your merchandise, but you're playing with fire. You don't know how someone will react. Be very careful before you falsely accuse someone of shoplifting. The cost to defend yourself against a case like that can be more than the value of the stolen item. Yes, you can win the case, but it could cost a fortune. A professional shoplifter knows more of the rules than you do. That's why you must get the police involved.

What if I see someone trying to put merchandise under a coat or in a bag, but the person sees me watching and puts it back? There isn't much you can do. The police don't arrest people for contemplating shoplifting.

What should I do if the person with the concealed merchandise leaves the store? See where the person goes. See whether you can get a license plate, and yes, you can ask for your merchandise back. And of course, you should contact the police so that there will be a record of the incident.

What if I suspect that an employee is stealing money or merchandise? Confront the employee, but first get advice from your attorney. You can be walking on real thin ice if you're wrong. The bottom line is that the employee must go because you'll never trust her again. That doubt will always stay with you. By letting the person go, you're ensuring that you won't have any repercussions later, such as a lawsuit for pain and suffering.

What if someone tries to rob me? First, understand that robberies last less than one minute, but they seem like forever. Always do what the robber wants. Do *not* offer information and be careful of any sudden moves. If someone is behind the robber, let that person know you don't want anyone startled because sudden moves could cause serious harm. Push the silent alarm only if doing so doesn't place you in jeopardy. Try to get a good description of the robber in your mind, and after he leaves, call the police and lock the door because you're now at a crime scene. Most robbers are more frightened than you are, so be careful. If the robbery is a drug-related incident, normal reason won't work.

What if my cash register is short on a regular basis? Review your closing procedure. Start reviewing cash register tapes. See whether the losses occur when certain employees are working. Most cash shortages are *not* from internal theft but from internal sloppiness in cash management — giving too much change or ringing in the wrong amount. Cash register overages are just as bad as shortages.

What if my phone lines go down, I lose my connection with the credit card processor, or I lose power while trying to process a credit card sale? Have a store policy pertaining to communication loss for credit card processing. It really depends on where your store is located. If it's in a higher crime area or an area that has a higher than ordinary share of credit card rejections, don't take credit cards during the blackout time period. But if you're in a neighborhood that has a more normal loss ratio of less than 1 percent, accept the card and get an authorization later.

What if someone has a medical emergency in my store? Immediately contact the police, who will arrange for an ambulance. Be aware that, as cruel as I may sound, this incident may be a scam. In my store once, a person faked a heart attack to distract employees enabling an accomplice could steal unnoticed. Please be compassionate in an emergency, but also be aware of a potential scam.

What if someone purchases merchandise, uses it or wears it, and then tries to return it to me? All the customer has to say to put the law on her side is that she thinks the merchandise is defective. Once a customer says that, you must take it back, but from a practical point of view, take it back anyway. As much as you may disagree with my advice, arguing with the customer isn't worth the hassle. Look at accepting this type of return as a cost of doing business. I know your tongue will bleed sometimes from biting it so hard, but not everything about this business is pleasant.

What if someone asks for an allowance (a price reduction) because the merchandise is slightly defective as a result of a scratch I saw the person put on it? You'll come across dishonest people like that in this business. This is a judgment call, but try not to let your emotions get in the way. I suggest that you offer a token discount. If they don't accept that, then say "I'll take it off the floor and send it back to the maker." The customer usually jumps for the token allowance.

What if someone tries to return something without a sales receipt? If you know the customer actually purchased the item because you or another employee saw the customer in the store, then don't hassle the person because of some store policy. Doing so will hurt you big time in the future. However, if you suspect the person is trying to return something she didn't actually purchase, issue a store credit but make sure that you get proper identification with a photo ID. If the person is lying, he won't want to show you a photo ID.

Part V

Spreading the Word Without Going Broke!

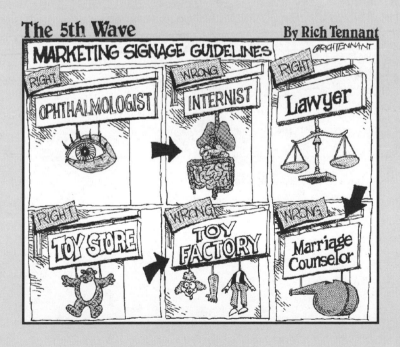

The 5th Wave   By Rich Tennant

MARKETING SIGNAGE GUIDELINES

RIGHT OPHTHALMOLOGIST   WRONG INTERNIST   RIGHT Lawyer

RIGHT TOY STORE   WRONG TOY FACTORY   WRONG Marriage Counselor

In this part . . .

This part talks about ways you can let the public know who you are and what you do. You'll be amazed at the number of options that are available. Many types of advertising are explored from local newspapers to direct mail, and electronic formats, as well.

You learn what it takes to generate word of mouth advertising — the very best kind of advertising there is. This part also covers the power of promotions and events that are not just price reductions, but rather celebrations designed to bring customers through your front door. It also tells you how to run a successful sale when you need to move merchandise out of your inventory.

Chapter 15

Generating Word-of-Mouth Advertising

● ●

In This Chapter

▶ Understanding why you have to WOW your customers

▶ Figuring out how to win customers

▶ Getting your customers to spread the good word

● ●

Twenty-nine years ago, my father had a heart attack, and my mother asked me to help out with our small family retail business. It was a 900-square-foot dress shop outside Boston. I was very happy working for Hertz in the marketing department, but I decided to help my family temporarily. Unfortunately, my dad passed away, and my temporary leave of absence lasted 25 years. I knew nothing about the retail business and nothing at all about the woman's apparel business. So I read whatever I could and observed and listened to everyone.

The one common theme in everything I read and heard was to listen to your customers. So I asked questions and even eavesdropped to hear what customers were saying about our store and our merchandise. I kept hearing a similar phrase over and over again. Little did I realize that one three-letter word, which seemed so insignificant at the time, would have such a profound impact on the way I did business for years to come.

The phenomenon occurred whenever a customer saw something she really liked for the first time. She would say, "WOW." The next phrase out of her mouth was, "That's different!" That was followed by "I love it," "I want it," "I'll take it," or "I'll try it."

I observed that the goal in retail (back then I thought only woman's apparel) is to get customers to say WOW. I then created the WOW standard. I asked myself and my staff, "Is that service a WOW? Is that merchandise a WOW? Is that display a WOW?" Everything we did had to be a WOW. If it wasn't a WOW, it wasn't good enough. The WOW standard built the business. It was the silver bullet to my success in retail.

Although Tom Peters, Sears, and many others have used the WOW standard, no one interprets it quite the way I do. I believe that WOW stands for Wonderful Opportunity to Win. As a retailer, you have a wonderful opportunity to win customers for life — to have them talk about you, fall in love with your store, and refer you to their friends and neighbors. It's about creating word-of-mouth advertising.

In this chapter, I talk about why you should strive to WOW your customers and tell you how to do so.

Why WOW?

Consumers are more demanding than ever before. They're also more challenging and aggravating because they're more knowledgeable than ever before. Many of your customers probably know more about what you sell than you do. The reason is simple: So much knowledge is readily available to consumers in the form of books, specialized magazines, and the Big Daddy of them all, the Internet. Today's consumers research their purchases because it's easy to do. As a retailer, you have to keep up and be on your toes.

Unfortunately, there's no room for error on your part, because your customers have choices that they never had before. You have more competition. There's always some fool who's willing to give merchandise away just to gain a foothold in the market. There's always a new shopping center or new shopping service starting up that wants business. As a result, you must WOW your customers every time they come into your store.

How to WOW

So how do you WOW a customer? First of all, doing what everyone else is doing is not a WOW. But doing what everyone else is doing, but better, *is* a WOW.

You can stand out from the crowd just by doing the basics better than anybody else — keeping the store clean, having presentable employees, greeting customers in a positive and friendly manner, thanking them for their purchases, not making personal phone calls while customers are in the store, having merchandise clearly priced, and having good values and consistent quality. These ideas aren't glamorous, but many businesses overlook them while they search for a silver bullet.

Technology isn't necessarily a WOW

Many retailers believe that technology is the answer to all their problems. Some say that technology is a WOW, but I disagree. Human contact makes the difference. Loyal customers build business. Ask yourself, are you loyal to an ATM machine? It does everything right: It knows your name, it suggests new services, it isn't too pushy, and it knows everything about you — even how much money you have in your bank account. But would you drive out of the way to go to your favorite machine? I don't think so. But you *will* drive out of your way to visit your favorite teller who you joke with or just plain like.

The neat thing about the WOW standard is that it's not hard to attain. The little things often turn out to be the biggest WOWs of them all. Following are some examples:

- ✔ Going the extra mile for a customer by delivering something or carrying a package to his car
- ✔ Tracking down a special order to make sure that the item comes in on time
- ✔ Calling a customer to tell her that something that you think she might like just came in, or that something she had looked at was just marked down
- ✔ Asking a customer for his opinion

WOWing is about being different and exciting. However, be prepared to fail from time to time. Sometimes different is just too different. But that's okay. The rewards will far exceed the occasional slips. The winners are always the people who fall down, get up, and try again. And after a defeat, people expect a little less from you, so it becomes even easier to WOW 'em. After all, WOWing is exceeding expectations, and if the expectations are lowered, then the WOWing is easier.

Using the ten building blocks of good customer service

For the last ten years, I have had the pleasure to work with one of the leading authorities in the infrastructure of customer service, Margo Chevers from Massachusetts. We've worked together on various projects, and I've always been impressed with her insight on the inner workings of customer service and its potential impact.

I asked Margo for the ten most important parts of creating a strong foundation for customer service. This was her reply:

- **Hire people who have a service attitude.** Some people simply enjoy serving others, their organizations, and their communities. The spirit of service dominates their personality. This attitude of service has nothing to do with money or background, and people who have this attitude are not necessarily the most outgoing or bubbly. But this type of person will move your business forward. These people make the best salespeople as well.

- **Make the customer's time with you an experience.** You have but a few short moments with customers. You don't have time to complain about your day or anything else. Ask yourself, "How can I make their experience better? Can I refer to them by name, and how can I ask without being too aggressive? How can I control the environment in the store? How am I affecting their five senses?" Exceed their expectations just a little by stimulating their senses and by having an attitude to serve and please, and you will have created a compelling and memorable experience.

  Of course, all you really have to do is shop at other stores, see what they're doing, and then top them. Is that cheating? No, that's comparative shopping.

- **Regularly inform all your employees about what's going on in the store.** Employees need to know what's happening. What new lines have you bought? When will they be coming in? What kind of advertising will take place in the next month? Will any physical changes be happening to the store? The more they know, the better they can serve your customers.

- **Make every decision with your customers in mind.** Ask yourself questions such as, "Do our customers like what we're doing?" and "Would our customers like this type of promotion?" Change the way you look at things — instead of centering it around yourself, focus on whether your customers would approve.

- **Make your customers an agenda item at every staff meeting.** Present their point of view and ask these questions: "What would the customer think of this? Would this move be fair to them? How can we serve our customers better or differently?"

- **Empower your employees to do the right thing.** And don't hold it against them if the situation doesn't turn out perfectly. That means giving employees the power to do whatever has to be done to make a customer's experience a WOW experience. For example, allow them to take something out of the window or off a display for a customer, to order something special, or to deliver something personally to a customer's home.

- **Continually ask yourself how you can improve and add value.** If you don't keep asking and pushing yourself, you'll start to slip behind the competition.

✔ **Create an atmosphere of excellence.** Let it be known that everything you and your employees do has to be the best, and you won't accept less. Doing so is difficult for many humble and shy people, but remember that winning organizations are always raising the bar.

✔ **Continually do the unexpected.** Have the reputation for doing the unexpected, and customers will always expect something different and exciting from your store. These are the things that customers talk about, which generates more business for you.

✔ **Never let an untrained employee have customer contact.** Your employees represent you, your store, and your brand. Working with customers is the most important thing an employee can do, so make sure that every employee who serves customers has been trained to do so and can do it well.

Rick's Random Rule #26: People forget good service, but memories of exceptional and horrible service last a lifetime.

Turning negatives into positives

Although the ideal is to WOW your customers with positive experiences, negative experiences do create WOW opportunities. By handling a customer's negative experiences well, you can turn that negative experience into a positive one and earn a repeat customer.

The loyalty exercise

Name a business that you have been doing business with for more than seven years. (It can't be a public utility.) Generally, the first businesses people think of are dry cleaners, supermarkets, and convenience stores. You will begin to realize the importance of convenience in the loyalty equation.

Then take the convenience factor out of the mix and think of a business with which you have done business for seven or more years that you have to go out of your way to get to. Ask your friends what businesses fit into this criteria for them. Usually, a business makes the cut because of the uniqueness of the products it sells, the level of service it provides, the personal relationships it develops with customers, or trust in the reliability of its product.

For example, I go to a certain men's store because I love the people there. They work at defining service to me as a warm hello, a smile, and meaningless sports talk about how we don't like the Yankees. (Being a Boston Red Sox fan is almost like a religion here.) Just the thought of that store gives me a warm and fuzzy feeling and makes me think about what I need to spruce up my wardrobe.

Think about your list of businesses. Then ask yourself how you can apply their principles to your store to make it just a little more special.

Before you even think of changing a negative experience, you must realize that the negative experiences you deal with represent only a small percentage of the negative experiences that take place in your store. Survey after survey reveals that only 4 percent of customers complain when they have a negative experience. Most people feel that complaining isn't worth the effort.

What that means is that the complainers are giving you an opportunity to understand what they have perceived as negatives. A customer's experience may not seem like a negative to you, but if it's a negative to that one customer, others may also perceive it that way as well. Regardless of how trivial the complaint seems or what a jerk the complainer may be, always remember that complainers are doing you a favor. Appreciate their concern, thank them, reward them, and make it a challenge to win them over again. Some of the best customers come from negative encounters.

Rick's Random Rule #4: Even if you have all the bests — the best advertising, merchandise, prices, packaging, displays, fixtures, location, and everything else — it's all for naught if an employee ignores or insults a customer.

Owning the complaint

Train your employees to follow this motto: Whoever gets the complaint owns it for life. Nothing is more annoying than the buck being passed from one person to the next. If the problem requires your intervention, the salesperson should stay with the customer, letting the customer know that she cares, and follow up after the problem has been resolved.

I believe that the owner should rubber-stamp whatever the employee advises. Doing so gives the employee a significant level of responsibility and will impress the customer as well. The only exception here is if the employee is getting belligerent with the customer; in that situation, a cooler head must prevail.

Letting the complainer talk

The worst thing you can do is to fight with a customer, because if you do, you lose automatically. Just as bad is when a store employee won't let the customer explain the problem and get it off her chest. Let her talk, and talk, and talk, and then ask for more detail. Many times, that's all it takes. Then ask the customer what you need to do to improve the situation.

Often, complainers will ask for more than you can give, and many times they're flat-out unreasonable. Some people get caught up in the argument, while others are just trying to get as much out of you as they can, and being unreasonable is the tactic they use. Go as far as is reasonable and fair, but never compromise your beliefs or values for any customer. That's why it's important to decide before these situations occur how far you would go, what you think is reasonable, and what actions are in alignment with your sense of ethics. You're going to lose some customers even if you do everything right — there's no way around it. You can't be and do everything for everybody.

Addressing the problem immediately

The longer a complaint festers, the worse it gets. Whatever you do, don't waste time in correcting a customer's problem. Give whatever you have to give, and fast. Have a sense of urgency — the customer will appreciate it. Never say that you'll get back to her next week. You must respond that afternoon, or the next morning at the latest. Also, give a good offer early, because the longer you wait, the larger an allowance you'll have to make.

You want your allowance to be a WOW. If it is, you'll restore the customer's faith in you. Be sure to recognize the lifetime value of your customers (see the following section).

To smooth over a customer's problem, I offer a gift certificate to the store before I give additional money back. If I can get the customer into the store again, at least I have a shot at making her happy. If you just give cash back, you will never see that customer again, because either she'll be embarrassed because she exaggerated her claim (which people do all the time as they get into their complaints) or she'll feel stupid patronizing a store that she put down.

Thinking of the lifetime value of a customer

Never look at a customer only as someone who buys something from you for $19.95. How many times does that person buy something for $19.95? How many years can he shop at your store, how big is his family, is he active in organizations, and does he have friends who can shop in your store? These are all measures of one customer's worth. When you add up all those potential sales, you may be looking at a $100,000 customer.

Treat everyone like a $100,000 customer. If you do so, your attitude toward WOW service changes quickly.

How to Turn WOW into WOMA

Word-of-mouth advertising (WOMA) makes a business grow and flourish. It builds a business on a solid foundation of personal referrals. There's nothing better than referrals. Every business in the world would love to run itself just on referrals because doing so is cheaper, easier, and more fun, saving it from spending time and money on advertising.

Having one customer refer another customer, who refers another, makes your store like one big happy family — the place where "everybody goes." The following are some of the best ways to accomplish that feat.

Selling experiences

Because consumers can get merchandise from many different sources, including the Internet, you have to do more than just sell merchandise — you have to sell *experiences* to distinguish yourself from your competition. How do you make your customers feel? What kinds of experiences are your customers having in your store? Are you creating a compelling and memorable experience that will keep them coming back? You want your customers to have those experiences that make them say, "WOW!" — and that they talk about with their friends, families, coworkers, and so on.

Good service, a good selection, and fair and competitive prices are no longer a WOW. Customers today want it *all:* nice, convenient stores; great assortments of merchandise; knowledgeable salespeople; the ability to return what they don't like when they feel like it; and appreciation for their business.

Delivering outstanding customer service is what I call the great equalizer, the dragon slayer, the one weapon that can cut the biggest competitor down to size because it builds you up. Great customer service creates loyal customers, and these customers talk to their friends — word gets around about how terrific your store is.

How do you bring customer service to the point of loyalty? How do you make your customers loyal to you so that they'll drive out of their way, past other stores that sell what you sell, to shop in your store? You exceed their expectations.

Getting into the expectation management business

You may not realize it, but you are not only in the retail business. *You are in the expectation management business.* All customers come into your store with a set of expectations. They have a perceived impression in their minds as to what the store is all about.

You may be saying to yourself, "Not me! I wander into a store with my mind open." I don't think so! If a store were dark and gloomy or had offensive posters in the window, you wouldn't even walk in. Small, subtle details affect us subconsciously, and we process them in our minds the same way a computer processes data.

So every customer has a set of expectations. If his experience in your store falls below those expectations, that customer will be turned off and will never return. However, if you exceed his expectations, you create a WOW. A WOW is your goal — it is the home run, the hat trick, the daily double, and the sugar and spice and everything nice. People talk about WOWs. They love to share WOW stories. WOW makes WOMA — word-of-mouth advertising. If you want to create WOMA, you need to give your customers something to talk about. Exceed their expectations in some way in every encounter.

Rick's Random Rule #16: Customers are like elephants. They always remember your bad attitudes, your broken promises, and how you handle misunderstandings.

Chapter 16

Advertising Vehicles: What to Include in Your Arsenal

In This Chapter

▶ Understanding the basics of advertising

▶ Choosing newspaper advertising

▶ Finding inexpensive ways to use TV advertising

▶ Using radio advertising effectively

▶ Advertising via direct mail

Great advertising will make you a lot of money, but you have to create a message exciting and provocative enough to make people walk through your front door with a desire to buy. You can communicate your message and build your business in many ways, but in this chapter I focus on advertising. I define *advertising* as any service or vehicle for which you pay money that communicates your name and message. Advertising costs are variable — you can spend a lot or a little. Your task is to determine how much is too much and how much is too little.

This chapter introduces many ways to spend your advertising budget. But remember that advertising is more than just spending money. The best form of advertising is still word of mouth. However, in order to generate word-of-mouth advertising, you have to continuously give people something to talk about — get your message out there.

Rick's Random Rule #34: The days of saying, "Half of my advertising doesn't work; I just don't know which half," are over. Learn how to advertise well, and *all* of your advertising will work.

Mastering the Basics of Advertising

The two most important features in any ad, regardless of what advertising medium you use, are telling the audience *who you are* and *what you are selling*. Mentioning this almost sounds too elementary, but look at the number of ads that give readers no idea what the store is selling or even what the store actually is. I believe that the most important parts of any ad are the name of your store and a brief slogan, a signature line, and a positioning statement that explains what the store is all about. (See Chapters 2 and 3 for more information on signature lines and branding.) If you have a Web site, include it in every ad.

Rick's Random Rule #64: Ads don't have to be big; they just have to be good.

Following is some additional advice about ad content that can help you make your advertising stronger and more effective:

- ✔ **The more specific the ad, the better it will pull.** Too many times, retailers forget the importance of good ad copy. For example, if an ad says, "Coat Sale," it will work, but if it says, "Petite Coat Sale," it will work even better. And if you qualify it even more and say, "Petite Coat Sale by Calvin Klein, regularly $300, on sale for $149," the ad will pull that much better.

- ✔ **Features tell, but benefits sell.** The problem that most retailers have when they write ads is that they think about things that are important to them, but not to their customers. They think about the features, not the benefits. When you create an ad, you must ask yourself, "How will this ad and the product I'm trying to sell benefit the person reading the ad?" A retailer who writes in an ad that he is having the biggest sale in history is talking only about himself, not the benefit to the customers.

- ✔ **If the merchandise is better, the ad must be better.** Stores must be in alignment with their advertising. That means that your advertising must reflect your store's appearance and merchandise. For example, everything in a Mercedes Benz ad, either newspaper, magazine, or TV, screams out sophisticated and expensive. This is accomplished by using icons or symbols that indicate wealth or success. Mercedes' ads are in alignment with the merchandise.

- ✔ **Beautiful, award-winning ads don't always pull.** People often fall in love with beautiful ads and assume that because they're so beautiful, they must work. Unfortunately, that's not always true. Pretty, clever, and cute ads aren't always the ads that sell merchandise. Remember, the best ad is the ad that pulls customers who want to buy into your store and reinforces your store as a brand.

> ✔ **You'll get tired of the ad, concept, style, or font at least six months before your customer does.** Many retailers are quick to change the style of an ad long before the customer is ready for them to change it. The reason: Retailers look at the ad so many times before their customers have seen it even once. Before you jump at the opportunity to "refresh" your ad, remember that most of your customers may not have seen it more than a few times. As to how long an ad can be run, it really depends on the type of ad. The same institutional ad can run for years, while an ad for a specific event can be a one-shot deal.

Producing Ads

Producing ads means actually constructing them. Most media outlets are more than happy to help you with the production of your advertisement. Some will charge and others will do it for free. The problem is some of these media can produce terrific ads while others are simply pitiful. Keep in mind that the purpose of the advertisement is to project a positive image about your business and to attract people through your front door. If a media's production department has the ability to accomplish this goal, then don't spend the money on outside vendors.

Thinking through the advertising agency dilemma

Many, many advertising agencies are ready and willing to take on the business of small retailers. You may have considered this option, but before you sign up, read this section.

The problem that retailers have with advertising agencies is that some retailers don't have budgets that are big enough to make using an agency mutually profitable for both themselves and the advertising agencies. If the average retailer spent 4 percent of total sales on advertising, a store that did $1 million in sales could spend only $40,000 on advertising. That means that the average advertising agency would make approximately $6,000, which is a commission of 15 percent on the account. Even if the retailer spent 8 percent on advertising, the advertising agency would still receive only a $12,000 fee for the year. Keep in mind that the store is doing $1 million in business. Where does that leave a retailer who has a healthy business, makes a good living, and does $600,000 in sales? This retailer can't even consider using an advertising agency and should look for other alternatives.

If you need help designing your advertising, you don't necessarily need a full-service advertising agency. What you do need is a good graphic design person and a good copywriter. Advertising for a smaller independent retailer is not that complicated. Plenty of good graphic design people offer this type of service. Review their work first to make sure that you like their style and feel comfortable working with them.

A good source for inexpensive graphic design talent is junior colleges. Many of these schools have strong graphic design departments and look to the community for live projects to work on.

Creating your own ads

Computer software is getting so sophisticated today that many people are creating their own ads. I warn against doing that because many times home-made ads lack that professional look. What I do suggest is to design your ads to the best of your ability and then bring in a graphic designer to finish them for you. You might also want to look for freelance copy writers, layout people, and art directors who can save you money because they don't have the high costs of running an agency. Check out *Small Business Marketing For Dummies* by Barbara Findlay Schenck with Linda English (Hungry Minds, Inc.) for some tips on creating effective ads.

Advertising in Newspapers

Whenever I speak to a group of retailers, the one common problem they share is that newspaper advertising just doesn't pull the way it used to. My question to them is simply "How can it?" Newspapers are no longer the only source of advertising. We used to receive most of our news from the newspaper. Now we get information from other sources such as television, radio, the Internet, magazines, and direct mail. Newspapers are no longer the power-houses they once were — but they still work. You just have to know how to use them effectively.

Years ago, almost any newspaper ad worked. If you look at the newspapers from the early 1900s, you see ads that are about as creative as my grocery list. Back then, those types of ads worked, but not today. There's no room for error. You have to pick your strategies and places wisely.

Here are a couple of rules that work regarding newspaper ads:

✔ **Never plan on good position.** The best place to have an ad in any newspaper is on the upper right corner of page 3. If you're selling things to men, then the upper right corner of the equivalent to page 3 in the sports section is just as good. The problem is simple: Everybody wants that placement in the newspaper. The likelihood of your ad ending up there is usually slim to none.

A good ad must be strong enough to stand on its own. That means that you should always prepare your advertising by thinking that you're going to be crowded and on the worst page of the newspaper, with ugly ads all around yours. Knowing that before you start is much better than being disappointed later. To prepare for the worst position, you must consider the kind of borders you put around your ads and where the readers' eyes will focus when they look at the ad. Strong headlines work well, and powerful graphics make you add pop from a page thats crowded with ads.

✔ **Be consistent with your fonts.** Every store must select the fonts it uses for signs, advertising, and even a special font just for sale time. You want your customers to be able to recognize your store just from the fonts in your ads.

Running the right type of ad

Although I'm not a big supporter of newspaper advertising, I do believe that three styles of ads are very effective.

Rick's Random Rule #47: Every ad you use must support your store brand.

Specialty ads

The one style of ad that always works is what I call the *specialty ad.* These ads are very small — either two columns wide x 2 inches deep or one column wide x 4 inches deep. Their purpose is to simply say this is what we are and this is what we do.

I have run this style of ad for more than 20 years. As I mention throughout this book, my specialty was selling mother of the bride dresses. You may be wondering how any store could be that niched and how I got into that type of business. It was all because of this style of ad. When I was first starting out as a retailer, I worked with a young advertising student who gave me the idea. I mentioned to him in passing that we sold a lot of mother of the bride and mother of the groom dresses and would love to expand that area of our business. He said, "Why don't you just run an ad that says, 'Mothers are our specialty'?"

We did exactly that. Underneath the headline "Mothers Are Our Specialty" was a short paragraph that told about our store and our unique specialty. At the bottom of the ad, we used our regular signature name, address, and so on. From the day we first ran the ad, we became the experts in the area of mother of the bride and mother of the groom dresses. Customers came to us for our expertise.

The obvious question is, how does becoming a specialty store affect business, especially if you sell more than one specialty? No one is saying that you can't have more than one specialty. Plenty of stores have run an ad highlighting two or three different specialties. For example, hardware stores use gardening as a specialty in the summer and then become foul weather specialists in the winter.

A specialty ad helps define your store. We live in a time of experts and specialists. Customers want to do business with a professional. Another benefit is the focus away from price and on expertise. By running an ad such as this, customers will start asking your advice in the same way that they ask their doctor. This simple little ad can change your business as it did mine and make the business even more enjoyable.

Don't try running a specialty ad for just a short period. They must be used over a long period to be successful.

Q&A ads

The Q&A ad has many of the same qualities as the specialty ad. It's small, works very well to define your business, creates expert status, draws the focus away from price, and works well over the long term. The Q&A ad is simply a 3- to 4-inch one-column ad. The secret to its effectiveness is that you have to run it in a local paper once a week.

The top line of the ad states, "Ask the _____ pro." Insert your specialty in the blank. For example, if you sell wedding gifts, you're the wedding pro; if you sell swimming pools, you're the swimming pool pro. The line underneath the headline states your name and your expertise, for example, "Sue Smith, the wedding expert." To the right of these lines, insert a small photograph or caricature of yourself. Remember, this is only a one-column ad, and the picture will be tiny. Some retailers are embarrassed about having their picture in the paper, but it's worth it. The rest of the ad features a question and your answer with your store's signature (name, address, and Web site).

Q&A ads are one of the most effective and inexpensive ways to advertise. Because you run the ad weekly for a year, you'll probably be able to sign a 52-week contract with the newspaper at a significantly lower cost than occasional ads. Some stores can run Q&A ads for as little as $15 a week.

Don't worry about not being able to come up with enough questions. Just ask your customers — make it a fun project within the store.

Profile ads

The profile ad is one of my all-time favorite styles of advertising because it helps create a bond between you and your customers. This is how it works: You select one of your customers. You don't have to choose one of your best customers, but the person should be one of your better-known customers in your community, such as the mayor or the mayor's spouse, an executive from a local company, a popular politician, a school principal or teacher, or a judge.

Obtain a picture of the customer and insert it into a three- or four-column ad that's 4 or 5 inches high — 4 x 5 is a good size. On the right side of the ad, you profile the customer with the following categories: profession, educational background, professional accomplishments, awards, favorite charities, favorite author or book, and favorite expression. The last item in the customer profile is a statement that the person buys his or her clothes, gifts, hardware supplies, swimming pools, or whatever you sell at your store.

When you submit the ad to the newspaper, ask for two ad slicks. *Slicks* are clean, crisp copies of the ad on shiny paper. Frame these nicely — they must look first-class. Give one to the customer and hang the other in your store. You start to create a gallery of customers. When people come in your store, they love to look at these slicks. They become like celebrity endorsements of your store. Profile advertising is a combination of community involvement with just a little splash of glitz. You don't have to run this ad every month, but do it at least four times a year.

Looking at the different kinds of newspapers

You have a multitude of choices when it comes to running newspaper ads, starting with a large metropolitan newspaper and going to the smallest of local weekly publications. Each one of these publications has a sales rep who will probably be calling on you. Each one of them will present a compelling reason to advertise in their publication. It is important to know the different options that are available in your area so that you can make an informed choice as to your advertising options. Your best bet is to try a couple and see what works best for you.

Large metropolitan newspapers

Your store's location determines whether a large metropolitan newspaper is even an option for you. My store was only 7 miles from downtown Boston, but even if it had been 30 miles away, most of my customers would still have read the *Boston Globe,* the large regional newspaper in the area. However, I had two problems in advertising there:

- Readers could get lost in the paper because it was so big.

- Advertising was too expensive because the paper covered such a large metropolitan area, and all media charge by how many people they reach. The larger the audience, the higher the price of ads.

Even with these problems, I decided it would be beneficial for me to advertise in the *Boston Globe*. I just had to be careful to select the right sections and to take advantage of special rates in order for it to be cost-effective.

The ways to advertise in a large regional newspaper vary. The following three are the most effective and most economical. Better rates are always available if you sign a longer-term contract with a commitment of ads.

- **Regional zones:** Many newspapers have introduced *zone editions* (often north, south, east, or west), which are generally delivered only on Sunday. These sections of the newspaper are much cheaper to advertise in and cover only the areas you want covered. These zone sections have a loyal following and are gaining in popularity across the nation. Just ask for the zone rates. Many times, the rep won't want to mention zones to you because the commissions on zone ads are much lower.

- **Special sections:** Sunday newspapers often feature special sections such as home, garden, wedding, travel, and so on that only occur a few times a year. These sections are a must-buy if you're involved in selling products that the section features. If you're in the bridal business, for example, you must have a presence in the wedding planner section of the newspaper. If you have a garden shop, make sure that you're in the garden section.

  Yes, ads in these sections are very expensive, but they help position your store as a player in the field. The ideal is to have a display ad, but if you can't afford that, put in a small space ad. Don't expect traffic to start to flow in immediately, because it won't. Seeing results from your ad takes a little bit of time because you're building your brand.

- **Weekly sections:** Most newspapers have separate pull-out magazine sections that appear every week on a regular basis. They are less expensive but still powerful. Furniture and home stores generally do well in these sections. These sections are image-building and brand-building vehicles. Don't expect an immediate hit, but an ad in this type of section will build a business on a solid foundation.

Small retailers will find it too expensive to use all three of these media. You have to decide what's right for you and what's strongest in your area.

Newspapers design longer-term contracts for the number of times you will run an ad, not necessarily how big the ad is. If you can afford to run only four ads a year, you could sign a six-time contract and run what is called a *rate saver* ad. This ad is usually a line or two that holds your reduced rate. I know it seems silly, but it's something that has been done for years. It's just one way around high prices.

Local newspapers

Every town has a local newspaper — and some are stronger than others. The best way to determine the strength of the local newspaper is by looking at the ads and seeing who's running in the paper. If the paper is strong and healthy, you'll see lots of ads that represent the majority of the businesspeople in the community. The best thing about the local newspaper is that it covers information that the readers can get only from a local paper.

The type of ads that work best are the specialty ad, the profile ad, and the Q&A ad, all described earlier in this chapter. Everyone has different opinions of the ways to spend advertising money, but I recommend a strategy that works very well in a local newspaper:

- Four profile ads a year, one for each quarter
- Two sale ads a year, one for your winter clearance and one for your summer clearance
- No specialty ads
- No display ads
- 46 Q&A ads run any week in which a sale or profile ad isn't running

With this strategy, you're in the local newspaper every week. If your local rates are $5 per column inch, you would spend approximately $920 for the 46 Q&A ads, $400 for the 4 profile ads, and $400 for your sale ads (a 4-column x 10-inch ad, which would be a 40-inch ad, a very good size). Your total advertising expenditure for the local newspaper would be $1,720 for the year. Even if I'm off on the cost per inch, this is still a small price to pay considering the exposure and the overall benefit you get. If you have more than one local paper, you can divide your ads between them. Obviously, you won't be able to get the 52-week rate, but a 26-week rate is still pretty good.

Regional newspaper groups are another solution to the dilemma. They generally offer wonderful deals and enticements to have you purchase ads in multiple newspapers. These deals are appealing, but remember that newspapers are not the strongest source for retail advertising, and you really don't want to spend the majority of your advertising budget on newspaper ads.

Shoppers

The numerous weekly (mainly advertising) publications are referred to as *shoppers.* Examples of these are *The Thrifty Nickel, The Local Shopper,* and *The Thrifty Shopper.* These free publications may have different names in your area, but they are usually a one-man show, meaning that the local owner of the publication is the same person who solicits ads from you.

Some merchants are highly successful advertising in this type of publication. However, the people who read this type of paper are usually value-conscious shoppers. If your store attracts that type of customer, weekly shoppers are a great place to advertise. But if you sell better-quality merchandise, avoid this type of publication unless it's during sale time. Even then, advertising in shoppers hurts a better store.

Advertising on the Radio

In rural or resort areas, radio is the most important advertising medium you can use. Running the station costs much less in these areas, and therefore the cost of the advertising is much less. (Don't confuse these local stations with a "local" station located in a metropolitan area. These local stations are different because they have too much competition from larger radio stations that cover the same market.)

Radio advertising is less effective in or near a metropolitan area because metropolitan areas simply have too many radio stations. The biggest problem with metropolitan radio advertising is that all the radio stations are competing for the same audience.

A radio advertising salesperson may come into your store and try to dazzle you with facts about how many people are listening to his station. He may get excited when he tells you that he has a 10 percent market share. Remember that this really means that 90 percent of the people listening to the radio *aren't* listening to that station.

Still, radio is a powerful medium if you follow two simple rules:

✔ **Be important to one radio station.** You just don't have a budget big enough to be meaningful to two stations. Every station has its audience, and you want to own that audience.

✔ **Create the same sound for your all your commercials.** Consistency makes radio ads work. Make sure that you have the same opening and closing in all your ads.

Sometimes just a word said differently makes a commercial memorable. A local furniture storeowner does his own spots, and he has the corniest way of saying "fantastic" that gets everybody's attention. Another local automobile dealer built his reputation by constantly repeating the words "come on down." The little things done differently become memorable.

The major advantage to radio is that because radio paints a larger-than-life picture and the spots are cheap to produce (yes, you can spend a lot of money if you want to, but it's unnecessary), you can become a "personality" very quickly if you do your own radio spots. I know that some of those spots are corny, but they work.

Making a long-term commitment to one station

Small retailers can do well with radio, but the first thing you have to do is determine which radio stations the majority of your customers listen to. One way to do this is to ask your customers what stations they listen to. Another way is to ask the stations what type of customers they target and match their targeted customer to your ideal customer. Then use the same strategy that you use in small-space newspaper ads — long-term consistency. You must make a long-term commitment because radio ads generally take a little time to sink in. Customers don't respond immediately after hearing the first ad unless the ad is for a major selling event, and even then the ad works much better if the store has been advertising on the radio station for a while.

Talk radio is a powerful way to advertise because it generally requires fewer spots than an all-music station. You can be successful running 10 to 15 spots per week on a talk radio station as opposed to the 30-plus spots that are required on all-music stations.

Radio rates are negotiable. Most radio reps are quick to tell you that they must go by the rate card, but that's nonsense. A long-term contract with a radio station holds a lot of power. So negotiate hard.

Donating prizes

There's another way to use radio even if your store is small and you don't have the money to pay for commercials. Instead of dealing with a radio sales rep, contact the promotion manager of the station and say the following: "I love your station and would love to be on your station. However, I'm a very small store and could never afford your advertising rates. I noticed that you need prizes to run different promotions and contests. I would love to donate some prizes from my store if you would mention my store on the radio." They'll love you for that. Because radio stations often use the same advertisers over and over, having prizes from a new source can be a refreshing change.

You can give merchandise, but gift certificates generally work much better. Write up a little article about the store to familiarize the station with your business. Interestingly, a majority of the gift certificates that are given out as prizes don't get redeemed. Understand that the reason you're doing this is for the publicity which you accomplish, whether or not the gift certificate is ever redeemed.

Sponsoring a regular feature

Another way to use radio advertising effectively on a small budget is to sponsor a feature on a particular program. For example, I advertised during a radio contest called "Battle of the Sexes" every Friday morning. Even though my ad ran only once a week, people thought I was on the radio station all the time!

The inappropriate radio commercial

Controversial or negative ads can be unbelievably effective if you can handle the uproar that may result. For seven straight years, my women's apparel store ran 12 spots per week on a talk radio station in Boston. One ad was about two women in church at a wedding. The women were talking about the mother of the bride, and not in the kindest of ways. Frankly, they were being catty. One said to the other, "I wonder what she's going to look like?" The other one replied, "Do you think she got anything good to wear? She always looks so dumpy in those cheap clothes she wears." The other woman responded, "I saw her the other day at Ruth's. I'm curious if she got anything there." "I doubt it, and they'd have to be miracle workers there," she replied.

Then you hear wedding music in the background, as one of the women cries out, "Oh my God! Look at her! She looks terrific." "That's the dress she had on at Ruth's. Maybe they are miracle workers," the other woman answered.

From the time that radio spot started to run, the phone didn't stop ringing. We got calls from every woman's group complaining to us that we were depicting women in a negative way. I decided to pull the ad, but that weekend, we had a 43 percent increase in sales. People came to complain, but they ended up buying. One woman told me what a despicable ad we were running. She went on to say that she hadn't been in the store for over eight years, but because of that ad, she had to come in to voice her opposition. That woman spent over $1,600 in the store that afternoon. She jokingly said, "I'm really glad you ran that horrible ad. I almost forgot how good you folks are."

No, I never ran the ad again. I wasn't even tempted. But I kept thinking of other controversial ads that I could run. Controversial ads can draw business, but don't even think about doing it unless you're the type who can handle the pressure.

Advertising on Television

I think of television as the ultimate advertising medium. But it's expensive, and you'll have to produce a quality commercial (I recommend professional help for this). When you're ready to run your commercial, you have two choices: network TV and cable. This section presents a few strategies for getting around (or under) the huge expense of television advertising.

Network TV

CBS, ABC, NBC, and Fox television networks are the granddaddies of television. For years, they were the only show in town, and they have been able to build large and powerful companies with the best of talent and technology. Because of the quality of the programming and the amount of viewers that they can track and deliver, the costs to advertise on these stations is prohibitive unless you're in a very rural area with more reasonable fees.

Prime time (evening television) is simply out of reach financially for any small business. I just can't help you there. However, when it comes to daytime network television, which features shows such as *Good Morning America, Today,* and *The Oprah Winfrey Show,* there are two ways to get around the high-cost issue and save significant amounts of money:

- ✔ **Use a media buyer.** Media buyers work like travel agents — they know the market; they know how far they can push people on price, and they know the availability. Their job is to be able to find you the lowest possible price, and they work on a commission. Every major metropolitan area has media buyers. Just check in the Yellow Pages or search the Web.

- ✔ **Use a media-buying service.** Buying services negotiate with the local affiliate of a major network to purchase all the excess time the station has at 5 p.m. on the day before the spots will run. By this time, there's little chance of selling the spots for full price, so the station offers them to the buying service at a reduction. A media buying service can keep one of your commercials on file so that it's ready to use on short notice.

My store used a media-buying service for three years with wonderful success. We were consistently on *Good Morning America* and *The Oprah Winfrey Show,* running beside other advertisers that were paying over ten times what we were paying. Check the Yellow Pages for buying services in your area.

Cable TV

Cable television is affordable, and like network TV, cable stations have unsold commercial time every day. Know that the cable sales rep's rate card is only the starting point in price negotiations. Many cable stations give you extra spots rather than lower the cost of each spot. Many times, the spots they give you are from midnight to 5 a.m., but you can negotiate for any time you think you can get.

Advertising on Billboards

Of all the forms of advertising, billboards are probably the least used and the biggest mystery. Billboards build businesses and brands almost subconsciously. Billboards make business names household names. Passersby become aware of products because of billboards, but many times they don't even know where they heard of those products.

If you're interested in a specific billboard, you can find the name of the company that owns the billboard on the billboard. Just give them a call and ask about the billboard's availability. Billboards are usually rented for a month at a time. Again, the same rule applies here as it does for other media — the more people who drive by the billboard, the higher the cost to rent it will be. The average billboard ranges in price from a low of $2000 per month to a high of $160,000 for prime space in Times Square, New York.

The sign in front of your store is also a sort of billboard. Make sure that it's clean, crisp, and always well lit.

Window signs are also billboards. The most important element of any grand-opening or store-closing sale is the signage in the store windows. Too many retailers just don't appreciate the value of their windows and the signs they put in them. Look at your store as a customer would look at it.

Telemarketing

A *giant* groan is usually the response I hear when I mention telemarketing in my workshops. Yet in survey after survey, customers rank receiving a short, friendly, informative message from a retail store they frequent as one of the highest levels of service one can receive. The problem is that we think of telemarketing as something that high-pressure home remodeling companies use to sell siding. When *you* call customers, you aren't trying to sell them anything; you're just trying to do one of two things:

- Make them aware of an event that is taking place at your store
- Let them know about a specific type of new merchandise that you thought they might be interested in

Here's the real secret to great telemarketing for retail stores: Call people when they're not home! Most people today have an answering machine or voice mail. All you really want to do is leave a 15-second message. If you think about what you're doing, it's the same as a 15-second radio commercial specifically designed for one customer.

The biggest event of the year for my store was our annual sidewalk sale. In addition to placing a large ad in the local newspaper, we decided to call all our customers and inform them of the upcoming sale. On the first day of the sale, all we heard from our customers was, "Thank you, thank you, thank you. That was so nice of you to call. I really appreciated it." Don't disregard this form of advertising. You might hate it, but your customers love it.

Advertising in Magazines

Many magazines actually have reasonable advertising rates. One reason is that more and more magazines are creating regional editions to attract smaller advertisers. If your business is in New England, you wouldn't want to waste your advertising dollars in a national magazine.

First, I recommend that you find out what magazines your customers are reading — just ask them. Then contact appropriate publications and ask whether they have regional rates. While you're on the phone, you also may want to ask whether the magazine sells mailing lists of its subscribers in your area. Most of them do, but be sure to ask the price per thousand names.

I don't recommend that you buy the lists directly from the magazine. Instead, go to a list broker to have her negotiate, but knowing the price that the magazine is selling the list for is good information to have to make sure that the list broker is treating you right.

Using Direct Mail

The number one type of retail advertising today is direct mail (which includes e-mail) because it's generally the most cost effective and highest producing advertising vehicle. Direct mail is the one media where you are able to target only customers who have an interest in buying what you are selling. But there are two different types of direct mail: *smart* direct mail and *stupid* direct mail. *Stupid direct mail* means that you collect names of people who walk into your store and sign up for a mailing list, and you send them a mailing piece about something that you don't know whether they even like or care about. That's just creating junk mail.

Smart direct mail is when you know the customers so well that you can send them a message about merchandise they like and can afford, written in a way they understand.

Every retailer knows that some customers are more valuable than others. For example, suppose that one of your customers spends $1,000 every time she comes in. Compare her to a customer who rarely buys anything, and if she does she usually returns it the next day. You know which one of those customers is more important! That's why you pinpoint your advertising to target your best customers. One of the most effective ways to do this is through establishing a *preferred customer program*.

Preferred customer programs are the hottest things in retail advertising today because they work. Direct mailings allow you to send coupons, discounts, special notices of upcoming events and sales to only those people who have an interest in your store or in what you sell. They also decrease advertising costs while improving sales and customer satisfaction. You simply invite your best customers to participate and then target your direct mailings to them. That's the closest thing to a silver bullet I can think of.

When you're ready to set up a preferred customer program, check out the Database Management folder on the CD for a sample customer profile form. You also find tips on ways to get customers to sign up as well as suggestions for deciding what types of advertising to send to program members.

Chapter 17

Promoting for Fun and Profit

In This Chapter

▶ Introducing competitive and noncompetitive promotions

▶ Discovering the elements of a successful promotion

▶ Recognizing the importance of fun in a promotion

▶ Seeing the value of a promotion checklist

*P*romotions are essential for the success of a retail business. But what exactly is a promotion? Well, it is not a sale. The purpose of running a promotion is to develop customer interest in what you are selling and then to convert this interest into action. In this chapter I show you how to do this — how to bring people (lots of people) to your store without marking down your merchandise. Unfortunately, too many retailers believe that the only way to attract customers is by reducing the price of the merchandise they sell. Sure that works, but other techniques work just as well.

Successful promotions accomplish the following:

✔ Create curiosity

✔ Give information

✔ Entertain customers

That is why when a new store first opens, it always gets a surge in business. People are curious about the store. They want to get the scoop or information about what is happening, and new store openings are always a fun event. Stores try to attract extra business because the more customers who visit the store, the better the chances are that they'll see something that they like and buy it. Similarly, when retailers make a change in their store or add a new feature, customers are curious and want to be informed of what's going on. But the surest way to get people to come is to entertain them.

Rick's Random Rule #96: Any idiot can mark it down and give it away, but the real merchant can maintain the markup and sell just as many.

Exploring Promotion Ideas

Promotions are the best way to get your customers and potential customers talking about your store. The more interesting the promotion, the more they're going to talk. In this section, I've broken down promotions into two categories — competitive and non-competitive.

Competitive promotions

Some of the best promotions are related to some type of competition. We live in a very competitive world. We love winners and even put champions on cereal boxes. The entertainment industry hands out the Tony awards, the Emmys, the Oscars, and the American Music Awards. In sports, athletes receive honors for being named an MVP, the best offensive player, and best defensive player. Even restaurants can earn awards. People can never get enough of awards. Everyone loved them, and they make for great promotions. The following are some of my favorites.

The bests

The "Why My Mom (or Dad) is Best" promotion is a wonderful promotion that costs very little and will establish your store as a top store — liked, respected, and talked about. Here's how the contest works: Contact all the elementary school teachers in your town and inform them that you're having a writing contest titled "Why My Mom (or Dad) Is Best." The teachers can use it as a class project and submit entries from their entire classes. The entries must be handwritten. Don't allow computer-generated stuff because it ruins the effect. As the entries come in, display them in your store window. Don't cover the entire window with the entries, however; you still want passersby to see your merchandise. If you can't fit all the entries in your window, display them on boards in your store.

Now comes the tough part — judging them. Consider forming a committee — ask a few civic leaders to volunteer. Offer a first, second, and third place, or name a winner for each of two categories, kids under and over 10. The Saturday night before Mother's Day or Father's Day, kids and their parents will crowd around your window just to find their entry.

Once you have selected a winner, notify the local newspaper of the event and ask whether it's interested in covering this story. If so, the paper may want to reproduce a copy of the winning entries. The reporter may end up thanking you for the story, and the paper may even want to cosponsor the promotion with you next year. Plaques and gift certificates to your store can serve as prizes. Your cost for this promotion? Not much at all. This kind of promotion works everywhere. You can also try the following variations of this contest:

- ✔ **The best teacher (or police officer or any other public servant) in town:** This promotion is a little more expensive because you need to run one or more small ads in the local paper to announce the competition.

- ✔ **The best garden in town:** This contest is appropriate for garden stores or nurseries. Promote this event in ads, news releases, and store signage. Entrants must submit a picture of their garden. Send a gardening expert (or a committee) plus a representative of your store to every nominee's garden for judging. The judging visits are a perfect time for networking.

- ✔ **The best ornament, egg, poem, or plate:** Craft and other specialty stores love these competitions. This promotion is announced the newspapers, but you can also run small ads in regional publications.

In search of the (name of your store) woman/man

With this promotion, you're seeking someone who best typifies your ideal customer. When I ran this promotion for my store, we had five finalists. We made people aware of this only with interior signs and an entry form and flyer describing the contest at the cash wrap counter. People nominated themselves or friends. Store employees served as judges. I placed ads in the local paper and in my store newsletter highlighting each finalist. After the winner was selected, I placed a newspaper ad that showcased the winner (and our store).

Competitive running and walking events

Sponsor a road race. Some stores sponsor annual road races and make the event one of their major community service projects of the year. Every time the road race is talked about, written about, or advertised, your store name will be mentioned. If your customers enjoy this type of activity, a run is the perfect type of event to sponsor. In addition to road races, consider sponsoring bicycle races, iron man competitions, or any other physically challenging contest.

Get sufficiently involved to make sure that the race is administered with the same standards you run your business. After all, your name and reputation are on the line.

Bed races

Chamber of commerce organizations, service clubs, or hospitals usually sponsor this type of event. The key to this promotion is that the money you raise goes to a local charity. Your involvement is to work with a charity and supply any of the necessary seed money, which generally isn't that much. This is a fun event that your customers will talk about for years to come.

Teams pay an entrance fee to compete in a bed race, which is held in a parking lot or on a street that's been closed to traffic. Five or six people make up a team, with one or two people lying in a bed on wheels and four people pushing the bed. As you can imagine, the event becomes hilarious to watch because participants fall out of bed as teams gain speed along the way. A team can't win unless someone is in its bed as it crosses the finish line. If you want word-of-mouth advertising, sponsor a bed race — it gives people something to talk about.

The ugliest gift competition

Consider promoting your store with an "ugliest gift I ever received" competition. Invite your customers to participate by bringing in the ugliest gift they have ever received. Offer the winner a gift certificate for your store and donate all the ugly gifts to charity.

If you don't want to deal with storage and clutter of the actual gifts in your store, ask participants to submit photographs of the items. Arrange for volunteers to pick up their ugly gifts and deliver them directly to the charity, many of which have their own stores where they can resell the items. This is another fun win/win project that can enhance your relationship with your community.

Art show or competition

Host an art show for local artists. Customers will appreciate your support of the arts. You can allow the art to be sold, but don't charge the artists anything. Just be grateful that they come and show their works. You want them to come back the next time you conduct such a promotion.

Select a panel of judges to award blue ribbons. One benefit to your business is that the award-winning artists will always refer to themselves as the "(your store) annual art competition winner." Also, consider sponsoring a similar competition for high school students. I actually like this contest even better because this event could significantly change the direction of a young person's life. Winning your event may give a kid the self-confidence to pursue a talent or dream.

Remember to invite members of the press to your store. To generate publicity for the event, contact the local arts councils for help in attracting artists and send a press release to the papers as well. Send a high-quality invitation to your customers and local dignitaries. You don't have to invite your entire customer mailing list; you can be selective.

You can find a sample press release in the Sales/Promotion Forms folder on the CD.

Rick's Random Rule #56: The promotions you choose define your store.

Noncompetitive promotions

The purpose of the noncompetitive promotion is the same as the competitive promotion — to increase public awareness of your business. Noncompetitive promotions are generally educational or information based. The more information you can give your customers, the better they will like you and support your business. It seems strange that education and information can be considered promotional events, but they are!

The survey

This type of relatively new promotion resulted from a consulting session I did with a retailer in upstate New York that sold dance and ice-skating costumes. The retailer made many buying decision based on the recitals and competitions of the dance and skating schools in their area. Because this business was relatively new, most of the schools had already established relationships with other stores. Therefore this store had to establish itself as an expert and a source that could be trusted.

More than 90 schools were in this retailer's marketing area, meaning that there was fierce competition among the schools for students. The store conducted a professional survey done by a respected marketing research firm, asking each school approximately 25 of the same questions. All the answers were then compiled to create a consumer's buying guide for dance and skate schools.

Questions covered the experience levels of teachers and questions about the facilities. Every school was invited to participate in the survey; however, those who didn't appeared in the buying guide with a "chose not to participate" next to their name. This store also offered the various schools advertising space in the buying guide. The retailer placed an ad in the local newspapers so that anyone could call to request a copy of the guide. The retailer also posted the ad on her Web site and sent it to all of the mothers clubs within her marketing area. By establishing a reputation as an expert, and the retailer was able to attract business from the schools.

A survey like this one is an interesting way of becoming a major player in the area in a very short period of time. The best part about this whole concept is that this promotion can run forever. And with enough advertising (which by the way makes a lot of sense for the dance schools because of the distribution and because the established schools with good reputations will score high so they want to participate), the cost to print the survey was not great. New schools also want to be involved because they get exposure that they couldn't get any other way. In a few years, this promotion will not only *not* cost the store any money but should become a major source of income for this business. Start thinking of surveys that you can do to benefit your customers.

Book signings

If you have any well-known authors living near your store, ask them whether they would consider doing a book signing at your store. Most of them will be more than happy to, providing the topic is pertinent to your business. Many trade shows include seminars led by people who have recently written a book that your customers would be interested in. If you meet such a person at a trade show, explore the possibility of them coming to your store for a signing.

Usually book signings don't last more than an hour, but from the retailer's point of view, they add credibility to your store. This type of promotion establishes your expert status with all of the benefits that brings.

Lunch at the store

If your business is an area with a lot of office buildings, many customers may shop on their lunch hour. If so, they're probably in a hurry and may not have time to eat. This promotion helps solve that problem. On the first Wednesday of every month, serve lunch at your store. The lunch can be as simple as small sandwiches and drinks, but it enables your customers to shop during lunch. You don't have to offer this promotion more than once a month. Whatever costs you incur are always offset by the extra sales that this promotion creates. Advertise this event with in-store signage and fliers at the front desk.

Lunch on the store

Retailers are often tempted to give a good customer, or someone who is buying a lot of merchandise, a 10 percent discount, or we might even throw something extra into the purchase. Don't do that! Instead, work out an arrangement with a local restaurant that allows you to buy $5 and $10 gift certificates at a reduced price. You can then say to the customer, "Thanks for buying so much. Let me buy you lunch or dinner" and present the certificate. Customers love this gesture — it spreads goodwill and saves you a lot of money.

Seminar marketing

Every store should conduct at least two to six seminars per year about topics that interest their customers. Bridal shops can present seminars about wedding planning. Gift stores can do seminars on the appropriate gifts to buy. Mother-of-the-bride stores can offer seminars on how to be the perfect mother-in-law. Woodworking stores can have demonstrations of techniques. These events reinforce your expert status, get people talking, and are good business. If you're going to be the pro, act like a pro.

Supply the meeting place

Organizations often need places to hold meetings. Sometimes an organization would rather not use a restaurant because it doesn't want to spend the money. So if you have space, even if you have to move some racks around on your selling floor so that you can set up a table, offer your store as the meeting place. The organization can meet after hours, before the store opens, or, if you have an extra room, during the day. You will be introducing your store to people who may never have thought of coming in, and you're showing your civic pride. Some businesses have used this opportunity to build wonderful relationships with people who became some of their best customers — people who never would have come into the store if it weren't for this offer. The fact that you offer your space is often enough to impress your customers.

Charity nights

This is an interesting promotion that isn't right for every industry but is extremely successful in apparel and gift areas. Charity nights are usually (but not always) held on a night that the store isn't regularly open. At these events, the store gives 20 percent of the proceeds to a specific charity. One employee runs the register, but all the other salespeople must come from the charity. The merchandise is sold at the ticket price, but at the end of the night, you total all the proceeds and donate 20 percent of the total sales to the charity. Obviously, the more business the charity can generate, the better for both of you.

These events usually run between 6 p.m. and 9 p.m. and some type of refreshments, such as wine and cheese, are served. You'll attract people who have never been in the store before but who come in and buy because of the charity. You may be surprised by how pushy the salespeople from the charity can be to make the sale. But it's okay because it's not you or your staff being pushy — and the pushiness is for a good cause. Do something for charity at least once a year.

Celebrity guest appearances

Consider paying a celebrity to come to your store to meet your customers and sign autographs. This event always works well with local sports heroes. Obviously you need a clientele, which is usually a younger customer, that will go crazy to meet a celebrity. My experience is that many of these personalities are much cheaper than you might think, but there are no hard and fast rules. Other local celebrities who draw crowds are local TV news anchors, weather forecasters, radio talk show hosts, and authors.

Radio station remotes

Most radio stations today are willing to set up a remote, providing that you give them enough advertising business. Yes, they generally will attract a crowd, but even if they don't, they keep on saying, "Broadcasting live from (your store)." The listeners will let their imagination go wild and just believe that hoards of people are showing up. When I moved the location of my store, I paid to have a remote broadcast of a talk radio station from the parking lot of the store. It was one of the best things I ever did, but if you asked the radio station, those folks thought it was terrible. Why? Because my customers didn't hang out by the broadcast van. They came into the store in droves, and they bought. Isn't that what they're supposed to do? I thought so.

Dress up or costumes

To enhance a promotion you're already planning, do something different, crazy, out of the ordinary! Ask all your employees to dress in costumes. You can celebrate a holiday such as George Washington's birthday by having everyone wear colonial attire. At Easter time, everyone can dress like bunnies. Let your imagination go wild. As for advertising and PR, don't make the costumes the main focus. They're only a way to enhance whatever promotion you're already doing.

Open house/demo days

The words "open house" convey the idea that something special is going on. You can guarantee that it is special by serving some type of food and offering demonstrations or presentations by experts about your merchandise. Some fields, such as sporting goods, electronics, computers, crafts, and even some areas of the gift market, lend themselves better to this type of promotion. The sound of this promotion says soft sale, information, and expert advice, so be sure that you have all three elements.

Displays in empty store windows

If a nearby store is empty, ask the landlord whether you can decorate the store windows. Doing so not only makes the store look more appealing for the landlord to rent but also gives you a free advertising area. It's another win/win situation.

Identifying the Characteristics of a Good Promotion

Before you fall in love with any promotion idea, answer the following questions:

- ✔ Will it increase sales?
- ✔ Will it increase awareness of the store? If you're a new business, this is just as important as increasing sales.
- ✔ Will you add new customers, the type who are good for the store?

✔ What kind of free publicity will it generate?

✔ How much will it cost? This is not about spending money; it's about how creative you are. Your goal is to spend nothing.

✔ Will it be fun for both the customers and the employees?

✔ Is it easy to understand? Promotions that are too complicated rarely work. Keep it simple.

✔ Will the promotion create curiosity?

✔ What is the news angle? Would a reporter write a story about it?

You may not be able to answer all of these questions about the promotion. That doesn't make the promotion bad; it simply helps you to focus on your goals for that particular promotion. Some promotions will be better than others, and that's okay. You just want your store to become a place where things are always happening. You don't want to motivate customers only by price.

Making It Fun

Seattle's famous Pike Place Market is home to a collection of independent stands of merchants selling everything from crafts to fish. But it's best known for a particular fish stand that emphasizes entertainment. There's even a documentary video about this fish stand that's used for business training.

Employees at this fish stand are constantly singing and chanting fun songs to help sell their fish. But they're best known for their flying fish routine. That's when a fishmonger in the front throws a whole fish to one of the slicers and wrappers 15 to 20 feet away in the back row as customers and onlookers wonder whether someone will actually catch the fish. They are promoting their product by using the concept of entertainment selling.

This video has been distributed to major corporations around the world. I first saw it when I was speaking for McDonald's. Think about it — McDonald's is one of the most successful retailers in the world, and yet it's learning from an independent fish stand. Just like the fish stand, you must look for ways to attract your customers by incorporating fun and entertainment into the mix. Making it fun pays off in the following ways:

✔ It creates an awareness of your store.

✔ It gets people talking about your store.

✔ It brings traffic into your store so that you do more business.

✔ It costs little or nothing to run.

Event showcases tresses and dresses

The promotion described here met all the criteria for a successful promotion. I consider it to be one of the best promotions ever.

When a downtown starts to die, certain stores remain, and those are generally the pizza parlor, the insurance offices, and the beauty shops. In my town, older women usually went to the beauty shop on a weekly basis to have their hair done. Those were the days of heavy spray and permanents. That was my customer, and the beauty shop was where they hung out. So I decided to create a competition for the best hairdresser in town. Models would show off hair designs while wearing clothes from my apparel store.

First, we invited Zonta (a women's organization) to cosponsor the event. We proposed to run a fashion show featuring models from the different beauty shops showing off their best hair designs. We explained that our goal was not to make any money and that all the proceeds would go to Zonta, but we needed the members' help in selling tickets. We reserved a conference hall, created beautiful invitations, and hand delivered them to every beauty shop in town. We wrote a press release and delivered it personally to the editors of the local newspapers and requested that they send a reporter to cover the event. All of the models had to come into my store to be fitted for the clothing that they would wear for the fashion show. We offered them a 20 percent discount if they decided to purchase anything that they modeled. We then contacted professional beauty school instructors from Boston to judge the competition.

Tickets sold out within a couple weeks. The reporters covered the story and took pictures of the winners wearing clothes from my store. The articles actually ran on the front page of two different newspapers — free advertising. Our sales from that event were close to $10,000. Our costs, including the invitations, the hall rental, the hours my staff put in, and the costs of the awards and gifts to the judges, all came out of the proceeds generated that night, which meant it cost us nothing to run.

This promotional event was truly a win- win-win-win event. The beauty shops won because of the exposure and publicity they received, especially the winners. The models won because they felt special and got a discount on store merchandise. Zonta won because the event became a fundraising event for which they didn't have to do much work. (I believe that the club netted over $5,000.) The community won because it seemed to bring everybody together with a common interest. And lastly my store won financially — immediately and for many years to come. I was able to present my merchandise to prospective customers who never would have shopped in my store otherwise. Many of the models went on to become very good customers.

Using a Promotion Checklist

The following is a checklist of questions to help you plan your promotions:

✔ What is the promotion idea? You should constantly be on the lookout for clever ideas. Look at industries other than your own. Read the paper for promotional ideas and innovative ways that other businesses promote. Usually a store that has one good promotion has other good promotions.

✔ What is the manpower commitment, and do you employ people that can execute the promotion?

✔ What is the lead time required? Make a timeline of all of the steps required from start to finish.

✔ What is the budget requirement?

✔ Where will the promotion take place?

✔ How will you inform your customers, employees, and new customers or prospects? What advertising and PR tools will you employ?

✔ What is the goal? What are you trying to accomplish?

✔ What kind of record keeping will you do to record the event history, and what ways could you improve the event for the future?

Obviously, this is a general list. The more promotions you do, the more sophisticated you can become in your planning process. Plan on constantly refining your process.

If you're looking for the bible of great promotional ideas, then visit your public library and browse through *Chase's Calendar of Events* (Contemporary Books). This annual publication is jam-packed full of those little-known holidays and birthdays that make great themes for promotions. What about celebrating Martha Stewart's birthday on August 3? It's a perfect holiday to celebrate if you have a craft or home decor business. If you own a sporting goods store, why not celebrate Babe Ruth's birthday on April 27? *Chase's* also has lists by date of some of the craziest holidays people, companies, and associations have created. Here are just a few:

✔ National Limerick Day

✔ Be Bald Be Free Day

✔ Be Late for Something Day

✔ Be Kind to Animals Week

✔ National Wildlife Week (I used this one when I bought too much leopard print merchandise for my store. Instead of marking it down, I used the excess material to celebrate this holiday with posters, window displays, press releases, and ads. We almost sold out every piece. What a fun promotion!)

Consider creating your own holiday and submitting it to *Chase's*. For example, if you own a shoe store, you could create "Be Kind to Your Feet Week." However, if you do submit a holiday for publication, be prepared to receive calls and letters from people wanting more information about your day. That's one of the nice things about Chase's — most of the listings have contact information so you can get more information about the day. Many listings will send you some cool, free stuff. This is a great source of fun, playful promotions.

Chapter 18

Setting Up Successful Sales

• •

In This Chapter

▶ Identifying reasons to run a sale

▶ Conducting a successful sale

▶ Getting help from a professional sale event planner

• •

Keeping stale and old merchandise on your store shelves puts you at a big disadvantage. Offering outdated goods slowly deteriorates the vitality of your business, and you start to lose customers almost silently. You can remedy this problem by having a sale event, which can help you to keep your merchandise fresh, clean, inviting, and current.

Like many retailers, I once believed that in order to have a sale you have to mark down everything in your store. You don't. You also don't have to make all your markdowns drastic. Some can be deeper than others. The purpose of this chapter is to explore some reasons for putting merchandise on sale and how to do it as effectively and profitably as possible.

Rick's Random Rule #921: It takes little fish to catch big ones.

Considering Some Reasons to Run a Sale

Too many retailers have sales without any idea why they're doing so, other than to generate more business. I don't recommend this approach! In order to run an effective sale, you must have a clear idea of your purpose so that you can select a name for the sale and plan it carefully. In the sections that follow, I present some common reasons for running a sale event.

To all those retailers who believe that a sale is the answer to all of their problems, it isn't. As a matter of fact, the bigger the sale event, the bigger the drop-off in sales after the event. Several professional sale and promotional consulting firms promise you large increases in sales during a major sale event, but they don't tell you what the effect will be after the event is over. Before you plan any sale event, please keep in mind the prospects of reduced business afterward. As a friend of mine says, "Beware of the stranger bearing gifts. You might have to pay for them later."

Opening a new store

When you first open your store, you want to introduce it to as many people as possible. "The stronger the opening, the stronger the store" is an old battle cry of seasoned merchants. The rationale is that the more that people talk about your store, the bigger your base of customers or at least potential customers.

Some people believe that a strong opening helps to pay for a big majority of the opening expenses such as advertising, additional payroll, and even some of the construction costs. But whether you believe this or not, the reason for running a grand opening sale is to generate cash and awareness.

You can find a grand opening checklist of things to do in the Sales/Promotion Forms folder on the CD.

Moving to a new location

If your store moves, you don't want to lose a customer. Of course, you want to add new customers, too, but many retailers tend to take the old customers for granted and focus only on the new ones. It's important to take special care of your existing customer base while you attract new customers.

Obviously, you want to run a sale to generate money to pay for the move. The real purpose of a moving sale, however, is awareness, which is more than just saying to your customers, "Here we are." Awareness also means letting your customers know what you can do for them. You have to change people's habits, and doing so isn't easy. You must give them a reason to travel to your new location.

Generating cash

The need for cash is probably the most common reason for having a sale, although very few retailers ever like to admit it. Having a sale for this reason is okay. Look at it this way: You probably need cash because you bought too much merchandise — albeit wonderful merchandise. In this situation, you need to turn the merchandise into cash as quickly as possible. As much as it may hurt, take your markdowns quick and deep and make this sale as short as possible. You don't want this type of sale to linger.

Making room for new merchandise

I believe that every retailer should be struggling because of inadequate space. If you're not, then you have too much space (or too little merchandise). Have fun with this sale, but make it short and deep. If you can't make money, at least make friends.

Stimulating business

If you find that you're not doing the amount of business you expected, you just may need to stimulate a little activity to ensure that you make your projections, goals, or last year's figures. Sometimes you may not even need a sale. Maybe all you need is a creative non-sale promotion. (Read Chapter 17 for ideas about promotions.)

Overcoming boredom

There comes a time in every store when the entire store, including the employees, get into a rut. That's the time to stir up the pot with something different. Celebrate the change with a sale. You may not have had any sale events for a few months and can sense that your customers are expecting something. A good retailer can feel when the time is right for a sale.

Adding names to your customer database

Your customer database or mailing list is the lifeblood of your business. Although you always like to make the register ring, one reason to run a sale is to gather customer names and information so that you can market directly to them in the future. This sale has a long-range goal, not just the joy of short-lived sales increases.

Letting the dogs out

The term *dog* refers to merchandise that has been hanging around your store that nobody wants to buy. This is merchandise that you once loved but nobody else did. When you have accumulated enough of these items, usually once a year, it's time to have a down-and-dirty sale just to dump the merchandise. You can just sell this merchandise off to a liquidator and be done with it, but you won't make as much money. Besides, you'll get a certain thrill about finally seeing it go out the front door. Keep in mind that while you're running this kind of sale, you'll also sell a substantial amount of your regular-price merchandise.

Marketing to a new area

Our store was located in a town near a very affluent town, but for some reason we rarely advertised in that market. Despite that, we noticed that we regularly attracted more and more customers from that town. When we ran a sale targeted at only that town's zip code, we added many names to our database, and the revenues from that sale were substantial. We called it our "01803 Sale." It was a great way to expand our marketplace.

Marketing to a specific group

If several of your customers belong to the same organization, think about running some type of joint promotion with that organization. You could declare a day (or weekend) "That Organization Day" and offer a special discount for organization members. If you try this event, every member of the organization will be saying nice things about your store.

Meeting competition

You can't let your competition consistently beat you on price. If those other stores are going to be your competition, then you must compete. A sale is just one way to compete. Use this tactic only when you're competing with a store your own size. Don't try to beat a huge store on price.

Announcing any change

Any time that anything changes within your business, such as remodeling your store or welcoming a new staff member, is a good time to celebrate with a sale. In retail, change is good, change is healthy, and customers love change. Change creates curiosity, and curiosity creates traffic — and do I have to tell you what traffic creates? Okay, sales. Take advantage of human nature and people's natural sense of curiosity.

Going out of business

The going-out-of-business sale is the most powerful of all sales. It is so powerful that all 50 states have enacted laws governing this type of sale. A certain magic draws customers to business when they see the "going out of business" sign.

The misery meter

The *misery meter* is the public perception that the more miserable the retailer is, the better the savings will be for them. One end of the misery meter is the going-out-of-business sale — the public believes that the retailer is so desperate that he's giving away merchandise just to get rid of it. On the other end of the misery meter is the not-so-much-off sale. One creates an excitement, and the other creates a yawn — maybe. Plenty of sale options fall between these two extremes. Just remember that when customers think they're getting something for nothing, they'll line up at your front door.

Running a Great Sale

Running a successful sale is both an art and a science. You must first capture the imagination of your potential customers and then execute the sale perfectly. Numerous factors go into making a successful sale. Some of the most fundamental include the following:

- **Promotable items:** Every sale needs one or two items that are well known and have a high-perceived value by the public. Be sure that you can purchase it from the vendor at a reduced price so you and your customers get a great deal.

- **Specific purpose:** If a sale doesn't make sense to the public, it won't work. That's why having a specific purpose for your sale and communicating it to the public are so important.

- **The timing of your sale:** Sales can't be too close to one another. Sales lose their effectiveness when the public can't differentiate one from another because your store seems to be running a continuous stream of sales.

- **Strong customer mailing list:** The stronger your customer list, the better the sale, because you can promote your sale directly to your customers. Consider keeping a separate list of sale customers. Ask people to register when they come in for sales.

- **Pre-sale shutdown period:** Prior to a sale event, close your doors for a few days to generate customer curiosity and give your staff a chance to get everything ready for the big event. You can even paper over your windows and use them as a billboard to advertise your upcoming sale. During the sale, you'll more than make up for any lost business during the shutdown period.

- **Careful planning:** Create a checklist and follow it to ensure that your sale runs smoothly. Create a folder for every sale event you ever have and include this checklist.

✔ **Sales promotions and giveaways:** Consider creating a bag stuffer — a flier announcing the coming sale that you'll insert into shopping bags before the sale. Also think about offering some shopping incentive, such as a tote bag, an umbrella, or a coupon, for the first 100 sale shoppers. You may even want to invite a celebrity to make an appearance. Include information about all of this in your folder, along with the details about any other thing you're using for the sale, such as renting searchlights, large balloons, or other attention grabbers.

You can find a sample sale checklist and a sample coupon in the Sales/Promotion Forms folder on the CD. While you're there, check out the sample sale meeting agenda, too.

The success of all sales is almost completely dependent on exceeding what customers expect when they walk through your front door.

Naming your sale

Never, never, never, run a nameless sale. Every sale is its own entity and has its own identity because every sale has a different reason for being. You must name — or, better yet, brand — your sale events to give your customers something to look forward to from year to year. The following questions are designed to help you start thinking about effective sale names:

✔ **Why are you having the sale?** Go back to the beginning of this chapter for some possible answers to this one.

✔ **Who is the target market for the sale?** Do you want only your sale customers? Do you want to attract people from a particular zip code? Thinking about who you want to shop at the sale will help you to come up with a name.

✔ **When are you going to have it?** Naming a sale for a time of year or season is very common.

✔ **What is going to be on sale?** How many coat sales have you seen? How many lawn mower sales have you seen? I can go on and on, but naming your sale after the type of merchandise you're featuring makes it easy for customers to understand what the sale event is all about.

✔ **What type of impact do you want?** Use the misery meter (see the related sidebar earlier in this chapter) to help you think of a name for your sale. Do you want the sale to sound like you're desperate, or do you want the sale to have a softer, friendlier feel?

✔ **What is the sense of urgency?** You want many sales to be quick, to the point, and over as fast as possible. The sense of urgency can dictate the name your sale. I have run many a sale called the "buy it fast before it's all gone sale." Another way to increase the sense of urgency is to advertise the ending date of the sale.

✔ **What are you offering?** What will you be offering that people just can't live without? What will draw them into your store? Whatever it is, include it in your sale name if possible.

✔ **Where will it be?** Remember the sidewalk sale? Not all sales are held within the confines of the store. The name implies the location. And that location implies something as well — cheap. You could have a parking lot sale, a tent sale, and even an off-site warehouse sale.

You can find a list of fun sale names in the Sales/Promotion Forms folder on the CD.

Choosing sale merchandise

A major factor in the success of any sale is the selection of merchandise presented to the customers. You need to have a mix of merchandise that cries out, "BUY ME!" The following are some factors to consider when you're deciding on which merchandise to actually put on sale:

✔ **The price wow.** Some merchandise is simply beautiful merchandise that will always grab buyers' attention. Other merchandise is just so-so or average — it's not exciting but eventually will sell. If you mark so-so merchandise down to the right price, it becomes a wow. The thing that motivates customers during a sale is getting that great buy. So be sure to consider the price when selecting the merchandise to go on sale.

✔ **Sufficient sale merchandise:** Make sure that you have a sufficient supply of sale merchandise to justify a big sale event. If you don't, consider just having a markdown table or area.

✔ **Range of merchandise:** Try to balance your sale merchandise between good, better, and best items and offer them at various markdowns. Don't think that everything should be in the low range just because it's sale time. You have three different levels of customers (at least), and you should offer each of them something on sale.

✔ **Merchandise matched to the type of sale:** Certain types of sales require different levels of merchandise. For example, a back room sale indicates better merchandise at a reduced rate, while a liquidation sounds like cheap, cheap, cheap. Be sure to match the name of the sale with appropriate merchandise.

If you're planning to return sale merchandise to original prices, think carefully before you write sale prices on price tags with a red pen. Reticketing everything will be a nightmare. Instead, try attaching separate sale price tags stapled to the original price tag. These can easily be removed.

Playing games with your prices destroys your credibility. Never mark things up only to mark them down. Yes, you can get away with this for a while, but when customers figure out what you're doing, they're likely to be furious. Whatever amount of money you make by doing this is not worth losing customers.

Advertising and promoting your sale

After you've decided on the type of sale you're going to run and given it a name, you have to decide how you plan to advertise or promote the sale. Although you can flip to Chapter 16 for specific information on effective advertising, the following list covers several ways to accomplish this task.

- **Direct mail:** This is the one of the best ways to advertise sales. And e-mail makes this a quick and inexpensive proposition. Create a special letter (known as modified long copy) that has your logo on the top, followed by four to five very short paragraphs about your sale (with key words underlined), and a salutation. Add a "P.S." to create some additional interest. Consider sending this information about your sale to the following:

  - Your entire customer list

  - A defined customer list (sale customers, big spenders, or anything in between, depending on the type of sale)

  - Registered customers (those customers who you've asked to sign up for the sale prior to the event — consider sending this group notification of further markdowns as your sale progresses)

  - Purchased lists, those customers who can be targeted by zip code, magazine subscriptions, and just about any other demographic element)

- **Telemarketing:** Make short, 15-second, informative phone calls to let your customers know that you're having a sale and when it will begin. You're not trying to sell them anything — just inform them.

- **Press releases:** For every interesting and different type of sale that you run, send out a press release to the surrounding newspapers. Rarely will a newspaper run a story on a summer clearance sale, but newspapers *will* run stories about sales that have additional news value to the community. If you come up with a creative name for a sale that has an interesting story behind it, present it to the papers. Remember that with advertising, you pay, and with public relations, you pray.

- **Tell your employees:** Meet with all your employees before every sale event and include as many as you can in the planning process. Having everyone involved does the following:

  - **Creates buy-in:** For the sale to be truly effective, your employees must believe in what you're doing — they must buy into the concept. Never try to get your staff to buy into something that is unethical or illegal. Employees want to work for people who always do the right thing.

- **Enables everyone to manage the sale event smoothly:** Discuss possible sale-related situations that are likely to occur. For example, what should employees do if a customer very recently bought something that you just marked down? What will the store policy be? Make sure everyone knows exactly what merchandise is on sale. Encourage employee input.

If you have a customer who has merchandise on layaway and now it is marked down, you better honor the lower price or be prepared to lose that customer. Discuss this type of issue with your employees before you run your sale.

You can find an advertising calendar, sample sale letters, a sample press release format, and sample sale ads in the Sales/Promotion Forms folder on the CD.

Preparing your store for the big event

The rules for setting up a successful sale are different than running your normal, everyday retail operation. If it doesn't look like you're having a sale, then you're not going to have a very successful one! This means that you should plan the sale layout of your store in a way that will stop people in the traffic flow with merchandise barriers that will draw many customers to one "buying frenzy" location.

Setting the stage

What is your store going to look like during the sale? The store must NOT look the same as usual — make it look different. Put racks in the aisles and remember that you don't get extra points for neatness. Customers want to see a live, happening place. Place sale racks near the front door to capture the customers' attention immediately. Planned confusion is the best term to describe what your store should look like. Create hustle-bustle, that feeling that lets customers know that something is different and happening. Your goal is to create a buying frenzy.

Creating interior signage

When running a sale, you must have bold interior signage. If you want your sale signage to have the effect of neon (but less tacky), make nice triangle signage with creative fonts and use a tasteful color specifically for the sale.

Use unique fonts — different from what you normally use for advertising — and use them only for sale time. Doing this helps brand your event. You want to train your customers to know that a sale is in progress when they see that font.

Making special sale tags

Using special sale price tags is a lot of work, but studies have shown that tagging every item creates significantly higher sale results. I recommend that you print sale tags with the name of the sale on the tag and place one on every piece of merchandise. However, if you don't use a separate tag, then go ahead and use a red pen to write markdowns on the original tag. Ensuring that the sale price is indicated on all sale merchandise is more important than avoiding the hassle of reticketing merchandise to the non-sale price after the sale is over.

You can find sample sale tags in the Sales/Promotion Forms folder on the CD.

Decorating for the sale

Balloons make any store come alive, so include them in most of your sale events. You can buy a small helium tank at party stores for about $20, and it's worth every penny. Balloons create a festive atmosphere and make it look like something is happening at the store and that customers can discover great buys. The name of your sale will suggest other decorating ideas.

Adding the fun

For some reason, sales are associated with fun. Don't try to change it; just go with the flow. During a sale, it's okay to do different, crazy things to get people in a festive buying mood. For example, have an early bird special that gives everybody an extra 10 percent discount if they shop in the store between 7 a.m. and 9 a.m. You can even have a pajama sale that offers customers an additional 15 or 20 percent off the reduced price if they come in wearing pajamas.

Analyzing the success of your sale event

When the sale is finally over, review the event. Doing so can help you plan future sales. Record your analysis in your sale folder (see the section, "Running a Great Sale," earlier in this chapter) to create a history, chronicling what worked and what didn't work.

I include a sample final analysis form with questions to guide your review on the CD. You can find it in the Sales/Promotion folder.

Using Professional Sale Companies

Depending on the situation, you may benefit from working with a professional sale planner. They're not cheap, but they do produce results. Many of these companies send a representative to your store to be there during the entire sale. You're buying an extra set of experienced hands that have been there before and know what to do. Other consulting firms will plan your sale for you, write all the ads, and do it for much less money. Decide what your needs are and how much work you want to do yourself.

When you employ a professional sales company, you commit yourself to a six- to eight-week contract. Some of these companies actually charge you a fee for their sales call. Expect some high-pressure sales tactics and be careful. But many of these consulting firms don't use that approach and do just as good a job.

Find out exactly who'll be working on your sale. If you get a top-notch consultant, you could have one of the best learning experiences you'll ever have in the retail business. However, if you get a bad consultant, you can waste a lot of money. The best criterion is simply the person's longevity with the company. If a person has been there less than two years, be concerned.

Part VI
Selling Made Simple

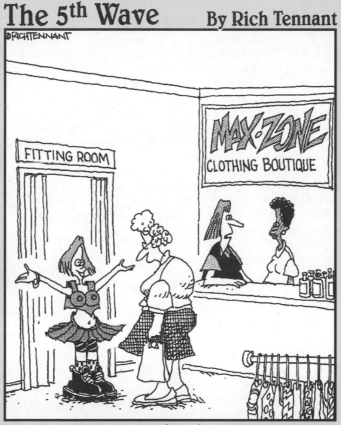

The 5th Wave   By Rich Tennant

FITTING ROOM

MAX-ZONE
CLOTHING BOUTIQUE

"The key to profitability is selling accessories. We sell tons of dark glasses to parents who don't want to be recognized."

In this part . . .

You realize that customers want to buy but hate to be sold to. This part also introduces you to selling strategies that have astonishing and instant results, including ways to play the game of selling the most amount of merchandise for the maximum amount of money. This part also includes a discussion on how to maximize your sales with effective visual merchandising.

But along with face-to-face selling you also explore the vehicle of electronic commerce that customers are demanding these days — the Internet. You learn how to make the Web work for you and why a Web presence is essential for every retail business.

Chapter 19

Selling the Soft Suggestive Way

• •

• •

Retailing is a business of selling. Everything we do is about having customers purchase merchandise from us. We make our stores look nice so that the customers will buy more merchandise. We advertise so that more customers will buy. We promote so that more customers will buy. But if we do everything right — we have the best displays, the best location, the best advertising, the best promotion, the best merchandise, at the lowest possible price — and an employee ignores or insults a customer, it's all for nothing.

Successful retailing depends on positive contact between the customer and store staff. Think of selling as providing a service. After all, that's what your customers want. The purpose of this chapter is to teach you how to sell so that it's enjoyable (and profitable) for you and your staff, and at the same time is helpful to your customers.

Recognizing a Great Salesperson

Great salespeople don't have a unique look — they just look like regular everyday people. But the one thing that they all have in common is their desire to serve the customer and put the customer's needs and wants before their own.

Ralph, the reluctant salesman

For three years, I was responsible for all Shell Oil dealer training in New England and New York. As part of my research, I even worked at a few stations. The employees often thought I was just a slow trainee from another station. One Saturday morning I met a fellow named Ralph. Ralph was the assistant manager of the station and had worked there for nine years. His goal was to become the manager of the station.

When I got to the station, it was already busy. I watched Ralph work and noticed that with every customer Ralph would say, "Don't forget Powerball tonight. It's at $42 million." The customer would respond, "Thanks Ralph," and then proceed to buy some tickets. He would say almost the same thing to the next customer, "Don't forget Powerball. It's up 42 mil tonight."

The customer would always thank Ralph and always buy tickets.

When business slowed up enough for Ralph and me to talk, he started telling me the things I would have to learn to be as fast at the cash register as he was. I asked him how many of those Powerball lottery tickets were sold since I had been there. He went to his lottery machine, hit a few buttons, and said proudly, "400, no 402 to be exact." Then I said something that made Ralph as angry as can be. I said, "You are quite the salesman." When I said that, his face turned bright red, and I could see the veins popping from his neck as he replied, "I'm not one of those salesman types. I didn't sell anything to anybody; *I was just taking care of my customers.*"

What are the characteristics of a great salesperson?

- ✔ They never ignore customers.
- ✔ They greet the customers by name whenever possible.
- ✔ They look professional. A professional appearance is vital to your store's image and helps build your brand. It also establishes the sales staff as people who customers can count on for expert advice.
- ✔ They understand the importance of serving customers.
- ✔ They're friendly and willing to listen to customers.
- ✔ They always suggest another item if the merchandise the customer wants is not available.
- ✔ They look at each customer as having the potential of buying multiple items.
- ✔ They always thank the customer.
- ✔ They always follow up and make sure that the customer was satisfied.

Rick's Random Rule #5: Selling is servicing. We all hate to be sold, but we love to be serviced.

Remembering Some Fundamental Rules of Retail Selling

One of the biggest mistakes many retailers make is to think that they're just selling merchandise. However, customers never buy the merchandise unless you sell some other things first, including the following:

- **Yourself:** Customers often judge the sales staff first. You need them to like you, respect you, or think you're a good person. If they don't like you, they won't buy from you.

- **Your store:** Customers must have confidence in the store before they'll buy any merchandise. If you say negative things about your store, customers will never buy from you regardless how much they might like you. Never say anything bad about the place where you work because you only make yourself look like a fool.

- **An experience:** You have to make sure that customers enjoy themselves in your store. If they don't, they won't buy anything. They can like you and like the store, but if they have an unpleasant experience, you may lose their future business.

Because customers form their impressions so quickly, there's very little room for error. This section offers tips on how to make all these impressions positive ones.

Turning lookers into buyers

Your challenge is to make merchandise look good enough to compel customers buy it. Every customer who comes into your store is just looking. Your job is to convert those lookers into buyers by tempting them with things they like in a way they enjoy. That's the secret to selling.

Practicing soft suggestive selling

The days of pushy, obnoxious salespeople are gone. Customers will not tolerate that type of treatment today. Instead, they want easy, hassle-free service. Traditional hard-sell tactics just won't work. To encourage people to buy, you have to counter all feelings of "I'm not in the mood to shop today." So how do you get customers in the mood? Here are some suggestions:

- Talk about what the customer likes to talk about.

- Focus on what they want, not what they need. Independent retailers today are making money on the want items — not the needs.

- Don't be judgmental.

- Never practice one-upmanship. Don't play the "mine is better than yours" game.

- Treat people the way they want to be treated. This is the platinum rule of retail. Everybody is different and wants to be treated differently. Later in this chapter I profile the major types of customers and tell you how to treat each type.

Getting people to like you

If someone doesn't like you, she won't want to do business with you. Selling people something is easier if they like you. And when customers like you, you can build their trust in you and your store. When customers like you, solving their problems is easier. There are many ways to get people to like you, but here I focus on the biggies.

- **Engage in selfless conversations.** Talk about the things the other person wants to talk about.

- **Be approachable.** Check your ego at the door. Customers won't like you if you're arrogant or present yourself as a know-it-all. Remember that you're there to serve, and sometimes you have to sacrifice your ego for the sake of the customer's.

- **Pay attention to details.** Customers appreciate the little stuff. Remembering their birthdays, observe holidays, and notify them about merchandise they may be interested in. Share some news or a good joke.

- **Extend sincere compliments.** Compliments make people feel good. Isn't it nice doing business with someone with a happy, bubbly personality? Of course it is. Why not tell your customers that it's fun to wait on them? You'll make their day. And if you tell that grumpy, hard-nosed customer that you enjoy taking care of people who know what they like, she'll melt faster than the Wicked Witch of the West. When a customer selects something, simply say, "Great choice." You'll be surprised at the wonderful reaction you get.

- **Laugh.** Laughter is the greatest social lubricant. Have some fun with your customers. People love to do business with people who laugh. The people we laugh with are the people we like.

Making a good impression

You never have a second chance to make a good first impression and judgement often starts the moment a customer enters your store. Everything sells and everything speaks — customers may make buying decisions based on the smallest of points. That water spot on the ceiling or the paper littering the floor tells them that you don't care about the details. But your friendly greeting and the fresh flowers at the cash register let them know that you *do* care about the little things.

As that customer crosses your threshold, you're formulating impressions, too. What kind of person are you dealing with? Is he going to be easy or hard to sell to? Is he in a hurry or not? You also form opinions in just a few seconds. The goal of the dance is to get the customer to start talking. Then they relax and can enjoy their experience.

Be careful not to stereotype. You never want to discount a new customer or treat her with any less enthusiasm than you would your best customer.

Realizing that customers buy with their emotions

Customers buy because they're depressed or because they're happy or maybe because they just want something different. The most successful store isn't always the one with best product. It's the store that makes customers feel good about doing business there. If you're looking for logic, a retail business is not the place to find it.

Rick's Random Rule #88: Today's customers don't buy things because they need them. They buy things because they crave change.

Avoiding LCR

LCR stands for "last customer residue." Don't take out your frustrations that the last customer caused you on the new customer who just walked in. It's show time every time a new customer walks in. Forget the last customer and focus on the next customer. I know you have a need to talk it out, but you can't do it with the next customer. Hold it, bite your tongue, jump up and down, but don't say a word to the new customer about what just happened. They don't care and will only think you're a jerk and won't want to do business with you or the store and may worry that you'll do the same to them when they leave.

The 4 percent rule

This rule is simple and sad. Four percent of all the customers who come in to every store in the world belong to the PLO: pushy, loud, and obnoxious. You will never please them. Don't drive yourself crazy trying to. The next time a customer gives you a hard time, look him in the eye and say, "You must be part of the 4 percent." He won't know what you're talking about, but at least it will make you feel good. I'M ONLY KIDDING! DON'T DO THAT! That was the comedy relief for this chapter. The point is, as hard as you try to sell to everyone, it's impossible. So don't beat yourself up if you lose a sale.

Knowing what not to say

Here's a list of phrases that drive customers away:

- ✔ "You couldn't afford that." How insulting!
- ✔ "We would need cash from you." What does this insinuate?
- ✔ "It's over there." Always go get things for customers.
- ✔ "All we have is out." At least offer to check in the back.
- ✔ "I only work here." You won't for long if you use this phrase.

Perfecting Your Sales Process

The sales process is made up of five components: the greeting, bonding or asking questions, making suggestions, overcoming objections, and closing the sale. Many times these steps occur so quickly that they almost blur together. You just need an awareness of the process and practice to master these steps.

Greeting customers

The first step of the sales process is the greeting — what you say when a customer first walks through your front door. Be sure to express gratitude. You could say, "Thanks for coming in!" or some modification of this. In doing so, you immediately establish a graciousness that is attractive to most shoppers. Try to make eye contact and be sure to smile.

If the store is really busy and you don't have time to properly greet everyone (days like this should happen more often), remember to at least acknowledge those people with a wave or a quick hello. Let them know that you or someone else will be right with them. Customers understand if you're busy, but they hate to be ignored.

Creating a bond

To sell to people, you need to know something about them — what they may want to buy and what they could be enticed to buy. Ask short questions and let the customers do the talking. The more you talk at this point, the less the customer will trust you. Get them to talk by asking some of the following questions:

- Who is it for?
- What is your opinion of this type of merchandise?
- Where are you planning to use it? Wear it? Store it?
- When do you want to pick it up?
- Which type do you prefer?
- How did you become so knowledgeable about these?

After you ask a question and get an answer, use an expander. These are questions or follow-up statements that expand the conversation. Memorize the following and use them freely within the conversation to get customers talking.

- Tell me about . . .
- Do you think . . .
- Which means . . .

Making suggestions

Use the information you get from conversations with customers to guide your choice of other merchandise to recommend. Try to suggest things that *they* may want — not necessarily things that you like. Look for buying signals — any movement or question the shopper makes that indicates she might be interested in an item. Show the merchandise with enthusiasm and style. Demonstrate product knowledge because customers expect you to know what you are talking about. In the end, if the customer doesn't like what you suggest, you have to be flexible. Don't take it personally.

I've discovered a simple little technique that not only will increase your sales and create add-on sales, but it's also easy to teach your sales staff. I call it "Did you see this?" This is how it works. An employee walks by a customer, points to a piece of merchandise, and says, "Did you see this?" then keeps on walking. The customer will want to know what the employee was pointing at. You've piqued his curiosity.

If your staff focuses on the "Did you see this?" strategy, you'll be amazed with the results. I used this approach in my store and the customer grapevine started buzzing with comments such as, "They are so nice there." "They aren't pushy; they suggest things." "They don't really have salespeople, just people to help."

Handling customer objections

When a customer starts to back off from a purchase, you need to know what to do. Here are two common objections customers give to making a purchase and how to respond:

✔ **Objections to price:** Find out what the customer is objecting to. Has she seen the same item in another store for less money? If so, you better think about adjusting your price to be competitive. Verify the validity of the claim and then make your adjustment. If it's simply a matter of something costing more than the customer wants to spend, show her something cheaper.

✔ **Objections to the product:** When a customer doesn't like one product, show her another one. Recognize that some customers need a choice and that some items look better when they're compared to another.

Always take merchandise that customers are planning to buy out of their hands and place it near the cash register. Doing so reinforces to the customers that they're buying those items and lets the customer shop with two hands.

Romancing your customers

Every retail business shares the goal of creating loyal customers. Not only do loyal customers provide you with sales revenue, but they also represent advertising opportunities. This list suggests some ways to court customers to keep them coming back to you.

✔ Be visually what the customer expects.

✔ Have an attitude of appreciation.

✔ Practice mutual understanding of both the good and the bad.

✔ Know as much as you can about a customer (this makes it easier to sell to them).

✔ Recognize that mistakes are opportunities.

✔ Be likeable so customers will want to do business with you.

✔ Remember the extras — the little things that differentiate you from your competition.

✔ Communicate with your customers by following up after a sale, checking for satisfaction, and just keeping in touch (out of sight, out of mind).

✔ Make shopping at your store fun for your customers.

The story of the candy lady

Twenty-five years ago, a 77-year-old woman (she told us her age) came into the store to buy a dress for her 60th high school reunion. She selected a prom dress, long white gloves, and a rabbit fur jacket to go with it. The other employees and I didn't want to sell it to her because we thought she looked stupid in it and if someone found out where she had bought it, we would be embarrassed. We tried to discourage her and suggested other things. But she had her mind made up. She told us that when she was in high school she couldn't afford to attend her senior prom. She now had more money than she could ever spend, however, and she wanted to go to that prom dressed the way she would have back then.

When we told her that people might laugh at her, she said, "I am not doing this for anyone other than myself." Then she looked me straight in the eye and, with a fierce determined look, said, "Sonny, let me tell you something you need to know about business. In business, you give people what they want, not what you want, or what anybody else wants." It turned out that she and her husband had started a very famous candy company. She said, "If we had given people what they needed and should have had, we would have been out of business years ago."

Closing the sale

Keep in mind that over 40 percent of the customers who walk through a specialty retail store actually buy something. However, you can use some specific techniques to increase this percentage. The following list includes some of the best closes you can use to finish off a sale:

- ✔ "Did you see this?" This is the best close (say it as you show another piece of merchandise). You keep trying until the customer determines that the sale is finished.

- ✔ If a customer says, "Let me think it over," respond with "No problem." Just ask customers what they would like to think over. Generally, their hesitation concerns money — either they're afraid they don't have enough or they think your price is too high.

- ✔ You can encourage the customer to buy something by simply saying, "Why not?" Let them tell you why they shouldn't.

- ✔ You can guide a wishy-washy customer who can't make up her mind by saying, "Let's do this," then selecting the merchandise for her.

- ✔ Just by saying, "Everyone's buying it" you can convince a status customer that she can't go home without something.

Tools for measuring your sales

ATS — Average Ticket Size. This represents the dollar amount of an average transaction. Even a slight increase in your ATS, for example from $80.00 to $85.00, can be significant. In order to come up with your ATS, just average all of the transactions or sales for the week. You can measure the ATS for each of your employees in the same way if you want to see how they compare with each other.

UPT — Units Per Transaction. This measure shows you how many units or items were sold per sale. You can measure your UPT over a period of time, for example a week, to determine your store's average. Just average of the number of items per sales receipt. You can also use UPT to evaluate your sales staff by monitoring their UPT averages. The higher the number, the stronger the sales person.

Regardless of the strategy you use to close the sale, be sure to collect some information about your customer that you can add to your customer database — the sale isn't finished until you do. You might even think about offering incentives to get customers to sign up.

Dealing with Challenging Customers

All customers might have been created equally, but some of them were dropped on their heads when they were very young. The following represent a few customer types with the more recognizable and common traits that you will have to deal with. Being able to recognize these traits is really the first step to successfully dealing with these challenging customers.

The know-it-all

The know-it-alls are the customers who try to make themselves feel important by making everyone around them feel inadequate or stupid. Don't be tempted to play one-upmanship with these people or you'll never sell them anything. The best approach is to be as professional as possible and give them as many compliments as you can. Doing so makes them feel good about themselves, and then they might buy something.

The whiner

Whiners are eternal pessimists. They want the people around them to be just as miserable as they are. Misery does love company. The best way to deal with whiners is to first offer a compliment and then try the 3F approach: I know how you *feel* about buying that item, I *felt* the same way when I had to make a decision, but I *found* after I bought it that I felt so much better.

The number nerd

Number nerds are comparison shoppers. Take advantage of their information. Ask them what they know about other products (and retailers), and they'll gladly share it with you. By expressing some interest, you can win them over. Offer these customers statistics, graphs, charts, manuals, or other statistical information to convince them to buy from you. Make sure that you have your most analytical staff member wait on them. It will be like two Martians talking.

Mr. Wishy-Washy

Wishy-washy people can't make up their minds or are afraid to make decisions. They may ask questions like, "What if my wife doesn't like it? Will I get my money back?" or they may say, "I'll have to sleep on it." Or they may ask what everyone else does. The best way to sell to these customers is to make the decision for them. Tell them, "This is what we are going to do." As strange as it may sound, they'll appreciate you for this approach. You'll see the relief come over them once they get past the decision process.

The possessor

Do you know someone who loves to say, "He's *my* accountant" or "That's *my* auto mechanic" or "I bought it at *my* gift store"? Once you initially win these customers over, they'll think they own you. This can be advantageous to your business because they'll refer lots of other people to your store. Try to think of it as free advertising.

The best approach is to involve them in decisions. Ask them what they think about different pieces of merchandise. You can even ask them whether they know someone who might like something in your store. They're likely to drag someone in to buy it. Ask them whether they think you have the right merchandise. Ask them to look around to see whether you should be carrying lines that they've seen in other stores. These people can provide you with great information. Do everything you can to hold on to them.

The butterfly

Psychologists refer to this personality type as the *socializer*. What you sell is secondary to the relationship the "butterfly" has with you. Many times socializers don't come into the store to buy; they just stop by to say hello. They love parties, events, or anything exciting that you do in the store. Be sure to keep your butterflies informed of what is happening at the store. Send them newsy newsletters and call them when merchandise you're sure they'll like comes in. If you ever need someone to give you a testimonial, use these customers because they'll overflow with praise.

Chapter 20

Visual Merchandising for the Artistically Deprived and Financially Handicapped

*V*isual merchandising is displaying what you sell in a way that compels people to buy it — taking special care with the way you stack the apples, the way you arrange the candles on the shelves, the way you hang the dress.

Every retailer has to pay attention to displays — they aren't limited to high-fashion boutiques or department stores. And display doesn't just mean decorating the store windows — it also refers to how you visually feature your merchandise to the public. Any time that you reposition a piece of merchandise to make it more appealing to a customer, you're working on your displays. Your displays can define your business and differentiate you from your competition.

Displaying the Goods

I want you to want me! I know that sounds a bit tawdry, but it's the truth, isn't it? Don't you want every display to make the merchandise wanted? You want customers to be so excited that they can't wait to buy it.

Currently, simplicity reigns supreme. The idea is that minimalist displays best show off fantastic merchandise. But remember, simplicity is a style — it, too, is a display technique. Anything you do to present your goods is some form of display technique. There are five considerations in planning any type of display:

✔ What merchandise do you have to feature?

✔ What is the season and/or the theme of the display?

✔ What type of mood or feeling should the display portray?

✔ What props do you have to work with?

✔ How will the space be utilized?

Featuring certain merchandise

Do you feature your fastest selling items, or do you highlight your slower selling items because they may need a little help to be sold? This question has been debated for generations of retailers. Both approaches are right at different times.

Another question is, do you feature your most unusual merchandise or do you feature the more basic everyday sellers? Again, both approaches are right depending on what your store is like. However, my personal preference is to feature the unusual over basic everyday because different is what people remember and talk about. Displays of unusual merchandise are more effective in selling other basic merchandise than displays of the basic merchandise itself. An unusual item may be what catches the customer's eye, but the practical side takes over and the basic item sells.

Use themes or sale seasons to define your displays. Of course, winter, summer, spring, and fall all offer opportunities for seasonal sales. Other seasonal themes could include graduations, outdoor entertaining, gardening, home repair, and golfing. If you decide to use a seasonal display, you must always be in anticipation of the season. Customers may think that retailers are rushing a season when they set up displays weeks ahead of a holiday. But retailers know that better customers tend to buy early. And besides, part of the job of a display is creating the mood of the season.

Giving a display a title (and no, I didn't name every display I did) makes them seem even more important and special. You may want to consider naming your displays to make them more fun and memorable. The following is a list of my all time favorite window themes. Have fun and use them in your store or use them as a springboard to start thinking about other themes that may work better for your particular business.

✔ **On the Trail of a Sale:** Carry out this theme in your window by featuring a Sherlock Holmes figure with a brimmed hat and magnifying glass. Use footsteps throughout the display (you can use contact paper) that follow a trail with signposts saying "Sale." The footsteps are the props that will help direct customers' eyes to the focal points of your display.

✔ **Set My Heart on Fire:** This Valentine's Day classic uses hearts and flame props to feature romantic merchandise.

✔ **Hot Deals:** This sale theme uses painted flames made from foam board strategically placed throughout the window, creating a fun, effective display.

✔ **Sneak Preview:** Use this theme at the beginning of any season. Cover your windows with brown paper and tear holes in it to allow passersby to view the new arrivals.

✔ **Right Up Your Alley:** Use props such as trash cans, lids, old tires, old street signs, old license plates, and even a few empty bottles scattered around to re-create an alley scene. Almost any type of merchandise works here.

✔ **Winter, Spring, Summer, or Fall:** This simple theme not only highlights the new merchandise season but also features the best of the season. You're pushing the style of the merchandise, not the price.

✔ **Jump Through Hoops:** With this theme you only need a bunch of hula hoops. Show them falling from the sky and lying on the ground and around the merchandise. The hoops create a whimsical mood that's especially appropriate for spring.

Puns intended

Calliope is a very small children's store (maybe 800 square feet) in Harvard Square in Cambridge, Massachusetts, that sells stuffed animals and children's apparel. However, the emphasis is on stuffed animals. Calliope has a very small window, but it is located on one of the busiest downtown streets in America. Owner Ann Lerner literally built her business by using themes for her windows. But she went after a very special type of theme around which to create her window. Ann loved puns, so she created one pun a month for her windows. Her windows are the talk of the town, and she was the recipient of the Visual Display Award in 2000 by the Retail Association of Massachusetts. And this all was because of her themes. The following are just a few samplings of 15 years of puns:

✔ **Peas on Earth:** This Christmas window featured a stuffed fur globe of the world with a stuffed fur peapod that had peas coming out of it, falling on the globe. It was a showstopper.

✔ **Much To Do About Mutton:** This window showcased a collection of stuffed lambs and sheep.

✔ **Gorillas in the Mix:** Stuffed gorillas and monkeys were surrounded by bamboo poles.

✔ **Nay Sayers:** This window showed toy horses at play.

✔ **Pearls Before Swine:** A collection of pigs wearing costume pearl jewelry decorated this window.

These little touches of creativity make a business stand out from the pack.

Creating a feeling or mood

Have you ever walked out of a store just because it doesn't feel right? Have you ever gone to a supermarket where you normally don't shop, and you feel uncomfortable and can't wait to go back to your regular store? You're most likely reacting to the feeling or mood that store has created with its displays.

Every display creates a feeling or a mood, ranging from the classic, timeless quality of every Brooks Brothers display to a whimsical or humorous feeling that a children's store might employ when using cartoon characters in a display. The more a display reflects real life, the better it is. Because life is made up of moods and feelings, people respond to them. Your task is to decide what feeling you want customers to come away with and then design a display that creates that mood. As you look through the following list of feelings and moods, see whether you can associate each with a display you've seen:

- Confident
- Sophisticated
- Defiant
- Carefree
- Rebellious
- Joyous
- Offbeat
- Conservative
- All-American
- Foreign intrigue
- Whimsical
- Manly
- Sweet
- Romantic
- Funky
- Humorous
- Outrageous
- Mysterious

Your job is to produce a display that evokes the emotions or feelings that you want your customers to have when they view the merchandise. Some retailers focus on the benefits to the customer. For example, a display of man resting on a hammock beside his new power grass cutter lets customers know that this lawn mower will give them extra time to relax.

No matter how effective your displays are, you have to change them. You want consumers to see your displays and think the magic words, "That's different," which really means they like it. If your last window display was a classic vintage-era look with antique chairs, old lace, and bookshelves, shake things up a bit with high-tech materials to create a slick contemporary look and feeling. Change is good because it piques interest. Just make sure that your displays are consistent with your brand. For example, don't use cheap display materials if your store is higher end. However, if yours is a discount store, inexpensive materials used in creative ways will appeal to your customers.

Check out the Daily Operations folder on the CD for some images of effective window displays.

Working with props

The variety of props you can use for displays is virtually endless — your greatest limitation is your imagination. Obviously the type of prop you use depends on the type of business you're in. The following list presents universal props that can be used in many different industries:

✔ **Foam board:** Foam board is a type of Styrofoam with a smooth paper covering and you can make almost any prop you can think of out of it. All you need is a utility knife and some creativity. You can find it in any art store.

✔ **Papers:** Paper comes in many different varieties and its uses can be just as diverse. You can use tissue paper to pad apparel items or fill shopping bags; wallpaper to create great backgrounds; seamless paper (heavy construction paper that comes in rolls and can be purchased at display supply houses) to make backdrops and separations. Computer paper, blueprints, and wrapping paper can make great window accents.

✔ **Photographs:** Use photos that emphasize your brand. Computer-altered images are especially effective. For example, a local bagel shop uses old-fashioned photos in which bagels substitute for bicycle tires, earrings, and so on to create a whimsical mood.

✔ **Picture frames:** These functional and decorative accents are perfect in a variety of situations. You can even use them to frame your merchandise.

✔ **Mini lights:** These little decorations aren't just for Christmas anymore. They can make the most boring display come alive, either inside the store or in the window.

✔ **Shopping bags:** Your own shopping bag or ones created out of foam board can be a powerful prop to showcase new arrivals or sale items. Don't forget the power of your own packaging and its power to build your brand.

✔ **Fabric:** Let your imagination go wild. Fabric can be draped, hung, placed on the floor, or stretched. You don't need expensive fabrics to make this effect work.

✔ **Movie paraphernalia:** Many movie rental stores throw out boxes of great prop material weekly, and you won't believe some of the creative ways you can use this stuff. Get friendly with your video store staff.

✔ **Trees and branches:** Yes, go out and cut a few branches. You'll end up using these display staples over and over again.

✔ **Baskets:** You can fill baskets with almost anything — from flowers for decoration to the merchandise itself.

✔ **Chairs:** Chairs come in handy for themes such as summer cookouts or football tailgate parties. Chairs are very versatile props.

✔ **Cylinders:** Cylinders are fabulous props because of their versatility. They come in many diameters, and you can cut them to any height. They're made of compressed layers of paper that you can cut with your trusty utility knife. You can decorate them and use them as buildups, which I discuss in the section "Uncovering Tips and Tricks of the Trade."

I've put a prop inventory list in the Daily Operation folder on the CD.

Before designing your display, figure out how much space you're working with and how you want to use that space. You don't have to use all the space you have, but make sure whatever space you have is planned.

Uncovering Tips and Tricks of the Trade

Retailing is an old profession. You may as well learn from the experience of others who have come before you. This section offers miscellaneous tidbits to help you make the most of your displays — both interior and exterior. Here are some factors to keep in mind:

✔ **Reflecting sunlight:** Extreme sunlight reflecting off your windows can make it nearly impossible for people to view your window displays. Obviously, having north/south windows are the best way to avoid this problem, but if you have an east/west exposure, make sure that the glass in your windows is treated glass — tinted much the same way as a car's windshield to protect from the sun's rays. If you don't, anything you put in those windows will fade, and your merchandise will be ruined.

✔ **Viewing distance for window displays:** Your window displays must be visible not only to pedestrians but also to motorists. Something that looks great up close may not even be visible from a distance. As a general rule, the farther the viewing distance, the bolder the display should be.

✔ **Window lighting:** If you have a perfect color-coordinated window display but terrible lighting, you end up with only an average window display. But an average display with dramatic lighting effects can make the display spectacular. Think of it as theater — set your retail stage with lighting.

Also be sure that you turn on your window lights when it starts to get dark. The easiest way for your store to look closed when it's not is keeping your window lights off after dark.

✔ **The positioning of interior displays:** The height of an interior display affects the power and visibility of the merchandise. Items near the floor just don't sell as well. That is why buildups (explained later in this list) are so important.

✔ **The lighting of interior displays:** Lights come in all different types, including floodlights, spotlights, and very small, highly focused tensors. They can be on tracks on the ceiling, built into the floor, or free standing on the floor. The challenge is to make your interior display lights stand out against the general lighting of your store.

✔ **Interior signage:** Use signs to direct customers to specific areas of your store or to present descriptions of merchandise. Regardless of their function, make sure that all your signage looks professional and reflects your brand.

✔ **The power of eye level:** When you create your displays, consider where your customers' eyes will most naturally focus. Place the strongest element of your display there. If you don't, customers may not notice things you want them to see.

✔ **Angles:** Position displays so that most customers can see them face on. Most of your displays should face the path that shoppers will travel through your store. However, some customers will come from a different direction, so always position a few displays for that viewer.

✔ **Clean windows:** Keep your windows spotless. This is the most basic of all the rules of display, and yet it gets broken everyday. A dirty window is a turnoff. Before you ever change a window display, *please* clean the glass.

✔ **Color:** The best displays are the displays that use color effectively, regardless of the type of product you're selling. Props are very important, but color is the number one attraction in any type of display.

✔ **Legends:** These are the names for your window displays. Make them street art. To create a buzz, name your windows.

✔ **Buildups:** Displays are the most effective when merchandise is at different levels and heights. You can use anything from a brick to a box of any size to create the structure. Cover it with fabric and voila!

✔ **Understatement:** Less is more. Focus on just a few things so that you don't dilute the impact of your displays. Also be wary of getting too cute or too clever.

✔ **White space:** Don't be afraid of wide-open space. Unfilled space helps direct the customers' eyes.

✔ **Incongruities:** Mismatched elements can make great themes. We once created an effective Halloween window by putting ugly masks on beautiful mannequins.

Rick's Random Rule #76: Great lighting can sell anything. Even the Brooklyn Bridge looks better at night.

Hiring a Visual Merchandiser

Professional display artists can make your merchandise come alive. You can find these specialists by asking your sales reps for names of people who do this kind of work. You also can get referrals from other retailers. Also don't be afraid to ask a retailer for the visual merchandiser's name if you see a great display in her store. Stores are more than happy to share this information.

There are two other sources for finding a professional display artist. You can check with any of the display companies that sell props, mannequins, or window decorations. You can find hundreds of these companies on the Web by using the keywords "retail store display." The second source is to read your trade journals because they usually contain advertisements for free-lance visual display artists.

Chapter 21

Selling Online: It's an E-World

● ●

In This Chapter

▶ Considering the basic rules of doing business online

▶ Finding a Web site designer and a Webmaster

▶ Choosing a domain name

▶ Selecting the elements for your site

▶ Marketing via e-mail

▶ Figuring out the cost

● ●

*T*he most recent competition within the retail industry has come not from an influx of new brick-and-mortar shops, but from computer chips and wires. Early predictions for the Internet invasion were staggering, and they sent chills of apprehension up the spines of retailers worldwide. Retailers believed the predictions because every week on Wall Street a brand-new dot-com retailer was born, making instant millionaires (on paper at least) of nerdy, geeky kids who knew nothing about retailing.

Although the dot-com frenzy didn't turn out to be as far-reaching as people originally thought, you still can make money by selling merchandise over the Internet. The Internet is here to stay, and the Web will be a significant force in retailing in the future. The difference is that traditional retailers won't be competing against Web merchants because they themselves will be the Web merchants. In this chapter, I show you what you need to do to maintain the business you have and expand it into new markets. The Web is the key, and it will add significant dollars to your bottom line as long as you approach it the right way.

Recognizing the Importance of Having a Web Site

Every retailer must have a Web site. This rule is *not* negotiable. Many retailers believe in what is referred to as the "feel-and-touch philosophy," which maintains that their customers won't buy anything online because the customers actually need to see and hold the products in person. While this may be true for some purchases, customers today are using the Web as they used the Yellow Pages just a few years ago, so you have to have an online presence.

Because the Internet today is used primarily as a research vehicle, customers who have a lot of questions and little time want to do as much research as possible online. Your challenge as a retailer is to make sure that customers can find the answers to their questions on your Web site. Because your site serves as your store's brochure, be sure it offers the following information:

✔ Contact information including address, phone, fax, and e-mail

✔ A description of who you are and what you do (your specialty)

✔ Directions to your store

✔ Store hours

✔ Your targeted clientele

✔ A list of manufacturers whose products you carry

✔ Information about related services (for example, alterations for an apparel shop) and associated fees

✔ What credit cards you accept

✔ Shipping options

Customers also want to know about other services and products you offer that they *might* need — maybe even things they haven't thought of yet. You have to be sure that your store's Web site provides valuable information to customers and entices them to buy from you instead of a competitor.

The younger the customers, the more Internet savvy they are. (However, surveys and studies report that the fastest-growing group of people getting online is senior citizens.) People want information, and many times they want it at 11 p.m. or, in my wife's case, at 6 a.m. If your store doesn't have a Web site today, people are likely to believe that your business isn't up to date, and they may be reluctant to do business with you.

Can you create a Web site on your own? Sure. Plenty of user-friendly software programs are available to help you design your own Web site. But I don't recommend doing it alone, for the following reasons:

 ✔ Designing a Web site takes a lot of time that you could better spend in other ways.

 ✔ You may not have a clue about the many details of creating a Web site, how to get your site listed with search engines, and how your site will look on different computers operating at different speeds. But a professional Web designer already knows all about these things and can get the job done faster, too.

Just as I recommend that you shop as many stores as you can when you first get started in retailing and constantly after that, I recommend you do the same thing when you're thinking about creating your Web site. Look around at other stores' sites, especially those whose business is similar to yours. Write down all the features you like and all the features you don't like. Notice the little things that make the site special and the dumb annoyances that you never want on your site. Spend a Sunday afternoon just searching sites. You'll become a pro in no time.

Although I hate the animated sites with cute little balls bouncing or things twirling, some of the things that I *do* like about a site include the following:

 ✔ **Careful organization:** You have to make finding things easy for the user.

 ✔ **Good navigation:** You need to make it easy for customers to get around (and get back to where they started from!).

 ✔ **Photos:** Just don't include too many — they slow things down.

 ✔ **Testimonials:** I think this is the most important element of a retail Web site.

 ✔ **Video clips:** Just think how exciting it could be if you were a fashion store and could put a fashion show on your Web site.

Choosing a Web Designer and a Webmaster

When you're looking for a person (or people) to develop and maintain your Web site, try to find someone who has worked in the retail industry and who understands your business. Use your retailers' network — ask around and see whether anyone can refer you to a great Web designer.

One designer I know has taken the time to learn and understand the retail industry — to become an expert in the industry. He attends all the trade shows to stay current with trends. No one has to teach him about collectibles, gifts, or a retailer's mind-set. He is a part of the industry and works with retailers every day. Look for a designer like this.

Creating a Web site requires two different types of skills: artistic talent to design the visuals and layout and technical expertise to make the site work. A Web design firm can usually take care of both of these needs — although they may need to put two different people on your project. You'll also need a Webmaster to keep your site up and running once it's in place. Choose this person carefully because you're going to be together for a very long time. That's why you don't necessarily want a local high school kid as your Webmaster. You want someone who is going to be around.

Avoid going to an ad agency that subcontracts Web site development work out to two people. This practice only costs more money.

Designers often sign their names to the sites they work on — like an artist signs a painting. If you can identify some other retailer's sites you like, look around and see whether you can discover the name of the designer. Many times the name is actually a hot link that enables you to jump right to the designer's site.

Selecting a Domain Name

A domain name is your address on the Internet. It is where someone goes on the Internet to find you. The Grand Poo-bahs of the Internet have added extra domains other than .com, .org, or .net — seven in fact. I'm sure that in due time these new ones will become very popular, but until that time .com is the suffix to get. (If you need more general information concerning the Internet, I recommend that you pick up *The Internet For Dummies,* by John R. Levine, Carol Baroudi, and Margaret Levine Young, published by Hungry Minds, Inc.).

You want your domain name to be the same as your store's name, or as close to it as possible. Remember that you can't use any punctuation or spaces in your domain name, so you wouldn't be Smith's Store.com. You would be smithsstore.com. Oh, in case you didn't notice, you don't have to capitalize either. Your Webmaster can register your domain name for you, but if you want to see what names are available, you can do your own search, by going to www.register.com. This reliable resource maintains a list of registered domain names, and searching this list doesn't cost anything.

Unfortunately, not everyone can spell or type very well, and some stores have names that are always misspelled (like my last name — some spell it Segal or Siegel or countless other ways). For those reasons, you may want to reserve another name that customers may visit inadvertently. Names do go fast, so reserve your name as quickly as possible. And if you have reserved your name but haven't done anything with it for a while, you may want to check to see whether your name is still secured.

Designing Your Site

Remember that your Web site may be the first point of contact for many customers. Make sure that your site makes a favorable first impression. I have visited countless Web sites and come up with the elements that I believe are absolutely essential for an effective Web site. In addition to the basics I list earlier in this chapter, consider including some of the following on your site:

- ✔ Your business's mission or vision statement
- ✔ A brief history of your business and/or your staff
- ✔ A photo of your store or the people working there
- ✔ A photo or detailed description of what you sell in your store
- ✔ An explanation of why someone should buy from you
- ✔ A site map or some other type of navigational tool
- ✔ Testimonial letters

Some people believe that testimonial letters are optional, but I believe they're a must. They are what sell your site. Get quotes from your customers telling you how great your store is and how wonderful your staff is. People love these letters, especially the quotes that tell about a problem that you went the extra mile to correct. This type of testimonial makes you human.

Re-creating your store's look and feel online

Why do you make your store windows look inviting? So that people will come into your store. For this same reason, you want to be sure your Web site looks inviting. Ideally, it should present the same look and feel as your store because you want your customers to have a consistent experience when doing business with you. This consistency helps to develop your brand (Remember brand? Go back to Chapter 3 if you need a refresher.) Here are the two Web site design tools that I think are the most important:

- ✔ **Color:** Color sets the tone for your entire site. It took me a while to figure this out because the issue of color is subtle. Don't underestimate its impact. Use the same colors on your site that you use in your store.
- ✔ **Fonts:** Fonts, or typefaces, are important in any of your printed material. But they're especially critical on your Web site because they'll be viewed on a computer screen, where eyestrain and monitor size come into play. Be aware that many people who create Web sites are techies with a limited sense of artistic design. They often just tend to slap all text into Ariel or Times Roman, not even thinking of the impact of a different font.

Optional items to have on your site

In addition to the essential elements that I list in the section "Designing Your Site," your site should include other features to enhance your customer's experience. Read through the following section to identify some elements that may be right for your site.

A shopping cart

Every retailer should at least offer a few things for sale, for no other reason than to test the waters to see whether you can actually sell merchandise from your Web site. Experiment with selling a few items at first, maybe five or six, and see what kind of response you get.

Always include your store's telephone and fax numbers on your Web site. You want to make your store as accessible to customers as possible.

Catalogs

Once you've determined that you can sell through your Web site, you're ready to create your own online catalog. Smaller stores could never get into the catalog business before because of the cost. The Web makes it easier to have a catalog. As for photographs, you have three options:

- ✔ Ask your manufacturers for pictures to scan.

- ✔ Download pictures from a manufacturer's Web site. Many manufacturers today are starting to have a section on their Web site just for this purpose. Some of them even write copy that you can download for your catalogs.

- ✔ Use a digital camera to take your own pictures of your merchandise and post them to your site.

Affiliate programs

Many companies will pay you a commission if a customer buys something from their site because of a link from your site. The leader in this type of marketing is Amazon.com. But Amazon is just one of thousands of affiliate programs you can have on your site. If you're interested in this type of program, go to www.referit.com. It lists many of the popular affiliate programs that are out there.

Ads

Your site can include a section where you place the ads that you run in the paper or circulars that you send out.

Coupons

Coupons are valuable whether you mail them or offer them on your Web site. Some stores have fun contests or little quizzes on their sites and use coupons as the prizes. In reality, everybody wins something.

New products section

This part of your Web site gives you a place to introduce new items that your store will be stocking. If the show rules allow photography, take your digital camera to a trade show and snap some shots of you holding the merchandise, or just give a written preview of new merchandise.

Bulletin boards

This section of your site gives your customers a place to leave questions or comments. A bulletin board can become a very active area of your site, especially if you sell a type of merchandise, such as collectibles, that has a loyal customer base.

Book reviews

Your commentary on a new book about your industry can be a nice touch. A book review can do a lot to establish you as an expert in the minds of your customers. Many customers appreciate this feature, and some may even put you on a higher pedestal than maybe you deserve. Your customers will value the opportunity for a little online education, and status customers will love the element of snob appeal associated with a book review by their favorite store owner.

Feedback

Every Web site must have a means for customers to send you an e-mail message from your site. This is almost standard operating procedure today.

Links

Other than affiliate programs, think about other sites you want your customers to be able to access from your site, such as your chamber of commerce or your shopping area. If you're in the woodworking business, you may want a link to the Web site of Norm Abrams, the guru of home repair. If you're in the golf business, a link to the PGA calendar of events site may be worthwhile. If you're in the fashion business, consider linking to fashion consultants or interior designers. Look for sites that would be helpful for your customers.

Regardless of how simple or fancy your Web site is, update it regularly. Doing so is not an option. If you create a site and forget about it, you're not tapping into its true potential. Sites have to be updated if you ever want customers to return. Would you go back to the same store if it displayed the same merchandise for a year or two? No way, so don't do it on your Web site.

Recognizing the Benefits of E-mail Marketing

E-mail marketing is the cheapest way for retailers to advertise. It has the same effect as sending out a piece of regular mail. With e-mail, however, the cost is much cheaper and the speed is 100 times faster. Think about how nice it would be to write a quick e-mail note to a good customer telling her a great outfit that would be perfect for her came in today. Then you snap a picture on your digital camera, download it, and attach it to your e-mail. From start to finish — including taking the picture — you've spent less than 15 minutes. Anytime you can discover a new way to do something that is better for both you and your customers, increases service, and costs less, just do it.

Consider producing an electronic newsletter (an e-zine) for your store. Because these are cheap to do, they're very popular. The problem is that people are starting to get an information overload, and rather than reading all of them, they're deleting them from their mailbox. If you do decide to do an e-zine, I recommend that you make your stories very short and to the point.

Calculating the Cost of a Web Site

Doing business over the Internet is still relatively new for most independent retailers. Strategies and procedures are changing all the time, but a few things that won't change are what is required to make Internet commerce work. If you decide to invest in creating a Web site for your store, understand what it's going to really cost you in the following areas:

- ✔ **Time:** Budget your time to make the Web a part of what you do and who you are. This is one case where time is far more valuable than money. Including research and implementation, creating an effective Web site takes a lot of time.

- ✔ **Commitment:** You have to believe it'll work — that investing in a Web site is worth the commitment. Have the attitude that you're going to make it work regardless of what it takes. Remember that lesser retailers than you have wonderful success stories of how well it works. Don't let all the headlines of the dot-com bust bother you. Some retailers didn't look at their Web site as extra business; they looked at it as their only business. And that approach is dangerous because they needed to build the infrastructure that you already have.

✔ **People:** Assign one person in your store or outside your store to be the champion for your Web site project. The administration of your Web site can't be an afterthought or something you will get to after everything else is done. Managing your Web site must be someone's top priority.

If you choose to invest the necessary resources in creating a Web site for your store, everyone will benefit. Your customers will enjoy the convenience, and you can enjoy more business. Once you start to establish regular Web-related routines, it will become the way you always did business.

Just because you have a Web site doesn't mean the cyber world will flock to it. Therefore, it is important to include your Web site address on everything that you print, such as shopping bags, register receipts, and all forms of advertising. In essence, you're starting a new business.

Part VII
Taking Care of
Business

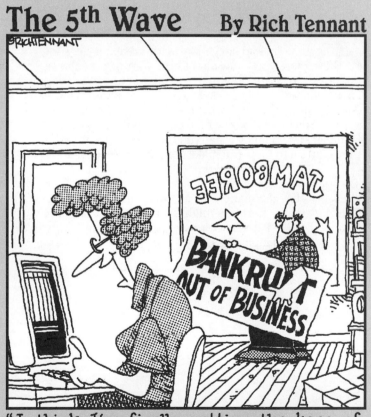

The 5th Wave   By Rich Tennant

"I think I'm finally getting the hang of this accounting system. It's even got a currency conversion function. Want to see how much we lost in rupees?"

In this part . . .

Accountants and lawyers provide great services but the more you know about how your own business operates the better off you'll be. You don't have to become an accountant, but you need to be able to understand some basic accounting principles that effect your businesses. You need to know how to read and interpret basic financial statements so that you can use the information they contain to help you make good business decisions.

This part introduces you to some computerized software packages that can make your accounting tasks a breeze. This may be the part you might be tempted to skip but PLEASE DON'T! It's a matter of making money or losing it. I promise it will be painless.

Chapter 22

Money Matters: Accounting for Money Coming in and Going Out

● ●

In This Chapter

▶ Accepting different types of payment

▶ Finding a computer system that suits your needs

▶ Choosing a payroll service

▶ Calling in your accountant

● ●

*T*his chapter is about the flow and the tracking of the money that comes into your store. It covers ways to collect money through credit cards and checks, ways to account for it with computerized accounting and merchandising systems, and how to disperse some of it — in the form of paychecks to your wonderful staff. It also introduces you to the benefits of payroll services and tells you when you need to utilize the services of your accountant. This chapter is devoted to making you a better business person.

Bringing the Money In

A common expression says that we live in a plastic economy, which means we have become extremely dependent on the use of credit and debit cards. Every retailer accepts credit cards today and there is an ATM machine on almost every street corner. Checks have always been a way of life for retailers, but their importance is diminishing with the advent of the debit card. But the point is to bring the money in. Let's see how it works from the retailer's point of view.

Dealing with credit cards

I believe that every retailer should accept at least four major credit cards: Visa, MasterCard, American Express, and Discover. However, Diners Club is making a major initiative to become a contender in the charge card arena. One of the biggest differences in these cards is the amount they charge merchants.

The companies that process credit card purchases are referred to as *processors* since their job is to electronically communicate information from your terminal to the charge card company. The money flows through the processor and the processor charges the retailer a percentage of each purchase for the use of this service. And they, in turn, pay the charge card companies their percentage fees. The processor is the middle man. Generally, American Express charges a percentage point or two more than the others. MasterCard and Visa's rates vary depending on the processor.

Debit cards provide another convenient way to accept payment. To a merchant, a debit card looks and acts the same as a credit card, but the money comes right out of the cardholder's bank account. The merchant usually pays the same percentage to the processor as with a credit card, although some processors charge a little more to accept debit cards. However, accepting debit card payment offers a couple of bonuses:

✔ Many of the people who liked to use checks are converting to debit cards because they duplicate the function of a check. For retailers, this means fewer checks will be returned for insufficient funds.

✔ Customers still tend to buy more with a credit card than with a check. Many debit cards allow you to transfer amounts to a loan account, which essentially makes it a credit card.

Rick's Random Rule #45: A customer with a credit card spends more than a customer who doesn't have one.

Finding a processor

If you don't know where to go to find the best rates — or even to find a processor — check with your state retail association or the National Retail Federation (www.nrf.com). Both organizations have programs and recommendations.

The only caution is to read the fine print when it comes to rates. Many processors advertise low rates, but watch out for the following issues:

✔ **Is there a monthly charge, and how much?** Many processors add a $7.50 or $10 monthly charge as a statement fee. You may find a processor that doesn't charge this fee.

✔ **How much are the transaction fees?** Many processors are quick to tell you that their rate is 2.1 percent, but they "forget" to tell you that they charge an additional 10 or 20 cents per transaction. (To me, that makes the rate more than 2.1 percent.)

✔ **Is there an additional charge for debit cards?** This charge can be an additional 0.5 percent.

✔ **Is there an additional charge for corporate cards?** I've seen charges of an additional 1.1 percent.

✔ **Is there an additional charge for foreign cards?** This charge can double the rate with a surcharge of 2.4 percent.

Many of these companies avoid telling the truth about their real rates, and you must ask what additional charges are assessed. A processor that charges a base 2.8 percent can often be much cheaper in the long run than another processor that offers 1.8 percent but tacks on a lot of extra charges.

Understand that credit card processing is a highly competitive business and rates charged by processors vary greatly. Shop around and don't be afraid to negotiate. Also check with your State Retail Association and big box warehouse stores for discounted rates. Just make sure you're comparing "apples to apples".

Read the fine print and make the sales rep sign a letter that states what you believe you're going to be charged. If the sales rep hesitates to sign this letter, you'd best reread the contract.

Considering private-label credit card vendors

A private-label credit card is a very viable option. Some credit card companies will issue credit cards with your store's name on them. The bills go out with your store's name on them, and customers can even come to your store to make payments if they wish. This option brings the customer into your store, giving them a chance to buy something else.

Private-label credit cards work really the same as any other credit card. The only difference is that the fee charged is generally higher than a normal card rate by 1 or 2 percentage points. The only problem is that many of the companies that provide this service require minimum total retail sales per year or a minimum number of credit card sales for processing that are sometimes higher than new store can generate.

The following is a list of companies that offer this type of program:

Household Retail Services, 2700 Sanders Road, Prospect Hill, IL 60070; phone 847-564-5000; Web site www.hrsusa.com

Multi Service, 8650 College Boulevard, Overland Park, KS 66210; phone 913-451-2400, fax 913-451-3690; Web site www.multiservicecorp.com

Shoppers Charge Accounts, 1000 MacArthur Boulevard, Mahwah, NJ 07430; phone 800-877-7467, fax 201-818-4310; Web site www.shopperscharge.com

Wendover, P.O. Box 26903, Greensboro, NC 27419-6903 or 725 North Regional Road, Greensboro, NC 27409; phone 800-436-1030 or 336-668-7000; Web site www.wendover.

Rick's Random Rule #77: One thing is better than a customer with a credit card; that's a customer with a credit card with your store's name on it.

Working with checks

Accepting checks used to be one of the scariest parts of doing business because you could make a big sale, have someone hand you a check to pay for it, and you would have no idea if there was money in the account to cover it. An out-of-state check made it even scarier! But now there are check guarantee services such as TeleCheck (www.telecheck.com or 800-835-3243) that, for a fee, will guarantee payment when they approve a check and in some cases the money is deposited into your account within 24 hours. You simply run a check through a terminal, enter the amount, and receive authorization (or not). The peace of mind you get from knowing that the checks you accept are good is worth every cent.

Choosing a Computer System to Manage the Flow

Computers have come down so much in price, and so much great, easy-to-use software is available that there's no reason for anyone not to use a computerized system. Computers can help you maximize efficiency (and accuracy) in nearly every business function (both accounting and merchandising), including keeping track of inventory, recording orders for new merchandise, maintaining a customer database, generating financial reports, and creating price tags — just to name a few. Even if you're afraid of computers, you have no excuse not to use one, because if you do everything manually, you still probably use a calculator, and today's software is as easy to use as a calculator.

Before you purchase a computer system though; talk to vendors, talk to other retailers who use them, and get a sense of what the systems can do. Then look at the costs involved and ask yourself the following questions:

- Will I do more business because of this system?
- Will I save money because of the system?

> ✔ How long will it take to justify the cost?
>
> ✔ Will my reports be more accurate?
>
> ✔ Will my customers get better service because of this system?
>
> ✔ Will I save time because of this system?

The type of system you choose depends on what you want it to do. Do you want it to help you keep track of your merchandise or your money — or both?

One of the biggest confusions that retailers have is understanding the difference between merchandise calculations and accounting calculations. Good merchandising practices create strong accounting numbers, but it's important to understand the difference.

Accounting focuses mainly on what has already taken place. The reports your accountant looks at are the net sales, the cash or credit card transactions. Accountants don't really care whether style number 1234 is selling; they care only about the money. On the other hand, merchandising focuses mainly on keeping track of your inventory.

You have the choice of either purchasing separate accounting and merchandising systems or taking the plunge and buying an integrated system that includes both. The following sections detail these options.

Exploring stand-alone accounting packages

A *stand-alone accounting package* is accounting software that is not connected to any merchandise system, such as your cash register or any inventory tracking system. There are two main reasons to buy a stand-alone accounting package rather than an integrated package:

> ✔ You may not need an integrated package if you're just starting out or your volume is very low.
>
> ✔ Stand-alone accounting software is cheaper than an integrated system. It's better to be financially prudent and then grow into your needs.

The two most popular stand-alone accounting software packages are QuickBooks and Peachtree. Others are just as good, but these two offer certain advantages:

> ✔ Every accountant is familiar with these systems, so you won't have to train your accountant on the idiosyncrasies of the system.
>
> ✔ If you have to hire a bookkeeper or a consultant to train you on how to use the system, more people out there are familiar with these systems than any others.

Considering a stand-alone merchandising system

Some businesses prefer to keep accounting functions separate from merchandising functions to avoid the risk of having an error automatically duplicated in other parts of your system. Another advantage to keeping your accounting and merchandising systems separate is that it provides a means of checks and balances between these two areas. What can a stand-alone merchandising system do for your store? Among other things, it can

- ✔ Record your sales

- ✔ Track your stock keeping units (SKUs) to tell you what's selling and what's not selling

- ✔ Control your database of customers and make it easy to store information about and keep track of your customers

- ✔ Become your credit card terminal

- ✔ Tell you what you have on order

- ✔ Log in merchandise and even create your price tags

The first question to ask the vendor is, "Can I implement separate parts of the system at different times?" Even better than that, ask whether you can buy the packages in modules. Why pay for something if you aren't going to use it for a year?

The following are some other questions to ask prospective vendors:

- ✔ How long have you been in business?

- ✔ How many systems do you have installed and up and running?

- ✔ What size businesses do you specialize in? (Go with someone who works with stores your size.)

- ✔ How long does it take the average store to be operational? Proficient?

- ✔ How often are updates added? How much do they cost? Will you include the first three updates in my initial fee? (Many times you can get software vendors to throw in updates for free.)

- ✔ Is tech support included in the initial fee? If not, for how long is it free?

- ✔ What are the hours of tech support and where is it located?

- ✔ What type of guarantees come with the system? And how long do I have to get my money back? (Hopefully at least a couple months.)

- ✔ Do I have to buy a computer separately? Or can I buy or use my own computer?

- ✔ How fast can your system cash out a customer?

✔ Do you have on-site installation?

✔ What functions does your system perform? Possibilities include

- Customer lookup

- Vendor lookup

- Price lookup

- Report generation (accounting and sales)

- Credit card processing

- Database management

- Ticket creation

- Sign creation (for racks and displays)

- Special order processing

- Gift registry setup

✔ Can you give me three references of stores of my size that have been using your system for more than one year?

Then check their referrals. Ask the other stores that use the system some of the following questions:

✔ Are you happy with the system? (If they all say yes, look for the holes in the story.)

✔ Is the company responsive to your questions and your needs?

✔ Are any tech support people better than others? (Get them to share names.)

✔ What kind of hardware are you running?

✔ How many terminals do you have?

✔ How much of the system are you using?

✔ Do you plan to add more modules? If so, when?

✔ What is the biggest surprise about the system?

✔ What should I avoid that you wish you had?

✔ What is the best/worst part about the system?

✔ What other systems did you look at before you bought this one?

The best places to go to find companies that sell computerized merchandising systems are the Web sites for your local state retail association and the National Retail Federation (www.nrf.com). From the NRF home page, go to Retail Info and then to Online Software Directory. The NRF is an excellent source, but your state association may work with someone local who is very responsive.

Choosing a fully integrated package

You can also buy a totally integrated software package that includes such things as point-of-sale systems, merchandise receiving and ticketing, and inventory control, as well as all your accounting functions.

Here's how a typical integrated system works. When a sale is rung in, the information is electronically divided in two. The accounting side determines whether the sale was cash or credit and posts it to a daily journal, which increases the cash account that allows you to pay bills with the money. That in turn reduces your accounts payable, increases your sales, and eventually makes it to your financial reports as sales in the P&L and as an asset in the balance sheet.

While all that is going on in the accounting side, on the merchandise side, the stock keeping unit records that the item was sold. If other items with the same SKU number were sold, that SKU number may show up in a hot selling report, or it will create a sales report for the category or class of the merchandise. It may initiate an automatic reorder if your system is programmed that way. It will reduce the amount of that item in your inventory. The system may analyze how well you have done with a supplier based on that sale. A merchandising system can generate countless reports, but they all relate to the flow of the merchandise. The accounting side, on the other hand, is concerned with the flow of the money.

These packages are more expensive than either the stand-alone accounting or merchandising packages. The accounting packages that they include are good, but generally not as good as the stand-alone accounting packages. Another possible disadvantage is that if you make a mistake in one area of a fully integrated system, it's automatically repeated in many different places.

Integrated systems don't all need the latest computer hardware, but the manufacturers are always coming out with upgrades that use the latest technology, and some retailers end up buying more expensive systems than they really need. After reviewing all the integrated systems on the market, you have to decide whether the benefits outweigh any downsides. I'm sure that you'll be happy if you choose a good integrated system.

My advice is to open your store with the least amount of expense and hassle — introducing technology represents both. Introduce your system slowly so that it's easy for you and your staff to absorb. Create a master plan that may take three years to implement. Running a marathon can seem just as horrifying, but if you train a little bit every day, it's not that bad. Do the same thing with a system. Get proficient in one area before you try the next part. This approach takes more time, but it's worth it. Have fun asking questions.

Consider purchasing all of your computer needs (hardware, software, installation, and training) through one vendor if possible. This way it only takes one phone call to get things repaired when they go wrong.

Selecting a Service to Dole Out the Paychecks

One of the biggest parts of the money going out of your store is payroll. To expedite the process you can use a payroll service. A payroll service calculates the amount of pay an employee receives, writes the payroll checks, generates reports, and calculates the payroll taxes. It can even deduct the tax amounts from your bank account and then pay the taxes when due.

The average costs for a business with fewer than 10 employees is generally about $20 per week — a bargain. Your accountant may already work with a service that she prefers, but if you aren't sure who to use, I suggest either ADP or Paychex. Their the biggest companies and their reports are easy to read and use.

> Paychex, 911 Panorama Trail South, Rochester, New York 14625; phone 716-385-6666; Web site www.paychex.com

> ADP Corporate Headquarters, 1 ADP Boulevard, Roseland, New Jersey 07068; phone 973-974-5000; Web site www.adp.com

Rick's Random Rule #82: The most important thing to any employee is the paycheck. Don't ever fool around with that.

Knowing When to Use Your Accountant

Although this chapter is in the part about things you shouldn't leave to your accountant, several business factors require the expertise of an accountant. The following list presents a few situations where you really do need the help of an accountant.

- ✔ Your accountant can review your company's financial data. Your accountant can question the numbers in your accounting reports and bring issues to your attention, but it is up to you (or your bookkeeper) to get to the source of the data.

- ✔ A good accountant advises you on what systems and reports you should review. If you have a problem understanding what the figures mean, call your accountant for clarification; but don't depend on your accountant for the data to begin with.

✔ Accountants prepare tax returns and schedule when tax payments should be made.

✔ Accountants should always be involved during the following activities:

- Financing your business: An accountant can advise you on the impact of different types of financing options and even which financial institutions to use.

- Selecting a payroll service: An accountant can help you find a service that produces reports that are understandable and timely.

- Choosing a bookkeeper: After all, the accountant will be working with this person.

- Reviewing the bookkeeper's work: An accountant can help evaluate the job of the bookkeeper.

- Selecting software and computers: Your accountant needs to understand the system you're using.

✔ Your accountant should serve as the liaison between you and the IRS and state tax agencies. Never communicate with any tax agency without advice from your accountant. Your accountant and the tax agencies speak the same language.

✔ Ask your accountant to review your retirement plans. You need someone to understand the best way to go and the tax implications.

✔ Your accountant can help you avoid mistakes. A good accountant can save costly mistakes by just asking you some questions and ensuring that all financial matters are being attended to.

Chapter 23

Understanding and Using Your Financial Statements

. . . .

In This Chapter

▶ Establishing routines that supply the data for your financial reports

▶ Using your financial reports to help you understand your business

. . . .

1 wrote this chapter as a tool for you, a retail store owner, to tell you what you must do to be able to use the financial information in your accounting reports to guide your business decisions and keep your store profitable. I'm not saying that you have to do everything yourself, but neither do I mean that you should blindly hire a bookkeeper and tell her to do all the "accounting stuff."

Many troubled retailers tell me that they're buying the right merchandise and selling it, but they just don't understand why they're not making money, why they can't take a paycheck, or why they're paying their bills late. There is only one thing worse than not making money, and that is not knowing *why* you don't make any money. The information in this chapter helps you avoid this type of money problem.

Getting the Numbers for Your Reports

To gain meaningful information from your various financial reports, you have to establish systems or routines that supply the data to plug into the accounting software that generates these reports. The list that follows presents many bookkeeping tasks that every retailer must do — or pay someone else to do — to keep your financial figures current.

> ✔ Record your daily sales (a process also known as daily cash reconciliation). Have a daily sales envelope where you place the money, checks, and charge receipts at the end of every business day. Either print a form on the envelope or attach a form to the envelope. (Check the Accounting

Forms folder on the CD for a sample.) This form should itemize the contents of the envelope and describe the business completed.

Most modern cash registers can identify the type of transaction (cash, check, or charge). However, just because a transaction is recorded doesn't mean that you actually have the money. So always do a manual check to make sure that you actually have what you say you have.

✔ Enter the information from the daily cash envelope into your computer accounting program according to the categories on the envelope.

✔ Enter any invoices (bills) into accounts payable. Divide your accounts payable by category. For example, you can have a merchandise category, rent category, advertising category, and so on. Software packages make this task very easy and add and subtotal your monthly expenses by each category.

✔ Reconcile your bank statements monthly. If you can't do this, you need to get a bookkeeper.

✔ Pay bills in a timely manner. With a computerized system, paying bills is simply a matter of checking off what you want paid and then printing the checks.

✔ Outsource payroll functions. Use a payroll service that calculates and processes any state and/or federal income taxes for you. You simply report the wage per employee to the service, either as an hourly rate with the number of hours worked or as a salary. The payroll service calculates all taxes, issues checks to employees, prepares a payroll report, and withdraws the necessary funds from your account to cover the taxes. The payroll checks are written on your regular checking account and must be signed before distribution to your employees. When you receive the report from the service, enter the information into your accounting system right away to keep your records current.

✔ Monitor your sales tax. Although your overall tax responsibility depends on where your business is located, sales tax is almost universal. On a daily basis, you must keep track of the amount of sales tax you collect. You can find this information on the daily sales envelope. Pay this tax when it's due, or large penalties will follow.

✔ Stay on top of your financial reports. Using a computerized accounting package makes this a fairly simple task and enables you to generate a multitude of reports, allowing you to look at your figures in a number of different ways. At a minimum, you should run the following reports:

　　• Cash flow report

　　• Accounts payable report

　　• Balance sheet

　　• Profit and loss statement

> Run these reports at least every other week. You can use the information in them to compare your current year's business to the previous year, to prove that you've paid an invoice when a vendor has no record of payment, and to supply your accountant with the figures she needs to prepare your tax return.

You can find examples of a daily sales envelope, a profit and loss statement, a balance sheet, an accounts payable report, and cash flow reports in the Accounting Forms folder on the CD.

Making the Most of Your Financial Reports

Your financial reports are your management tools. They give you a snapshot of how your business is doing financially and what you can expect from it in the future. You need to be able to understand these reports so that you can better understand your business.

Learning from your cash flow report

A cash flow report tells you where your money is going and how much money actually came in to your business. If you know, for example, that your store did $10,000 worth of business, but your cash flow report shows only $9,000 received, you have to account for the discrepancy. Maybe a check bounced or a credit card payment wasn't deposited into your account on time. Or perhaps a C.O.D. delivery required cash. Your cash flow report can provide your first indication that you have a problem, so be sure to review it regularly and make sure that you really understand what the figures are telling you.

Reviewing your accounts payable report

Your accounts payable report tells you how much money you owe and when it is due. You may also need to look at this report to approve bills for payment. For example, if you know what bills are due for a certain time frame, you have to determine whether your business can generate enough revenue to pay them. If you can't pay, you need to be able to estimate when you can pay. The information in your accounts payable report can tell you when you need to adjust (postpone) new purchases that would only get you into deeper problems. But if you don't review this report, you'll never know.

Looking at your balance sheet

Your balance sheet provides the best picture of your business' financial condition at any given time. It's called a balance sheet because it is a simple equation that must balance — assets equal liabilities plus owner's equity. Your assets include everything your business owns — inventory, business machines, fixtures, furniture, cash, and so on. Your liabilities show who *really owns* these assets (or a portion of them) — creditors, banks, and vendors you owe money to. The owner's equity portion is what the business is really worth. If you were to sell off all of the assets and pay all off all the liabilities, the amount remaining would be the owner's equity.

One of the ratios that every owner should understand, because every banker checks this first, is the *net working capital ratio*. This is what you get when you subtract your *current liabilities* (bills due within 30 days) from your *current assets* (what you could turn into cash within 30 days). Here's an example of that formula:

Current assets ($100,000) – current liabilities ($90,000) = net working capital ($10,000)

Your net working capital represents your business's ability to meet short-term obligations. To determine whether you have a positive or a negative net working capital, divide your current assets by your current liabilities to get your *current ratio*:

Current assets ($100,000) ÷ current liabilities ($90,000) = current ratio (1.1)

Anything over 1.1 means that you have a positive net working capital. Your current ratio is important to banks when they're considering whether to offer financing. It's important to you, as well.

Understanding your profit and loss statement

Your profit and loss statement — sometimes called an income statement — is simply a tabulation of your revenues and expenses. Every profit and loss statement (P&L) has five elements:

- ✔ **Net sales:** The amount of sales during a specific time period.
- ✔ **The cost of goods sold:** What it actually costs you to have the merchandise available for sale.

Add your beginning inventory to your purchases to get your *total available goods* to sell. Then, subtract your ending inventory from total available goods to get your *cost of goods sold.*

✔ **Gross profit:** Net sales minus the cost of goods sold.

✔ **Total operating expenses:** A list of all your expenses.

✔ **Net income/loss:** Gross profit minus total operating expenses.

Your profit and loss statement tells you whether or not your business is making money. However, it doesn't tell you whether or not you actually have money in the bank because some expenses can be prepaid or depreciated over a number of years. Still, you can base many of your business decisions on the elements of the P & L because

✔ *Sales* tells you how much revenue is coming in and if it is acceptable for the size of your store, the length of time you've been in business, and the size of your inventory.

✔ *The cost of goods sold* portion tells you how good a buyer you really are. It tells whether you've bought too much or too little. It can tell you when you're showing a profit only because of an increase in inventory and whether you're selling your merchandise at full price or marking too many things down. And it can even show signs of theft. The cost of goods sold offers clues to what is happening with the inventory and the merchandise purchases in your business.

✔ *Expenses* tells you how much it costs to run the business.

✔ *Profits or losses* tells you how much money you're actually making — the "bottom line."

As you review your expenses on the P&L statement, you'll soon realize that you can control only three items on a monthly basis: advertising, payroll, and the cost of goods sold. Control these three, and your business will be a success.

Plan on spending between 2 percent and 10 percent of sales on advertising. The amount depends on whether you're in a good location that will bring you customers. If you're in an expensive mall with good traffic, you can probably get away with 2 percent. But if your location is way off the beaten track on a side street, with very low rent, then you may be looking at closer to 10 percent because you have to advertise more to bring customers to your store.

Payroll percentages vary depending on whether you include the owner's salary or not. If you don't include the owner's salary, payroll should be in the 10 percent range, and with the owner's salary, it can be up to 20 percent of your total sales for any given period.

Anticipating your expenses

To avoid getting into financial hot water, keep careful tabs on all your operating expenses. Most of your expenses are fixed expenses that you can't do a thing about, but still you need to be aware of them so that you aren't surprised when the bills come in. What follows is a list of possible operating expenses to keep in mind.

Accounting Services	Miscellaneous
Advertising	Motor vehicle
Bad debts	Payroll
Charity	Professional fees (Consulting services)
Credit card charges	Rent
Depreciation	Store supplies
Education	Taxes (payroll)
Insurance (business)	Telephone
Insurance (medical)	Travel and entertainment
Interest expense	Utilities
Legal Services	Window display

In general, if your total expenses go over 40 percent, your store is in trouble. Use this figure as a guide. This percentage may vary in some industries, but in most specialty retailing environments, whenever I see a store with expenses above 40 percent, trouble is either already there or on the horizon.

Pay careful attention to your cost of goods sold, because unless you thoroughly understand this figure, it can affect your P&L — making things look good when there are really major problems. A high cost of goods sold may make it appear that you have a larger asset in the form of inventory. The problem is that inventory depreciates. That's why you can't look only at the bottom line. It doesn't lie, but it doesn't tell the whole story either.

Another important ratio that your banker and accountant monitor closely is your *return on equity*. To find out your return on equity, divide your net income (from your P&L) by your owner's equity (from your balance sheet). The result is your return on equity.

Net income ÷ owner's equity = return on equity

Your business is your asset. In many cases, it's your livelihood. Evaluate it as an investment. How much is it returning to you? You know how much interest your savings account makes. Then you should know how much your business returns to you. Knowing this number allows you to analyze your own investment and determine whether it's a good one or not. Ten percent is generally considered to be a good return on an investment.

Part VIII
The Part of Tens

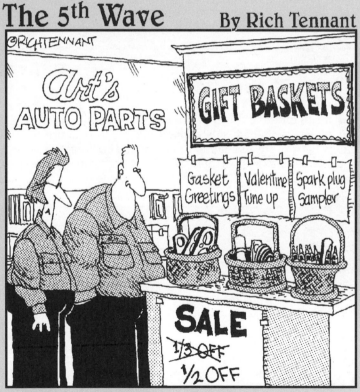

The 5th Wave   By Rich Tennant

"I don't know, Art. I think you're just ahead of your time."

In this part . . .

The chapters in this part provide a quick, rapid-fire set of lists that encapsulate the purpose of this entire book. Look at these chapters as a review that keeps you focused on the purpose of retailing and how you can be successful.

Ten Common Retailing Myths

From the outside in, things appear different than they really are. Those differences force you to make subconscious assumptions that are incorrect. The purpose of this chapter is to lay to rest some of those myths and misconceptions that can get even experienced retailers into trouble because they were afraid to ask, "Why?"

All Advertising Costs Money

The best form of advertising is word of mouth — and it costs you nothing! Give people something to talk about. Get involved in community events. Network at seminars and workshops. Call your local radio station and offer to donate merchandise or gift certificates to charity events — in exchange for promotional mentions, of course. Write articles for your local newspaper on trends in your industry. You can pursue plenty of advertising opportunities *before* having to loosen your purse strings.

Institutional Advertising Works Slowly

Most retailers want to advertise price cuts. They believe that if they put something on sale, customers will flock to their stores. But *institutional advertising* (advertising the business name or brand as opposed to advertising a specific promotion, price, or item) can attract customers just as much as discounts can — if your store can create sufficient interest by having a unique specialty, that is. Which ad do you think will draw more customers?

- ✔ "The Toilet Doctor . . . Any toilet fixed in an hour"
- ✔ "Joe's Plumbing . . . Toilet repairs 20 percent off this week only"

The first ad is definitely the runaway hit.

A Newspaper Ad Will Bring All the Business (or Help) You Need

If only this were still true. Unfortunately, people don't read the newspaper as often as they used to. According to surveys that I've distributed to retailers at my various presentations, newspaper ads rank fourth in advertising effectiveness. The most effective form of advertising is *direct response* (via direct mail or e-mail). Television comes in second — for those who can afford it — and radio is third.

You Must Work 60 Hours a Week to Be Successful

Hogwash! Working excessive amounts of overtime will just make you cranky — and you're likely to take your frustrations out on your customers. Spending too much time working is the primary operative in the formula for burnout. Although your store must be open a lot of hours, you can't possibly be there the entire time. It just doesn't work. Instead, surround yourself with a capable staff who can represent your interests (and your brand) in your absence. See Chapter 13 for more on finding and keeping an excellent staff.

Senior Citizens Work Slowly

The senior citizens of today aren't what they were 20 years ago. These days, the AARP (American Association of Retired Persons) sends you a membership card when you turn 50 years young. Also, more and more people are retiring early from one profession to go into retail as a second career. They love retail because they can be with people while working part-time. They're the perfect employees for retail because they're not looking for extra benefits, they don't have children at home to worry about, and their motivation for working is more than just money. So consider the advantages of hiring mature, experienced workers!

Find an Excellent Location and You'll Always Do Great

If only it were that easy. I've given more than 30 presentations in *vacant* stores — all of which were located in some of the best malls in the United States. Most were once rented by national chains, and their locations were selected by savvy business people. On the other hand, I've seen successful stores that were located downtown and had little or no parking. Location is very important — but if you combine the wrong merchandise with poor management, your business is doomed no matter where you set up shop.

You Should Never Sell Merchandise for Less Than You Paid for It

No one wants to sell merchandise at below cost — but if you have to do it, do it. If an item is gathering dust, turn that investment into something that's going to perform. Don't wait forever to mark it down. The sooner you recognize that it's a slow seller (a dog), move it out. Turn it into cash and buy something else with the money. Then sell that.

The Future of Retailing Is on the Web

Although sometimes it may appear that the Internet will replace brick-and-mortar stores, traditional retailing is here to stay. I've worked in just about every retail market and have listened to market researchers from the finest universities — and the one thing everyone agrees on is this: The maximum percentage of total retail sales that Web retailing will ever hit is 30 percent. Considering the number of e-tailers that went bust in 2000, I think that estimate is pretty optimistic. After all, only about 4 to 5 percent of retailers failed at the turn of this century. There's plenty of traditional retailing left to be done.

All Promotions Are Sale or Price Promotions

Some of the best promotions are non-sale promotions. The more people who come through your front door, the better your chances for doing more business. To bring people into your store, do something to start a buzz — and have some fun! Examples include celebrating Elvis Presley's birthday, having the ugliest gift contest, or holding a pajama sale that starts at 7:00 a.m. and awards the customer with the best pajamas a prize.

Promotions aren't just about giving merchandise away at a discount. Pack your store while selling merchandise at your regular prices! It can happen. Make buying fun, and the customers will come.

You Should Focus on Attracting New Customers Because the Old Ones Leave Anyway

A new customer is great, but an old one is better — keeping a customer costs 75 percent less than attracting one. Your established customers will leave only if you don't do anything to keep them. Focus at least 50 to 60 percent of your efforts on your established customer base. Don't treat strangers better than you treat the customers whose purchases have long paid your rent. But don't neglect the new customers either — you want them to become old ones!

Price Is the Only Thing That Matters

If this were true, most malls would go out of business. Top retailers would no longer be so successful. Store and fixture design would be a thing of the past. Additional store hours wouldn't be important, and sales and customer service training wouldn't exist. Long checkout lines wouldn't bother us, and nice packaging would be irrelevant. Retailing involves far more than offering merchandise at the lowest possible price. Price is important, but so is great merchandise, stellar service, an inviting store atmosphere, convenient hours and location — get the picture?

Chapter 25

Ten Keys to Retailing Success

In This Chapter

▶ Keep track of your customers

▶ Train and value your employees

▶ Stand in your customers' shoes

▶ Never quit learning

▶ Show professionalism and consistency

Successful retailers use certain elements over and over again. Some of them are actions, and some are attitudes. The one thing they have in common is that they must be practiced on a daily, weekly, and monthly basis. Are any of these elements silver bullets to success? Maybe. But by utilizing all of them, you will guarantee your business's success.

Practice Database Marketing

In the old days, shopkeepers lived in the same towns as their customers and knew every customer by name — knew their children, where they worked, and approximately how much money they made. All this information made it easy for the shopkeepers to market their merchandise to their customers. What was successful 100 years ago still works today; it's just done a little differently. Now, it's called database marketing (also known as one-to-one marketing), which simply means knowing who your customers are, what they like, when they like to buy, how much they want to spend, and how to communicate with them.

Today, great retailers gather information from their preferred customer programs and surveys and store it in computer databases. Then they can regularly communicate with their customers only about the things that interest them. Database marketing is powerful because it increases the level of service, creates loyal customers, and reduces advertising costs — all at once! It has the power to turn prospective customers into real customers and real customers into loyal friends, and it keeps the cash register ringing.

To learn more about this approach, check out *Small Business Marketing For Dummies* by Barbara Schenck (Hungry Minds, Inc.).

Invest in Training Your Employees

Everyone knows that training is important. But in retail, the store that constantly works with its employees in an organized fashion is more successful. These same retailers constantly work on their training methods and are always trying to improve the manner in which they present material to ensure its effectiveness. Customers can feel and sense the difference. You can immediately tell when you've walked into a store that has trained its people well. These employees know what to say and do in whatever situation they find themselves.

Many retailers say to me, "Why train them? They're only going to leave." My response is, "But what if they stay?" Yes, training is a constant battle. Yes, you may have to repeat the same messages over and over, but training is something that winners do and that employees as well as customers appreciate.

Think Like a Customer

Thinking like a customer is very hard to do. Retailers tend to think like retailers and forget why customers buy what they buy. Retailers are more concerned with the features of products than the true benefits to the customer. To be a successful retailer, you must change your way of thinking and stand back from your store and your employees — look at them in the same way your customers do.

Thinking like a customer means that you must shop for products the way your customers would shop. To be a good retailer, you need to be a good customer — so shop! Shopping at your competitors' stores or other stores in your category — even different kinds of stores — can give you lots of new ideas and fresh approaches to merchandising.

Update Your Financial and Marketing Plans Weekly

Know your percentages. I'm shocked at the number of retailers who really don't understand how they make money in the retail business. If you don't know how much money you make, how can you know how much you can spend on merchandise or advertising? Successful retailers plan and budget down to the penny. They know the effects of every purchase and how it fits into the plan. When you update your financial and marketing plans weekly, concerns that arise usually catch your attention early enough that you can make adjustments to correct them and avoid major disasters.

Successful retailers know how and where they're going to advertise and how much they're going to spend. They also plan what they expect from their marketing and advertising. These retailers consider weekly planning and reviewing as important as opening the store in the morning.

Work at Networking

It's not what you know; it's who you know. We've all heard that saying, but networking is more than knowing the right people. It's knowing other retailers in similar circumstances to yours. Similar challenges can make them friends. They understand what you're saying and thinking. Networking is so important simply to know that you're not alone. Other people are doing what you do, going through the same ups and downs that you are.

I once networked with a retailer who mentioned in passing that the state retail association had a wonderful workers compensation insurance program. I didn't even know that there was a state retail association, and I certainly didn't know that it offered benefits that I could profit from. That one lead saved me over $100,000 during an eight-year period. All those sharp retailers who think that they're better and smarter than everyone else aren't so smart if they aren't networking.

Attend Seminars and Keep Learning

I'm always baffled that more retailers don't take advantage of opportunities to learn. The retail industry is changing fast, faster in the last ten years than at any other time in its history. The issues of private labeling, profiling customers, TV shopping, suburban sprawl, downtown rebirths, and technology are topics that retailers must learn about. Yet some retailers never attend the seminars presented at trade shows. The winning retailers are there, though. They go to pick up an idea or two, or even to remind themselves of something they may have forgotten. You should, too!

Someone in one of my workshops once told me that if she would just use half the stuff she already knew, she would be twice the retailer she already is. We need those reminders. Go to a workshop expecting that you'll already know more than 90 percent of what is presented. But in addition to offering the reminder and a couple of fresh ideas, workshops or seminars can pay huge dividends.

Read your trade publication as well. Promise yourself that you'll read one long story a month — don't just skim the publication, but really read it. Great retailers know what's happening in their industry. Think about signing up for newsgroups on the Web, too.

Appreciate Your Employees

The number one problem in retailing today is attracting and retaining employees. It's a buyer's market, and employees can get jobs at any number of places. You must work to show your appreciation for them. To paraphrase former president John F. Kennedy, "Don't ask what they can do for you. Ask what you can do for your employees, especially the good ones." Be sure to remember their birthdays, anniversaries, and, most important of all, their names. Work to make your employees part of your business family. The great retailers have figured out that every single good employee they keep is the equivalent of five others they won't have to hire. That's because it usually takes five hires to find one good employee who stays.

Make Shopping in Your Store Entertaining

Make shopping fun, and people will come. Just about anything sold today can be purchased online for less money. We live in an entertainment-based society — we want to be entertained at whatever we do. For example, you can now buy gas while watching short videos at the pump, and you can browse at a bookstore while listening to a classical string quartet. Customers will stay loyal to your business if you make shopping fun. The best retailers acknowledge and address this reality. Look for ways to make your business a fun place to shop.

Demonstrate Professionalism and Consistency

Great stores do the same thing over and over again. They make sure that each customer has the exact same experience. The worst thing you can do for your store is to close up at irregular times when business is slow. Customers want to know what to expect when they head out to your store — every time. McDonald's built its business on its consistency. But along with consistency, you must exhibit professionalism. I combine these two terms because retailers must consistently act like professionals. You must be clean and neat and have everything in order (and absolutely no handmade paper signs adorning your store!).

Many franchise companies gained a foothold when they recognized that the industry lacked professionalism. For example, a new chain of flower shops called KaBloom has opened. KaBloom shops are beautiful — they're well lit and maintained, and the merchandise is attractively displayed. Employees wear smocks, aprons, or shirts with the KaBloom logo on them. That's the kind of professionalism that customers value, and that's what winning retailers offer.

Carry Distinctive Products

Every time you buy something to sell in your store, ask yourself, "Is this good enough? Is it different enough or special enough?" When you start to say, "That's good enough," it usually isn't.

I was waiting in line at an airport and started talking to a lovely older woman from Jackson, Mississippi. I told her that I was going to give a speech called "How Independent Retailers Can Compete with the Biggies." When I told her my title, she turned to me and said that all the independent stores have to do is carry something a little different from the large chains. She was right. Carry merchandise that isn't readily available in other stores, and customers will come for it.

Know Who You Are and Who Your Customers Are

The winning stores know exactly who they are, and they know their limitations. They don't try to be everything to everybody. They have a niche and stay with it. Follow their lead — don't try to be something you're not. Also, remember who your customers are and what they like. Good retailers go to great efforts to review their mission and share it with their employees so that they can pass it on to their customers.

Chapter 26

Ten Common Retail Mistakes

In This Chapter

▶ Learning what to avoid

▶ Taking cues from other successful retailers

As a consultant, I see retailers make common mistakes over and over again, just as successful retailers use common tactics and strategies. I could have called this chapter the "if only" chapter, because every time I work with a retailer who's in trouble, they use those words — "If only I hadn't cut back on my advertising" or "If only I hadn't delegated all the financial matters." The purpose of this chapter is to eliminate those "if onlys."

Cutting the Advertising Budget to Save Money

Running a retail business has two basic, variable costs: payroll and advertising. So when cash flow is tight, cutting back on your advertising budget (not your payroll budget — you need to keep your employees happy!) is very tempting. When you decrease your advertising, any increase in business may reassure you that you've done the right thing. But sales will slowly start to fall. If your business is "out of sight" for consumers, it will soon be out of mind as well. Instead of slashing your advertising budget, focus on one-to-one or e-mail marketing — the costs are minimal and the results are strong.

Underestimating the Power of Customer Contact

To stay in your office rather than mingle with your customers is the kiss of death for your business, especially if it's a relatively small business. Customers *want* to see The Boss; they *want* a knowledgeable person on the sales floor. More important, however, by maintaining a visible presence in your store, you can learn what your customers do and don't like — and why.

Delegating All Financial Matters

A surefire way to scare consultants and bankers alike is to let someone else handle all the bookkeeping — and not stay informed about it yourself. An accountant needs to handle certain aspects of your business, but you (and every retailer) must be able to handle the following questions about your business for yourself:

- How much inventory does my business have?
- Is my business profitable?
- What is my business's cash flow situation?
- What are my business's percentages for rent, advertising, payroll, and cost of goods sold in relationship to sales?
- What is my business's stock to sales ratio?

These basic issues don't take long to understand or keep up with. It's like exercising for 30 minutes three days a week — some people just don't do it, despite the benefits. Make sure that you're not one of those people.

Failing to Shop at Other Stores

Shame on the store that keeps its head in the sand! Shopping at other stores can give you information to guide your future business decisions.

Take a look around at competing businesses (go to another city or town if you need to). Get ideas about merchandise. See if you can tell what's selling and what's hanging around. Check the prices and pricing policies. Then check general store policies. What are stores doing to wow their customers, and why do customers keep coming back?

But don't limit yourself to stores in your field. How are people in other industries moving their merchandise? If you're a jeweler, go to a bookstore. If you own a bookstore, shop at an apparel store. Then apply what you learn to your own store.

Skipping Seminars and Workshops

Almost every trade show offers seminars or workshops. I'm amazed when retailers don't take advantage of these learning opportunities. Granted, not all speakers make spectacular presentations, but as my father used to say, "You can learn from a fool." Whereas a strong speaker may spark terrific new ideas, a weak presentation often serves to reinforce what you already know — and this just may be the impetus you need to put your ideas into action. A single idea can turn a business around.

Many times, the real learning comes from the other retailers you meet at the seminar. A significant amount of networking takes place before and after a seminar — for two reasons:

- ✔ Attendees have at least two common subjects to talk about: the speaker and the topic at hand.
- ✔ Attendees believe in continuing education and want to learn. They're the easiest people to network with because they want to learn from you as much as you want to learn from them, and almost everyone is willing to share ideas and information.

Being Undercapitalized

New retailers often have no idea how long it will take for their businesses to show a profit. And most are unaware of how much money running a business requires — especially when it doesn't do what they expect it to do. Most new businesses are very optimistic and generally surround themselves with positive people who believe in what they're doing. They never plan for bad times, and they don't realize how long it takes to build a critical mass of customers. Ask yourself, "What would happen if _____ were to happen to my business? How long could I survive?" Then make sure that you have enough money to weather you through that storm and others like it.

Taking Too Big or Small a Salary

I've been a consultant for stores that had serious cash flow problems and no one could figure out why. Everything seemed to be in line — the sales were good and expenses weren't too large. But all my questions were answered as soon as I looked at the owner's salary: He was taking home more than $100,000 — in his first year of business! Why? Perhaps he'd left a $75,000-a-year corporate job and, now that he was working more hours, expected at least $100,000 a year. Whatever his reason, he didn't know that if your business can't afford such a high salary, you can't either.

On the flip side, some owners work for nothing to build their businesses. Because it's too easy to become resentful of the demand when the compensation is low or nonexistent, businesses whose owners work for nothing just don't last. Don't end up hating your business. If you feel that you must work for nothing, consider your time as a loan to your business that it must eventually pay back.

To figure out an appropriate salary, determine how much it would cost to hire someone else to do your job. Pay yourself that amount. To succeed, you must be realistic about costs, salaries, and profits. Look at your business as if you were a Wall Street investor. You want to see a fair salary — not too high and definitely not too low.

Misjudging Your Real Rent Costs

New retailers often face this trauma early in the first year of business. They get the first bill from the landlord, and they're shocked to see, in addition to the expected charges, a bunch of extra charges they weren't expecting. Don't be taken by surprise — make sure that you understand what you'll have to pay for, including charges for upkeep on common areas, building maintenance charges, and taxes. Read your lease agreement carefully before you sign it, and don't forget what it says. Also, don't forget that the initial statements you receive concerning maintenance costs or your share of the tax burden may be only estimates. Be prepared to pay more when the *real* bill arrives.

You may have to come up with a big chunk of money at the end of the year — if your business does well, causing your sales to exceed your minimum for the year, you could get hit with an *overage charge* (additional money due the landlord when the store exceeds the agreed-upon sales revenue). To avoid such an unpleasant year-end surprise, make sure that you understand what your *real* rent costs are going to be. Before you sign a lease, go take it to a lawyer *and* have a retail leasing professional review it and explain it to you. See Chapter 6 for more on leases.

Assuming You Know Your Customers

If you don't know what the customer you're trying to attract is like, how is that customer supposed to know to shop at your store? You must know your prime customer's profile: income level, tastes, place of residence, and so on.

Buying What You Like (Even If Your Customers Don't Want to Buy It)

I believe that you should build your business with merchandise that *you* really like and believe in. Finding customers with tastes similar to yours, however, often takes time. To cater to the needs and wants of the customers who are within your marketing area, you had better sell what they want to buy — otherwise, you could lose a lot of money waiting. If you choose to wait, make sure that you know what you're committing yourself to.

Another option is to locate your business in an area with customers who like what you like. If you want to sell handmade pet toys, for example, set up in an area where pets are popular.

Forgetting to Think Like a Customer

When you become a retailer, don't forget what it's like to be a customer. Successful retailers understand what's going on inside the minds of their customers. If you consciously think like your customers would, you can anticipate or correct problems in your store.

One of the best examples of this involves the initial greeting to the customer. When customers enter your store, they're saying to themselves, "I'll try that store. I've heard good things about it." Or, "I'm always able to get what I'm looking for there." The customer is deciding to give you the opportunity to sell to him. Thinking like a customer tells you to say, "Thanks for coming in. We appreciate it." You're in alignment with the customer.

Another example is understanding the customer's motivation. If a customer is concerned about buying an appropriate gift for her boss's daughter's wedding, for example, and the salesperson talks only about price, the salesperson isn't thinking like the customer. In this instance, the appropriate gift, not the price, is what's important.

Chapter 27

Ten Reasons to Shop at Independent Specialty Stores

In This Chapter

▶ Outstanding service and staff

▶ Distinctive merchandise

▶ Security and convenience

There's more to retailing than selection and price. When you shop at an independent specialty store, you're looking beyond the lowest price and the largest selection. Listed in this chapter are the ten best reasons to skip the chain store and go to an independent.

Better Service

Customers generally believe that the smaller the business, the better the service. Customers expect that the owner will be on the premises and that the owner cares. They feel that small stores have to give superior service in order to survive, so they have come to expect it. Customers feel more important in an independent store because they are — every sale is important. A national discount department store giant can turn off 1,000 customers (not that they do) and not be affected, but a small store can't afford to lose a single customer due to bad service.

Contact with the Boss

Many customers love to shop in a store where the boss or owner is around — and for more than just good service. First of all, they like dealing with the boss because the buck stops with the boss. If anything has to be approved or negotiated, the boss can do it. Dealing with the boss also makes customers feel important. Some people love to name-drop, but they also feel more secure in dealing with the owner. That's why owners of small retail stores should never hide in the back room — it's the worst thing you can do to the business. Customers want to see you!

Knowledgeable Sales Staff

Who do you think knows more about a digital camera — the sales clerk at a top-quality camera shop or the high school kid working part-time at a local discount store? The clerk at the camera shop, of course. Customers frequently shop at independent specialty stores because they want expertise and believe they can find it there. That's why training your employees well is so important. Customers expect all staff in a specialty store to be expertly informed about the merchandise. You ruin an expectation, and you've lost a customer.

Unique Merchandise

Customers don't come to a specialty store to see the same merchandise they can find in a department store. Customers go to a specialty store so that they can feel special and buy special, different merchandise. The comments I hear all the time are "I shop here because I don't want to look like everyone else" or "I don't want to give a gift that everyone knows what I paid for it." Different is good — and it sells.

Customer-Friendly Store Design

Many customers love the intimacy and smaller size of a specialty store. They don't have to go to another floor or walk a mile to another department. In addition, they get better service because employees can bring merchandise to them more quickly. A smaller store also can take the time to create more interesting and helpful displays that make merchandise easier to find.

No Waiting at the Register

Customers hate to wait — especially when they're checking out. A specialty store just doesn't have that problem (although sometimes we wish we did). Many people believe that time has become the most important commodity we sell. Small retailers can do everything right, but if a customer has to wait, it's as bad as ignoring the customer. I've seen customers put merchandise down and walk out of a store because they refused to wait. If you have to keep a customer waiting, at least let her know why. Doing so will ease the pain.

Education Opportunities

Customers appreciate the growing trend among specialty retailers of offering classes that appeal to their customers. No matter what business you're in, you can find some relevant class to offer. My apparel store offered classes on new forms of weight loss. My customers loved it. And it had the potential to help my business because people always buy lots of clothes after they lose weight.

Most retailers think that they have to draw big crowds to make the classes worthwhile. Actually, the opposite is true. The smaller the group, the better — a class of three to five people is fine. Let people know that seating is very limited, so signing up early is important. Classes offer a wonderful time for you to bond with your customers and, of course, to give them another reason to visit your store.

Familiar Faces

"I know everybody there. They're like family." You want your customers to have this kind of feeling about your store. Just as an owner who maintains a presence on the selling floor helps keep customers coming back, the familiar faces of your sales staff work as a magnet to draw in your customers. Your employees may become some of your customers' favorite people — they provide a sense of security. I know the faces of all the employees at my favorite bagel shop. They make me feel comfortable, like I belong. See Chapter 13 for information on retaining your employees. Keep your staff with you as long as you can — doing so makes a difference to your customers.

Security

"I feel safe bringing my kids there." You want customers to say this about your store, too. Security is a much bigger issue in shopping than ever before, mostly because people hear so many frightening, crime-related stories in the media. I did work for a large oil company that had two almost-identical gas station/convenience stores, both in similar locations. Yet one did almost 30 percent more business. The company eventually realized that the difference in business came after sundown. Finally, a customer said, "I won't come here at night! It's too dark here. I don't feel safe." The lighting at the station was adequate, but it wasn't nearly as bright as at competing locations. Make your business safe enough for a mother with two small kids.

Personalized Service

"They ordered it special for me." Customers love to go to a store that buys just for them. No other store can compete with such service, even if they're quick to process a special order for a customer without any obligation. Sure, you may get stuck with the merchandise if your customer doesn't like it, but the positive experiences far outweigh any negative ones.

The best two ways to wow a customer are to anticipate what your customer wants and to inform her when merchandise she likes arrives at your store. This is not about sending slick advertising to everyone on your mailing list; it's about friendly reminders that let select customers know that you're thinking especially of them. A personalized note goes a long way.

Distinctive Packaging

Many specialty retail stores have built a brand name that cries out quality, and because of that, the packaging becomes a status symbol in itself. And some stores have built a business with their packaging alone. Customers feel proud to carry certain packaging. This is no place to cut corners — packaging pays for itself over and over again. Distinctive packaging is a quiet little differentiator that distinguishes you from your competitors and helps you attract customers.

I learned this lesson the hard way. I had very expensive and distinctive packaging until a packaging rep told me that he could save me so much money with something that would look just as good. It did look *almost* as good, but it wasn't the same, and my customers knew the difference. They were disappointed with the cheaper packaging, and you never want to disappoint a customer! I switched back to the more expensive, but familiar, packaging.

Chapter 28

Ten Ways to WOW a Customer

. . . .

. . . .

Service, selection, and price are no longer good enough to impress a customer. You must go beyond that to the point where you make customers say, "WOW!" When that happens, you have exceeded their expectations. Usually, the next thing customers say is, "That's different!"

I believe that WOW stands for *Wonderful Opportunity to Win* — to win customers to your business because you have created a brief moment of amazement. To do that, you must create a WOW standard, always raising the bar. In this chapter are the top ten ways to WOW your customers.

Be Visually Consistent

If you say that you're a professional and that you're the best, you'd better be the best. You'd better look like you're the best, act like you're the best, and have the best people working for you. The outside of the store should reflect your advertising, and the inside of the store should reflect the outside. Your packaging must reinforce the message. You must be in alignment; otherwise, customers will be turned off for good. See Chapter 16 to find out about consistency in advertising.

Have an Attitude of Appreciation

I want people to be happy that they're doing business with me and to appreciate doing business with me. That's why I believe that the best greeting in a retail store is, "Thanks for coming in." Appreciating the individual customer, and not just the business the person is giving you, is important, too. As a customer, I want to hear thank-yous with my name attached to them. I want a thank-you note if I make a purchase of over $50. I don't want to go anywhere where I'm treated like a number.

Make the Customer Feel Important

As a customer, I don't want to be ignored or treated like I'm in the store to steal. I don't want the salesperson talking about herself unless I'm interested. I want the salesperson to pamper me and treat me like I am the most important person in the world. Treat me like I'm the president of a major corporation — because I might be. Treat me as if you're waiting on a person who speaks and writes about customer service issues, and your experience will be written about and will grace the stages of the largest conventions in the world. If you treat every customer like that, you won't have to read any further.

The best way to make someone feel important is to adopt the attitude, approach, and mannerisms of a professional servant. You are there to cater to that customer's needs in the most polite and professional manner. It's not so much *what* you do, but *how* you do it that counts.

Know the Names

You can't WOW your customers unless you know them. The most important thing to know is their names. Do whatever you have to do to find out your customers' names. Ask them, write the names down, put a description beside each name — better yet, take a Polaroid picture and write the customer's name on the white border. Hang it up and make a customer photo gallery. Do whatever you have to do, but make learning names a priority.

Other important people to know

Just knowing your customers isn't enough anymore. You also have to know the following:

✔ **Your employees:** You have to know what motivates your employees, both positively and negatively. You have to take the time to care about them, because if you care about them, they'll care about you and your customers.

✔ **Your vendors:** You want your vendors to be your disciples. The more you find out about them and their likes, the better off you'll be.

✔ **Yourself:** People respect people who know their limitations and focus on the things they do well. To know yourself, you have to understand what your brand is and what your name means in the marketplace. Only a fool thinks that he can do everything well.

Think of Mistakes as Opportunities

Everyone makes mistakes — it's what you do about them that impresses people. Somehow, the best customers seem to come from situations that started off negatively.

Get People to Like You

You can't do business with people who don't like you. I don't care how good your prices are or how good your products are; if I don't like you, I'm not doing business with you. The key is to get customers to like you. If they like you, WOWing them is easier. Selling to them and taking care of their problems are also easier. A customer with a problem who doesn't like you is the most dangerous and feared customer of all.

So what's the best way to get people to like you? The following two suggestions always work:

✔ **Harness the power of a compliment.** Not a slap-'em-on-the-back politician kind of compliment; I'm talking about the sincere, honest type. Look for something outstanding or unusual about someone. Here are four things to look for:

  • **Material possessions — glasses, jewelry, handbags, cars, clothes, or anything else they own:** People spend big money on these items, and many of them do it to make themselves feel good. Why would you not at least acknowledge how nice they are?

  • **Physical appearance:** This one is controversial. We live in an era of sexual harassment, and you must be careful with everything you say, but what's wrong with telling customers that they look like they've lost weight or asking whether they've been exercising? (If someone told me I looked like I lost 8 ounces, I would buy anything from that person!) And what's wrong with asking a customer whether she has changed her hairstyle and complimenting that new style? Nothing is wrong with telling customers that they look good if you deliver your compliment with respect and dignity.

  If you're concerned about this approach, compliment on appearance only if you know the customer fairly well.

  • **Personality:** Isn't it nice to wait on a customer with a happy, bubbly personality? Of course it is, so why not tell him so? You'll make his day. If you're waiting on the toughest, most demanding customer around, why not tell him that you appreciate someone who knows what he likes? You might even say that such customers make you better and thank them. If you deliver this compliment right, the customer will melt faster than the Wicked Witch of the West.

- **Things they say or do:** Have you ever been served by a real professional in a good restaurant? What does this waiter always say after you order something? "Excellent choice." How does that compliment make you feel? Good, like you really know what you're talking about. Would it be a sin to compliment your customers on the choices they make? I don't think so. Try it!

✔ **Master the ability to listen — not just hear, but truly listen.** I believe that listening is a form of a compliment. It involves more than just paying attention. Here are four tips for listening well:

- **Look at people when they're talking to you.** Nothing is more annoying than trying to talk to a person who isn't looking at you.

- **Use reaffirming statements** — you know, those little nods, ahas, and yeahs we make when we're really listening to someone and want them to know that we're listening. Reaffirmations are very comforting to the speaker.

- **Acknowledge that you heard the speaker.** In the course of conversation, a customer may mention that he bought a new car, his wife had a baby, or his father is sick. If so, acknowledge it later with a "Good luck with the car (or baby)" or "I hope your dad is feeling better." People like to know that you were listening. By commenting in response to what a customer says, you're offering a compliment because you're saying, "Your words are important to me."

- **Use the word *understand*.** Hearing this word is reassuring to the listener, especially one who has a problem. Use phrases such as "I understand what you mean," "I understand where you're coming from," and "I understand how you could feel like that."

Rick's Random Rule #4: You can be friendly with someone who doesn't smile, but you can't be friendly with someone who doesn't listen.

Pay Attention to the Extras

WOWing is all about details. It's about the little things a business can do that make it memorable and give customers that warm, fuzzy feeling. Consider the hot baked chocolate chip cookies that the Doubletree hotels serve or the little envelopes in which Talbots puts customer receipts. In New Orleans, they call it *lagniappe* — the little extra thing a merchant gives you that says, "Thanks for shopping here."

You might offer a gift certificate for the next purchase or send a birthday or anniversary card to a customer. You could place a jar of candy at the front desk or even create a nice sitting area for the men who come shopping with their wives. Brainstorm with your employees and see what you can do that tells your customers you care.

Follow Up

After you make a sale of a certain size, follow up with a phone call, a card, or an e-mail to make sure that the transaction went well. (Follow up only on sales of over $75 or $100, or whatever amount is appropriate for your business.) Follow-up is one of the hardest things to do, but you must do it. It tells customers that you really care about them.

Many old-school retailers use the expression, "Let sleeping dogs lie." If you do that and a problem arises, you will have lost the customer. But if you catch the problem early by following up after the sale, it will be the start of something special because you will have WOWed the customer.

Keep in Touch

Regularly remind your customers that you're still alive and there to serve. You might try a phone call, a postcard, a newsletter, a fax, or an e-mail — anything that serves as a friendly reminder letting your customers know that you're thinking about them.

I once fell in love with an Army and Navy store located near my daughter's dance school. I used to drop off my daughter and go into the store to explore. I always bought something. The store sold casual wear as well, so finding something I liked or needed wasn't hard. It got so bad that my wife would tell me, "Don't buy anything else." I only went there three times a month, but this went on for about three years. Browsing through this store became my ritual. The owner was a terrific guy and a very good merchant. He knew his customers and always suggested the right thing — something that you didn't really need but couldn't live without.

After my daughter stopped dancing, I went back a couple of times but then drifted away. A year ago, I bumped into another father whose daughter went to the same dance school and who had his own love affair with the Army and Navy store. I used to see him in there a couple times a month. I asked him whether he had been back, and he told me that the store had closed. The owner tried to sell the business but couldn't because the landlord had raised the rent so high. He decided to close up and move to Florida, where he could live a lot cheaper on what he had. This father told me that he caught the tail end of the sale and said that the buys were unbelievable. I asked him how he found out about the sale. Did he get a notice or anything? He said, "No, my neighbor told me about it. He never did tell his customers."

Shame on him! There's no excuse for failing to keep in touch. A store will never WOW you in the long term if it doesn't keep in touch with you.

Make It Fun

Throughout this book, I talk about the benefits of fun and of playful behavior. Taking a lighthearted approach can help customers feel comfortable and relaxed. And a WOW that's muffled by the sound of laughter keeps customers coming back again and again. I learned it all from my mother, who always had a story to tell or a joke on the ready for that right situation that would brighten the day of every customer she met. We would tell her that she *was* the WOW, and she would reply, "No, I just have good stories."

Write down any good lines you hear and save them for the store. Your customers will appreciate your attempts at humor. Laughter, fun, and the attitude of not only selling to very customer but also entertaining them a bit can go a long way toward keeping customers happy. You see, when you humorize, you humanize, and the greatest WOW of them all is and always will be doing business with a human being who can laugh with and cares about you.

Appendix

About the CD

System Requirements

Make sure that your computer meets the minimum system requirements shown in the following list. If your computer doesn't match up to most of these requirements, you may have problems using the software and files on the CD.

- A PC with a Pentium or faster processor; or a Mac OS computer with a 68040 or faster processor

- Microsoft Windows 95 or later; or Mac OS system software 7.6.1 or later

- Some files require Microsoft Excel 97 or higher

- At least 32MB of total RAM installed on your computer; for best performance, we recommend at least 64MB

- A CD-ROM drive

- A sound card for PCs; Mac OS computers have built-in sound support

- A monitor capable of displaying at least 256 colors or grayscale

- A modem with a speed of at least 14,400 bps

If you need more information on the basics, check out these books published by Hungry Minds, Inc.: *PCs For Dummies,* by Dan Gookin; *Macs For Dummies,* by David Pogue; *iMacs For Dummies* by David Pogue; *Windows 95 For Dummies, Windows 98 For Dummies, Windows 2000 Professional For Dummies, Microsoft Windows ME Millennium Edition For Dummies,* all by Andy Rathbone.

Using the CD with Microsoft Windows

To install items from the CD to your hard drive, follow these steps:

1. **Insert the CD into your computer's CD-ROM drive.**

   A window will appear with the following options: HTML Interface, Browse CD, and Exit. Choose one.

   HTML Interface: Click this button if you want to view the contents of the CD in standard Dummies presentation. It'll look like a Web page.

   Browse CD: Click this button if you want to skip the fancy presentation and simply view the CD contents from the directory structure. This means you'll just see a list of folders — plain and simple.

   Exit: Well, what can I say? Click this button if you want to quit.

   Note: If you do not have autorun enabled or if the autorun window does not appear, follow these steps to access the CD.

2. **Click the Start button and choose Run from the menu.**

3. **In the dialog box that appears, type** d:\start.htm.

   Replace *d* with the proper drive letter for your CD-ROM if it uses a different letter. (If you don't know the letter, double-click My Computer on your desktop and see what letter is listed for your CD-ROM drive.)

   Your browser opens, and the license agreement is displayed. If you don't have a browser, Microsoft Internet Explorer and Netscape Communicator are included on the CD.

4. **Read through the license agreement, nod your head, and click the Agree button if you want to use the CD.**

   After you click Agree, you're taken to the Main menu, where you can browse through the contents of the CD.

5. **To navigate within the interface, click a topic of interest to take you to an explanation of the files on the CD and how to use or install them.**

6. **To install software from the CD, simply click the software name.**

   You'll see two options: to run or open the file from the current location or to save the file to your hard drive. Choose to run or open the file from its current location, and the installation procedure continues. When you finish using the interface, close your browser as usual.

Note: We have included an "easy install" in these HTML pages. If your browser supports installations from within it, go ahead and click the links of the program names you see. You'll see two options: Run the File from the Current Location and Save the File to Your Hard Drive. Choose to Run the File from the Current Location and the installation procedure will continue. A Security Warning dialog box appears. Click Yes to continue the installation.

To run some of the programs on the CD, you may need to keep the disc inside your CD-ROM drive. This is a good thing. Otherwise, a very large chunk of the program would be installed to your hard drive, consuming valuable hard drive space and possibly keeping you from installing other software.

Using the CD with Mac OS

To install items from the CD to your hard drive, follow these steps:

1. **Insert the CD into your computer's CD-ROM drive.**

   In a moment, an icon representing the CD you just inserted appears on your Mac desktop. Chances are, the icon looks like a CD-ROM.

2. **Double-click the CD icon to show the CD's contents.**

3. **Double-click** start.htm **to open your browser and display the license agreement.**

   If your browser doesn't open automatically, open it as you normally would by choosing File⇨Open File (in Internet Explorer) or File⇨Open⇨Location in Netscape (in Netscape Communicator) and select *RetailBizKit FD*. The license agreement appears.

4. **Read through the license agreement, nod your head, and click the Accept button if you want to use the CD.**

   After you click Accept, you're taken to the Main menu. This is where you can browse through the contents of the CD.

5. **To navigate within the interface, click any topic of interest and you're taken you to an explanation of the files on the CD and how to use or install them.**

6. **To install software from the CD, simply click the software name.**

What You'll Find on the CD

The following sections are arranged by category and provide a summary of the software and other goodies you'll find on the CD. If you need help with installing the items provided on the CD, refer back to the installation instructions in the preceding section.

Shareware programs are fully functional, trial versions of copyrighted programs. If you like particular programs register with their authors for a nominal fee and receive licenses, enhanced versions, and technical support. *Freeware programs* are free, copyrighted games, applications, and utilities.

Unlike shareware, these programs do not require a fee or provide technical support. *GNU software* is governed by its own license, which is included inside the folder of the GNU product. See the GNU license for more details.

Trial, demo, or evaluation versions are usually limited either by time or functionality (such as being unable to save projects). Some trial versions are very sensitive to system date changes. If you alter your computer's date, the programs will "time out" and will no longer be functional.

Sample Forms, Ads, and Reports

This section lists the various forms from the book as well as some extras thrown in especially for the CD. Each form is available to you as a PDF file and almost every form is available as a Rich Text File (.rtf). You'll need Adobe Acrobat Reader (available on this CD) to view and print the PDF files. You can use your favorite word processor to view, print, and edit the .rtf files.

There are also a few forms that require Microsoft Excel. Those particular forms have been marked below as Excel Documents. Excel is not included on this CD. For information about Excel, check out Microsoft's Web site `http://www.microsoft.com`.

You can find the items listed below on the CD in a folder called "Forms."

Accounting Forms

Accounts Payable Report (Excel Document)

Balance Sheet

Cash Flow Reports

   Detailed Cash Flow Projection

   Summary Cash Flow Projection

   Long-term Cash Flow Projection

Cash Refund Form

Credit Reference Listing Sheet

Daily Cash Receipts

Daily Sales Envelope

IRS Form #583 Excerpt

Petty Cash Form

Profit and Loss Statements
    Margie's Craft Emporium
    Jake & Izzy's Scrapbooks
    Annie's Stamps
Sales Report Introduction
    Sold Vs. On-Hand
    Vendor Summary
    Department Summary
    Best Seller Report

Advertising Forms

Advertising Calendar
Employment Ad
Profile Ad
Question and Answer Ad

Buying Forms

Buying Budget (Excel document)
Buying Schedule (Excel document)
Cancellation Notice
Markdown Forms
Markdown Reports (Excel document)
On Order Report (Excel document)
Open to Buy Form (Excel document)
Open to Thrive Forms
Planned Monthly Worksheet (Excel document)
Daily Worksheet (Excel document)
On Order Report (Excel document)
Actual Monthly Worksheet (Excel document)
Purchase Order Form

Daily Operation Forms

Alteration Form
Consignment Merchandise Form (Excel document)
Credit Slip
Employee Handbook
Gift Certificate
Gift Certificate Record (Excel document)
Gift Registry
Inventory Sheets (Excel document)
Layaway Form
On Hold Form
Price Tag
Receiving Forms (Two Samples)
   Sample A (Excel Document)
   Sample B
Return Authorization Form
Return Policy
Sales Management System
Sales Slip
Sample Window Displays
   At the Library
   Castles
   In the Mythical Woods
   Key-Butzing
   Lace Ladies
   Neigh Sayers
   Pianos from Heaven
   Say It With a Twist
   South of the Border
Special Ordering
Time Card or Sign In Sheet (Excel document)
Vacation Schedule Tracker (Excel document)
Visual Display Calendar (Excel document)
Visual Display Prop Inventory
Work Schedules (Excel document)

Database Management Forms

Anniversary Card
Birthday Card
Coupons
Customer Profile Form
Preferred Customer Membership Card
Preferred Customer Tag
Thank You Note

Employment Forms

Application
Employee Emergency Contact Form
Employee Recruitment Card
Employment Agreement Letter
Exit Interview
Interview Evaluation Form
Employee Review Form

Legal Forms

Long Commercial Lease
General Partnership Agreement
Real Estate Property Lease Check List

Miscellaneous Forms

8-Point Retail Filter
Nifty Fifty: What's Important to Me Test
S. W. O. T. Exercise

Sales/Promotion Forms

Advertising Calendar
Coupons
Final Analysis Form
Grand Opening Check List
Elements of a Newsletter
Sample Newsletter
Format for Press Release
Sample Sale Check List
Sale Meeting Agenda
Sale Names List
Sale Price Tag
Sample Ads (12)
Sample Sale Letters (2)

Software

Acrobat Reader

Evaluation version.

For Macintosh and Windows. Acrobat Reader, from Adobe Systems, is a program that lets you view and print Portable Document Format, or PDF files. The PDF format is used by many programs you find on the Internet for storing documentation, because it supports the use of such stylish elements as assorted fonts and colorful graphics (as opposed to plain text, or ASCII, which doesn't allow for any special effects in a document). You can also get more information by visiting the Adobe Systems Web site, at www.adobe.com.

Internet Explorer

Commercial version.

For Macintosh and Windows. Internet Explorer, from Microsoft, is one of the best-known Web browsers available. In addition to the browser, this package includes other Internet tools from Microsoft: Outlook Express 5, a mail and news reading program; Windows Media Player, a program that can display or play many types of audio and video files; and NetMeeting 3, a video conferencing program.

If you have a version of Windows 98, 2000, or NT that already includes Internet Explorer 5.5, don't install the CD-ROM version. Instead, go to Microsoft's Web site at `www.microsoft.com/windows/ie/download/windows.htm` and see what updates are available to fix errors and security problems in the version you have.

Mindspring Internet Access

Commercial verison.

For Macintosh and Windows.MindSpring is an Internet service provider (ISP) that has local telephone access from most areas of the continental United States. The software provided by MindSpring on the CD-ROM includes and easy-to-use interface to the Internet programs you will want to use, as well as some useful Internet client -programs. Visit the MindSpring Web site at `www.mindspring.com`

Before you sign up for an account with MindSpring, check whether it's accessible from your location as a local telephone call. You can check MindSpring availability in your area through their Web site or call their customer service department at 1-888-677-7464.

Mindspring has several plans you can choose from, depending on how much time you need to spend connected. At the time this book was written, MindSpring offered unlimited 56K dial-up Internet access for $19.95 per month. MindSpring also offers residential and business ISDN and DSL service.

If you already have an Internet service provider, please note that the MindSpring software makes changes to your computer's current Internet configuration and may replace your current settings. These changes may stop you from being able to access the Internet through your current provider.

Netscape Communicator

Commercial version.

For Macintosh and Windows. Netscape Communicator, from Netscape Communications, is one of the best-known Web browsers available. The CD-ROM installs Netscape Communicator Version 4.7. You also have the option of installing Real Player G2 (to play streaming audio and video files) and Winamp (to play MPEG3 files).

You can find information about Netscape Navigator from its Help menu or at its Web site, `home.netscape.com`.

Troubleshooting

I tried my best to compile programs that work on most computers with the minimum system requirements. Alas, your computer may differ, and some programs may not work properly for some reason.

The two likeliest problems are that you don't have enough memory (RAM) for the programs you want to use, or you have other programs running that are affecting installation or running of a program. If you get an error message such as Not enough memory or Setup cannot continue, try one or more of the following suggestions and then try using the software again:

- **Turn off any antivirus software running on your computer.** Installation programs sometimes mimic virus activity and may make your computer incorrectly believe that it's being infected by a virus.

- **Close all running programs.** The more programs you have running, the less memory is available to other programs. Installation programs typically update files and programs; so if you keep other programs running, installation may not work properly.

- **Have your local computer store add more RAM to your computer.** This is, admittedly, a drastic and somewhat expensive step. However, if you have a Windows 95 PC or a Mac OS computer with a PowerPC chip, adding more memory can really help the speed of your computer and allow more programs to run at the same time. This may include closing the CD interface and running a product's installation program from Windows Explorer.

If you still have trouble installing the items from the CD, please call the Hungry Minds, Inc. Customer Service phone number at 800-762-2974 (outside the U.S.: 317-572-3993) or send email to techsupdum@hungryminds.com.

Index

∙∙

• T •

Hungry Minds, Inc.
End-User License Agreement

READ THIS. You should carefully read these terms and conditions before opening the software packet(s) included with this book ("Book"). This is a license agreement ("Agreement") between you and Hungry Minds, Inc. ("HMI"). By opening the accompanying software packet(s), you acknowledge that you have read and accept the following terms and conditions. If you do not agree and do not want to be bound by such terms and conditions, promptly return the Book and the unopened software packet(s) to the place you obtained them for a full refund.

1. **License Grant.** HMI grants to you (either an individual or entity) a nonexclusive license to use one copy of the enclosed software program(s) (collectively, the "Software") solely for your own personal or business purposes on a single computer (whether a standard computer or a workstation component of a multi-user network). The Software is in use on a computer when it is loaded into temporary memory (RAM) or installed into permanent memory (hard disk, CD-ROM, or other storage device). HMI reserves all rights not expressly granted herein.

2. **Ownership.** HMI is the owner of all right, title, and interest, including copyright, in and to the compilation of the Software recorded on the disk(s) or CD-ROM ("Software Media"). Copyright to the individual programs recorded on the Software Media is owned by the author or other authorized copyright owner of each program. Ownership of the Software and all proprietary rights relating thereto remain with HMI and its licensers.

3. **Restrictions On Use and Transfer.**

   (a) You may only (i) make one copy of the Software for backup or archival purposes, or (ii) transfer the Software to a single hard disk, provided that you keep the original for backup or archival purposes. You may not (i) rent or lease the Software, (ii) copy or reproduce the Software through a LAN or other network system or through any computer subscriber system or bulletin-board system, or (iii) modify, adapt, or create derivative works based on the Software.

   (b) You may not reverse engineer, decompile, or disassemble the Software. You may transfer the Software and user documentation on a permanent basis, provided that the transferee agrees to accept the terms and conditions of this Agreement and you retain no copies. If the Software is an update or has been updated, any transfer must include the most recent update and all prior versions.

4. **Restrictions on Use of Individual Programs.** You must follow the individual requirements and restrictions detailed for each individual program in the "About the CD" appendix of this book. These limitations are also contained in the individual license agreements recorded on the Software Media. These limitations may include a requirement that after using the program for a specified period of time, the user must pay a registration fee or discontinue use. By opening the Software packet(s), you will be agreeing to abide by the licenses and restrictions for these individual programs that are detailed in the "About the CD" appendix and on the Software Media. None of the material on this Software Media or listed in this Book may ever be redistributed, in original or modified form, for commercial purposes.

5. **Limited Warranty.**

   (a) HMI warrants that the Software and Software Media are free from defects in materials and workmanship under normal use for a period of sixty (60) days from the date of purchase of this Book. If HMI receives notification within the warranty period of defects in materials or workmanship, HMI will replace the defective Software Media.

   (b) **HMI AND THE AUTHOR OF THE BOOK DISCLAIM ALL OTHER WARRANTIES, EXPRESS OR IMPLIED, INCLUDING WITHOUT LIMITATION IMPLIED WARRANTIES OF MERCHANTABILITY AND FITNESS FOR A PARTICULAR PURPOSE, WITH RESPECT TO THE SOFTWARE, THE PROGRAMS, THE SOURCE CODE CONTAINED THEREIN, AND/OR THE TECHNIQUES DESCRIBED IN THIS BOOK. HMI DOES NOT WARRANT THAT THE FUNCTIONS CONTAINED IN THE SOFTWARE WILL MEET YOUR REQUIREMENTS OR THAT THE OPERATION OF THE SOFTWARE WILL BE ERROR FREE.**

   (c) This limited warranty gives you specific legal rights, and you may have other rights that vary from jurisdiction to jurisdiction.

6. **Remedies.**

   (a) HMI's entire liability and your exclusive remedy for defects in materials and workmanship shall be limited to replacement of the Software Media, which may be returned to HMI with a copy of your receipt at the following address: Software Media Fulfillment Department, Attn.: *Retail Business Kit For Dummies*, Hungry Minds, Inc., 10475 Crosspoint Blvd., Indianapolis, IN 46256, or call 1-800-762-2974. Please allow four to six weeks for delivery. This Limited Warranty is void if failure of the Software Media has resulted from accident, abuse, or misapplication. Any replacement Software Media will be warranted for the remainder of the original warranty period or thirty (30) days, whichever is longer.

   (b) In no event shall HMI or the author be liable for any damages whatsoever (including without limitation damages for loss of business profits, business interruption, loss of business information, or any other pecuniary loss) arising from the use of or inability to use the Book or the Software, even if HMI has been advised of the possibility of such damages.

   (c) Because some jurisdictions do not allow the exclusion or limitation of liability for consequential or incidental damages, the above limitation or exclusion may not apply to you.

7. **U.S. Government Restricted Rights.** Use, duplication, or disclosure of the Software for or on behalf of the United States of America, its agencies and/or instrumentalities (the "U.S. Government") is subject to restrictions as stated in paragraph (c)(1)(ii) of the Rights in Technical Data and Computer Software clause of DFARS 252.227-7013, or subparagraphs (c)(1) and (2) of the Commercial Computer Software - Restricted Rights clause at FAR 52.227-19, and in similar clauses in the NASA FAR supplement, as applicable.

8. **General.** This Agreement constitutes the entire understanding of the parties and revokes and supersedes all prior agreements, oral or written, between them and may not be modified or amended except in a writing signed by both parties hereto that specifically refers to this Agreement. This Agreement shall take precedence over any other documents that may be in conflict herewith. If any one or more provisions contained in this Agreement are held by any court or tribunal to be invalid, illegal, or otherwise unenforceable, each and every other provision shall remain in full force and effect.

Installation Instructions

The *Retail Business Kit For Dummies* CD offers valuable information that you won't want to miss. To install the items from the CD to your hard drive, follow these steps.

For Microsoft Windows Users

1. Insert the CD into your computer's CD-ROM drive.

2. Open your browser.

3. Click Start➪Run.

4. In the dialog box that appears, type D:\START.HTM

5. Read through the license agreement, nod your head, and then click the Accept button if you want to use the CD — after you click Accept, you'll jump to the Main Menu.

6. To navigate within the interface, simply click on any topic of interest to take you to an explanation of the files on the CD and how to use or install them.

7. To install the software from the CD, simply click on the software name.

For Mac OS Users

1. Insert the CD into your computer's CD-ROM drive.

2. Double click the CD icon to show the CD's contents.

3. To launch the CD Interface, double click START.HTM.

4. Read through the license agreement, nod your head, and then click the Accept button if you want to use the CD — after you click Accept, you'll jump to the Software Menu.

5. To navigate within the interface, simply click on any topic of interest to take you to an explanation of the files on the CD and how to use or install them.

6. To install the software from the CD, simply click on the software name.

For more complete information, please see the "About the CD" appendix.

FOR DUMMIES
BOOK REGISTRATION

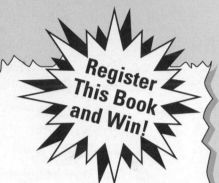
Register This Book and Win!

We want to hear from you!

Visit **dummies.com** to register this book and tell us how you liked it!

- Get entered in our monthly prize giveaway.

- Give us feedback about this book — tell us what you like best, what you like least, or maybe what you'd like to ask the author and us to change!

- Let us know any other *For Dummies* topics that interest you.

Your feedback helps us determine what books to publish, tells us what coverage to add as we revise our books, and lets us know whether we're meeting your needs as a *For Dummies* reader. You're our most valuable resource, and what you have to say is important to us!

Not on the Web yet? It's easy to get started with *Dummies 101: The Internet For Windows 98* or *The Internet For Dummies* at local retailers everywhere.

Or let us know what you think by sending us a letter at the following address:

For Dummies Book Registration
Dummies Press
10475 Crosspoint Blvd.
Indianapolis, IN 46256

...FOR DUMMIES™
BESTSELLING BOOK SERIES